Deborah Martin is Senior Lecturer in Latin American Cultural Studies at University College London. She has published widely on Latin American film, including *Painting, Literature and Film in Colombian Feminine Culture, 1940–2005: Of Border Guards, Nomads and Women* (2012) and *The Cinema of Lucrecia Martel* (2016).

Deborah Shaw is Reader in Film Studies at the University of Portsmouth, UK, where her key research interests are in transnational film theory and Latin American cinema. She is the founding co-editor of the *Transnational Cinemas* journal and her books include *Contemporary Latin American Cinema: Ten Key Films* (2003) and *The Three Amigos: The Transnational Filmmaking of Guillermo del Toro, Alejandro González Iñárritu, and Alfonso Cuarón* (2013).

'This exciting collection balances contextual analysis with close attention to individual films and the careers of more and less visible women working in different industry roles. A major contribution to not only film studies but also to current and future thinking about women's cultural production in Latin America.'

– Claire Williams, University of Oxford

'Focusing on the cinemas of Argentina, Brazil, Chile, Mexico, Peru, Venezuela, and the Hispanic US, the essays collected here are brilliant advocates for filmmaking by Latin American women. A timely reminder that the personal is still political.'

– Andrea Noble, Durham University

TAURIS WORLD CINEMA SERIES

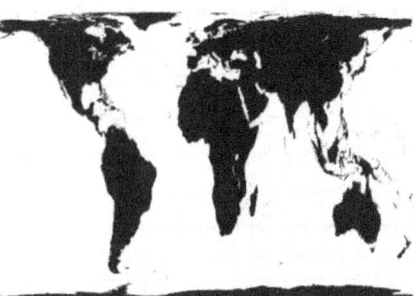

Series Editors:
Lúcia Nagib, *Professor of Film at the University of Reading*
Julian Ross, *Research Fellow at the University of Westminster*

Advisory Board: Laura Mulvey (UK), Robert Stam (USA), Ismail Xavier (Brazil), Dudley Andrew (USA)

The *Tauris World Cinema Series* aims to reveal and celebrate the richness and complexity of film art across the globe, exploring a wide variety of cinemas set within their own cultures and as they interconnect in a global context. The books in the series will represent innovative scholarship, in tune with the multicultural character of contemporary audiences. Drawing upon an international authorship, they will challenge outdated conceptions of world cinema, and provide new ways of understanding a field at the centre of film studies in an era of transnational networks.

Published and forthcoming in the World Cinema series:

Animation in the Middle East: Practice and Aesthetics from Baghdad to Casablanca
Edited by Stefanie Van de Peer

Basque Cinema: A Cultural and Political History
By Rob Stone and María Pilar Rodriguez

Brazil on Screen: Cinema Novo, New Cinema, Utopia
By Lúcia Nagib

The Cinema of Jia Zhangke: Realism and Memory in Chinese Film
By Cecília Mello

The Cinema of Sri Lanka: South Asian Film in Texts and Contexts
By Ian Conrich and Vilasnee Tampoe-Hautin

Contemporary New Zealand Cinema: From New Wave to Blockbuster
Edited by Ian Conrich and Stuart Murray

Contemporary Portuguese Cinema: Globalising the Nation
Edited by Mariana Liz

Cosmopolitan Cinema: Cross-cultural Encounters in East Asian Film
By Felicia Chan

Documentary Cinema: Contemporary Non-fiction Film and Video Worldwide
By Keith Beattie

East Asian Cinemas: Exploring Transnational Connections on Film
Edited by Leon Hunt and Leung Wing-Fai

East Asian Film Noir: Transnational Encounters and Intercultural Dialogue
Edited by Chi-Yun Shin and Mark Gallagher

Film Genres and African Cinema: Postcolonial Encounters
By Rachael Langford

Impure Cinema: Intermedial and Intercultural Approaches to Film
Edited by Lúcia Nagib and Anne Jerslev

Latin American Women Filmmakers: Production, Politics, Poetics
Edited by Deborah Martin and Deborah Shaw

Lebanese Cinema: Imagining the Civil War and Beyond
By Lina Khatib

New Argentine Cinema
By Jens Andermann

New Directions in German Cinema
Edited by Paul Cooke and Chris Homewood

New Turkish Cinema: Belonging, Identity and Memory
By Asuman Suner

On Cinema
By Glauber Rocha
Edited by Ismail Xavier

Palestinian Filmmaking in Israel: Narratives of Place and Identity
By Yael Freidman

Paulo Emílio Salles Gomes: On Brazil and Global Cinema
Edited by Maite Conde and Stephanie Dennison

Performing Authorship: Self-inscription and Corporeality in the Cinema
By Cecilia Sayad

Queer Masculinities in Latin American Cinema: Male Bodies and Narrative Representations
By Gustavo Subero

Realism in Greek Cinema: From the Post-war Period to the Present
By Vrasidas Karalis

Realism of the Senses in World Cinema: The Experience of Physical Reality
By Tiago de Luca

The Spanish Fantastic: Contemporary Filmmaking in Horror, Fantasy and Sci-fi
By Shelagh-Rowan Legg

Stars in World Cinema: Screen Icons and Star Systems Across Cultures
Edited by Andrea Bandhauer and Michelle Royer

Thai Cinema: The Complete Guide Edited by Mary J. Ainslie and Katarzyna Ancuta

Theorizing World Cinema
Edited by Lúcia Nagib, Chris Perriam and Rajinder Dudrah

Viewing Film
By Donald Richie

Queries, ideas and submissions to:

Series Editor: Professor Lúcia Nagib –
l.nagib@reading.ac.uk

Series Editor: Dr. Julian Ross –
rossj@westminster.ac.uk

Cinema Editor at I.B.Tauris, Maddy Hamey-Thomas –
mhamey-thomas@ibtauris.com

LATIN AMERICAN WOMEN FILMMAKERS

PRODUCTION, POLITICS, POETICS

Edited by Deborah Martin and Deborah Shaw

BLOOMSBURY ACADEMIC
LONDON • NEW YORK • OXFORD • NEW DELHI • SYDNEY

BLOOMSBURY ACADEMIC
Bloomsbury Publishing Plc
50 Bedford Square, London, WC1B 3DP, UK
1385 Broadway, New York, NY 10018, USA
29 Earlsfort Terrace, Dublin 2, Ireland

BLOOMSBURY, BLOOMSBURY ACADEMIC and the Diana logo
are trademarks of Bloomsbury Publishing Plc

First published in Great Britain 2017 by I. B. Tauris
This paperback edition published in 2021

Copyright © B. Ruby Rich, 2017

Copyright individual chapters © 2017 Sarah Barrow, Claudia Bossay, Constanza
Burucúa, Marvin D'Lugo, Catherine Leen, Leslie L. Marsh, Deborah Martin,
Lúcia Nagib, María-Paz Peirano, Deborah Shaw, Niamh Thornton

B. Ruby Rich has asserted their right under the Copyright,
Designs and Patents Act, 1988, to be identified as Author of this work.

For legal purposes the Acknowledgements on p. xiv constitute an
extension of this copyright page.

All rights reserved. No part of this publication may be reproduced or
transmitted in any form or by any means, electronic or mechanical,
including photocopying, recording, or any information storage or retrieval
system, without prior permission in writing from the publishers.

Bloomsbury Publishing Plc does not have any control over, or responsibility for,
any third-party websites referred to or in this book. All internet addresses given
in this book were correct at the time of going to press. The author and publisher
regret any inconvenience caused if addresses have changed or sites have
ceased to exist, but can accept no responsibility for any such changes.

A catalogue record for this book is available from the British Library.

A catalog record for this book is available from the Library of Congress.

ISBN: HB: 978-1-7845-3711-1
PB: 978-1-3502-4425-2
ePDF: 978-1-7867-3172-2
eBook: 978-1-7867-2172-3

Tauris World Cinema Series

To find out more about our authors and books visit
www.bloomsbury.com and sign up for our newsletters.

Contents

List of Illustrations	ix
Notes on Contributors	xi
Acknowledgements	xiv
Preface: Performing the Impossible in Plain Sight	
B. Ruby Rich	xv

    Introduction   1
    Deborah Martin and Deborah Shaw

I INDUSTRIAL CONTEXTS

  1 Beyond Difference: Female Participation in the Brazilian Film Revival of the 1990s   31
      Lúcia Nagib

  2 Through Female Eyes: Reframing Peru on Screen   48
      Sarah Barrow

  3 *Parando la olla documental*: Women and Contemporary Chilean Documentary Film   70
      Claudia Bossay and María-Paz Peirano

II REPRESENTATIONS

  4 Beyond the Spitfire: Re-visioning Latinas in Sylvia Morales' *A Crushing Love* (2009)   99
      Catherine Leen

  5 Intimacy and Distance – Domestic Servants in Latin American Women's Cinema: *La mujer sin cabeza* and *El niño pez/The Fish Child*   123
      Deborah Shaw

Contents

6 Women's Filmmaking and Comedy in Brazil: Anna Muylaert's *Durval Discos* (2002) and *É Proibido Fumar* (2009)   149
Leslie L. Marsh

7 Young Women at the Margins: Discourses on Exclusion in Two Films by Solveig Hoogesteijn   172
Constanza Burucúa

III KEY AGENTS

8 Re-Framing Mexican Women's Filmmaking: The Case of Marcela Fernández Violante   197
Niamh Thornton

9 Bertha Navarro and the Remapping of Latin American Cinema: Markets, Aesthetics, Cultural Politics   217
Marvin D'Lugo

10 *Planeta ciénaga*: Lucrecia Martel and Contemporary Argentine Women's Filmmaking   241
Deborah Martin

Index   263

Illustrations

1.1 *Terra Estrangeira/Foreign Land* (Walter Salles and Daniela Thomas, 1995). 35

1.2 *Crede-mi/Believe Me* (Bia Lessa and Dany Roland, 1997): a digital revelling in liquid modernity. 38

1.3 The painting 'Pas de deux', which came to existence during the filming of *Crime delicado/Delicate Crime* (Beto Brant, 2006). 46

2.1 Cayetana contemplates her future in *Las malas intenciones* (Rosario García Montero, 2011). 58

3.1 Macarena Aguiló editing *El edificio de los chilenos* (Macarena Aguiló and Susana Foxley, 2012). 85

3.2 Castillo and Aguiló watching the footage in *Calle Santa Fe* (Carmen Castillo, 2007). 85

4.1 Michelle interrupts Sylvia editing the documentary *A Crushing Love* (Sylvia Morales, 2009). 113

4.2 Dolores Huerta and her children at a meeting of the United Farm Workers (still taken from *A Crushing Love*). 115

5.1 Vero's in focus head fills the screen, while the boy looking for work is cast in shadow (*La mujer sin cabeza*, Lucrecia Martel, 2008). 137

5.2 Lala glimpses Mitay Pyra in the lake (*El niño pez*, Lucía Puenzo, 2009). 143

6.1 The carnivalesque scene of the crime(s) in *Durval Discos* (Anna Muylaert, 2002). 163

6.2 The 'Brazilian' wax in *É proibido fumar* (Anna Muylaert, 2009). 168

7.1 Macu's wedding portrait (*Macu, la mujer del policía*, Solveig Hoogesteijn, 1991). 180

List of illustrations

7.2 Maroa looking through a window (*Maroa, una niña de la calle*, Solveig Hoogesteijn, 2006).   185

9.1 Guillermo Del Toro on the set of *Cronos* with Federico Luppi (Guillermo del Toro, 1993).   228

9.2 Bertha Navarro receives the Ariel de Oro as a lifetime achievement award (public domain).   237

10.1 Watery worlds: Amalia (María Alché) in *La niña santa* (Lucrecia Martel, 2004).   250

10.2 Water and queer childhood desire: Jorgelina (Guadalupe Alonso) in *El último verano de la boyita* (Julia Solomonoff, 2009).   255

Notes on Contributors

Sarah Barrow is Head of Film and Media at the University of Lincoln. She has published on Hispanic cinemas in a range of edited collections and journals, including co-editing special issues of *Transnational Cinemas* and *New Cinemas*. She co-edited/authored *50 Key British Films* (Routledge, 2008) and the *Routledge Encyclopaedia of Films* (2014). Her specialist area is Peruvian cinema, policy and identity.

Claudia Bossay is a historian from the Universidad Diego Portales in Chile with a PhD in Film Studies from Queen's University Belfast (QUB). She holds an MA in Interdisciplinary Studies from QUB. She is currently a postdoctoral fellow in the Instituto de la Comunicación e Imagen (ICEI) at the Universidad de Chile. Her research interests lie in the crossroads between cinema and historical representation and Latin American cinema's relationship with its own memory.

Constanza Burucúa is Associate Professor in Film Studies and Hispanic Studies in the Department of Modern Languages and Literatures at the University of Western Ontario (Canada). Her research focuses on Latin American film cultures and she is also committed to the production of documentary films. She has published *Confronting the 'Dirty War' in Argentine Cinema, 1983–1993* (Tamesis, 2009), as well as a number of articles in edited volumes and different journals.

Marvin D'Lugo is Research Professor of Language, Literature and Culture at Clark University (Worcester, Massachusetts, USA). Former editor of *Studies in Spanish and Latin American Cinemas*, he is co-editing the *Routledge Companion to Latin American Cinema*. He is the author of books on Spanish filmmakers Carlos Saura and Pedro Almodóvar and is currently preparing a book on Mexican post-national film auteurs. His articles on Spanish and Latin American film auteurs have appeared in *Film Quarterly*, *Revista*

Notes on Contributors

Canadiense de Estudios Hispánicos, *Revista Iberoamericana* and *Journal of Spanish Cultural Studies*, among others.

Catherine Leen is Head of Spanish and Latin American Studies at the National University of Ireland, Maynooth, Ireland. Her teaching and research interests centre on Mexican and Chicana/o literature and cinema, and Argentine and Paraguayan visual culture and literature. In 2008, she received a Fulbright Scholarship to conduct research at the Chicana/o Studies Center at the University of California, Santa Barbara. Her most recent publication is a volume exploring the relevance of Chicana/o studies outside the United States, entitled *International Perspectives on Chicana/o Culture: 'This World Is My Place'* (co-edited by Dr Niamh Thornton; Routledge 2014). She is currently completing a monograph on Latina/o filmmakers and Mexico.

Leslie L. Marsh is Associate Professor in the Department of World Languages and Cultures and Director of the Center for Latin American and Latino Studies at Georgia State University (Atlanta, Georgia, USA). She specialises in Latin American Film and Media Studies, focusing broadly on questions of citizenship. Among other publications, she is the author of *Brazilian Women's Filmmaking: From Dictatorship to Democracy* (University of Illinois Press, 2012) and co-editor of *The Middle Class in Emerging Societies: Consumers, Lifestyles and Markets* (Routledge, 2016). She is currently working on a project that examines contemporary nation branding and Brazil and a special issue on the BRICS nations for the *International Journal of Communication* with Hongmei Li (Miami University, Ohio, USA).

Lúcia Nagib is Professor of Film and Director of the Centre for Film Aesthetics and Cultures, University of Reading. She is the author of *World Cinema and the Ethics of Realism* (Continuum, 2011), *Brazil on Screen: Cinema Novo, New Cinema, Utopia* (I.B.Tauris, 2007), *Nascido das cinzas: autor e sujeito nos filmes de Oshima* (Edusp, 1995), *O cinema da retomada: depoimentos de 90 cineastas dos anos 90* (Editora 34, 2002), *Em torno da nouvelle vague japonesa* (Editora da Unicamp, 1993) and *Werner Herzog: o cinema como realidade* (Estação Liberdade, 1991). She is the editor of *Impure Cinema: Intermedial and Intercultural Approaches* *to Film* (with Anne Jerslev, I.B.Tauris, 2014), *Theorizing World Cinema* (with Chris Perriam and Rajinder Dudrah, I.B.Tauris, 2011), *Realism and the Audiovisual Media* (with Cecília Mello, Palgrave, 2009) and *The New Brazilian Cinema* (I.B.Tauris, 2003), among others.

María-Paz Peirano is a Social Anthropologist from the Universidad de Chile and has a PhD in Social Anthropology from the University of Kent. She holds postgraduate degrees in both Documentary Film and Film Studies, from the Universidad de Chile and Pontificia Universidad Católica de Chile, respectively. Her research involves an ethnographic approach to film as social practice, focusing on documentary film and the construction of Chilean cinema in transnational settings. She is currently a postdoctoral researcher in Global Interactions at Leiden University.

B. Ruby Rich is a professor at the University of California, Santa Cruz, and Editor of the journal *Film Quarterly*. She is the author of *New Queer Cinema: The Director's Cut* (Duke University Press, 2013) and *Chick Flicks: Theories and Memories of the Feminist Film Movement* (Duke University Press, 1998). Her championing of Latin American women's cinema spans decades, including her work on Cuba's Sara Gómez in the 1970s, her participation in the *Encuentro* of Mexican and Chicana filmmakers in Tijuana in 1990, her writing on Ximena Cuevas's *El corazon sangriente* in the 1990s, and her *New York Times* feature on Lucrecia Martel's debut in 2001. With a long career in film exhibition, journalism and festival curating, she remains committed to discovery and explication as a life practice.

Acknowledgements

We would like to thank all the contributors for their efficiency and willingness to craft their chapters following our suggestions. We would also like to thank Ralph Footring for his eagle-eyed attention to detail, and the staff of I.B. Tauris for their work on and support of the volume, in particular Maddy Hamey-Thomas. Deborah Shaw would like to acknowledge the support of the Faculty of Creative and Cultural Industries at the University of Portsmouth, and to thank Mitch Lomax and Theo Shaw for their support and love. This work was supported by the Spanish Ministry of Economy and Competitiveness under Grant CSO2014-52750-P: 'The transnational relations in Spanish-American digital cinema: the cases of Spain, Mexico and Argentina'. Deborah Martin is grateful for the support of the School of European Languages, Culture and Society at University College London, and thanks Anna Poppa for her love and encouragement.

Preface: Performing the Impossible in Plain Sight

by B. Ruby Rich

My appreciation for this grand collection of texts is framed by an awareness that it is a volume which is an anomaly, simultaneously overdue and premature. It is a brave critical intervention that is at once urgent and only now possible, for this book must perforce stand in for the many volumes on the many films that are missing from screens and shelves because of the long cultural delay in supporting the production of women's filmmaking in Latin America and therefore inevitably postponing the possibility of scholarship on them as well. Happily, thanks to this anthology, the status of these filmmakers may now be declared forever changed.

For the reader who discovers here, for the first time, the world of Latin American women directors and producers, these essays will be a revelation. For this writer, steeped for a lifetime in the worlds of Latin American cinema and the struggles by several generations of women there to make their mark, this volume is a gift. In one generation, Latin American women's cinema has evolved from the singular achievement of isolated films, discovered and viewed only with difficulty, into a mature corpus of work that has created a field of its own. And yet, the history-making women of Latin American cinema remain outsiders to the Latin American and even Anglophone canon, under-recognised and still urgently need of champions. Thanks to this pair of perspicacious editors, Deborah Martin and Deborah Shaw, they finally have them.

1.

First, a bit of background to my relationship to Latin American film culture and Latin women's filmmaking. At the invitation of the Rockefeller Foundation, I spent a week at the Conference on High Culture/Low

Preface: Performing the Impossible in Plain Sight

Culture in Bellagio, Italy, with a group of colleagues that included several founders of the New Latin American cinema movement. Here I presented my ideas on the 'collective subjectivity' and aesthetic reconfigurations that were beginning to reshape the continent's revolutionary cinema in the post-dictatorship era. I had written a broadside on the topic two years earlier for the *Village Voice*, after first fighting my way up the chain of command to the editor to win permission and claim column inches for the never very popular subject of Latin American film, which I insisted was undergoing a historic transformation. At Bellagio, with supportive colleagues, I somehow found the courage to test these ideas on Julio García Espinosa, Nelson Pereira Dos Santos and Tomás Gutiérrez Alea, all seated there at the very same table. It was with tremendous relief that I received their blessing.

The conference year was 1989. Argentina's María Luisa Bemberg had not been invited, nor Brazil's Suzana Amaral, though they had taken the top two awards at Havana's International Festival of New Latin American Cinema three years earlier. María Novaro had just finished her first feature, *Lola*, but would not make the far more widely recognised *Danzón* for another two years; Lúcia Murat was not in Bellagio either, though her *Que bom te ver viva/How Nice To See You Alive* would be released in Brazil the very same year. The great Argentine director Lucrecia Martel, meanwhile, was barely out of film school – she had just made her first short and it would be another six years before her *Rey Muerto* would win the Coral for best short film at the Havana Film Festival, and another six before her brilliant *La cienaga/The Swamp* would burst on the scene.[1]

It is no coincidence that Havana is the common denominator for all these filmmakers: they all appeared there at one time or another, especially in the magical 1980s, when it seemed that all of Latin America held an annual reunion at the film festival every December, some arriving from exile to greet comrades unseen since military coups took over their homelands.

The 'Winds of Change' exhibition in Toronto, organised in the mid-1980s by my friend Helga Stephenson, took stock of the great works of Latin American film and brought a few generations of filmmakers to Toronto, where I got to meet many of them. It catalysed my thinking for 'An/other view of New Latin American cinema', an essay I am delighted to see has informed much of the thinking in this collection. But I had already been immersed in Latin American film and the politics of its circulation. I had travelled to Cuba the first time in 1978 to learn about Cuban film and look for any women who could be found. The feature director Sara Gómez was already dead (1974), but our group was granted a first look at *De cierta manera/One Way or Another*, then just being finished and readied for release.

In a time of hope, I went back again and again. In 1983, I was part of a group that brought *La otra cara*, a programme of US independent film, to the film festival.[2] Film figures from Connie Field to Richard Peña, the late Jacqueline Shearer to J. Hoberman, showed up for the historic event. In 1985, I returned again. I started to meet the women who would make a difference: Bertha Navarro was always in Cuba, making deals and introducing people to each other; I would see her in Mexico City, too. When I went back in 1986, Lita Stantic was there with Julie Christie to premiere Bemberg's *Miss Mary* and Suzana Amaral came with *A hora da estrela/The Hour of the Star*; the two films took first and second prize. That same year, there was a sort of Cuban summit on women in Latin American film; the great Delphine Seyrig, who championed video as a production medium, attended, along with many others. I still recall Delphine's shock at the gender dynamics of the eye candy on view at the award ceremony. Year after year I returned for the festival and reconnected with these women, forging connections that would lead me to Buenos Aires in 1987 and on to Guadalajara in 2002.

There is another event crucial to my thinking about new cinematic directions and sources that must be noted. One year after the Bellagio conference, the landmark 'Cruzando Fronteras: Crossing Borders' conference in Tijuana, Mexico, corrected the gender imbalance and brought together generations. There, on a panel on 'Estética de mujer y sexualidad' (the aesthetics of women and sexuality), I further developed these ideas about a new wave in Latin American cinema, this time in the company of María Novaro, Marcela Fernández Violante and the great elder getting her due, Matilde Landeta. Once again, I had to summon the nerve to deliver new theories of authorship in the presence of those very authors.

2.

Back in 1989–90, many of the filmmakers and films discussed in this volume were not yet present, or if they were they were not yet prominent or even recognised. Some, like Bertha Navarro, were already powerful insiders, producing important new films (today, her daughter Valentina Leduc Navarro is an editor and director). Others were already well known publically; for instance, Lita Stantic was known as the producer of María Luisa Bemberg's films, and eventually for her own, then decisively as the *madrina* of the filmmakers creating a new Argentine cinema. Women working outside of the Mexico–Brazil–Argentina nexus were little known, with the exception, back then, of Venezuela's Fina Torres. Few were able to amass an oeuvre; many were able to produce only one or two films.

My claims for a new kind of cinema, so kindly hailed by this volume's writers and editors, were an attempt to finesse an entrance into the Latin American cinematic pantheon for a distinctive approach that could create a space where women directors' contributions could be recognised and contextualised by a new breed of scholars. I went on to write about the works of María Novaro, Fina Torres, Guita Shyfter, Lucía Puenzo, Lúcia Murat, Lucrecia Martel and the other brilliant filmmakers who emerged in the 1990s and new millennium. But I was able to do so only one by one, as films were released, and sometimes not at all. Even when a film managed to attain a brief release, like Guita Shyfter's *Novia que te vea/Like A Bride*, it would often vanish again. Subsequent changes in viewing formats have made it even more difficult to track much of this work, as films have fallen once again out of circulation. Only writing keeps history alive. Only criticism can create a place for these works in today's memory, today's curricula, today's filmographies.

The women filmmakers in this volume were performing the impossible in plain sight. They should have been hailed as a movement long ago. Now, finally, they can be.

3.

This volume's editors and authors accomplish the hard work of analysis and research to position these works as a field, congruent with its filmic strategies, analysing its hard-won cinematic and digital texts, probing underlying conditions and recognising their implications and consequences. The decision by *Las Déboras* to 'stage post-script encounters between the authors' and thereby 'place their chapters in conversation with each other' is a wonderful one that is well suited to the subject. Indeed, this volume offers a case study for all scholars in how to approach bodies of work without exposing them to either a nationalist or an auteurist reduction. The essays push the emergent regionalist approach in film studies and cultural studies, adapting it to encompass gender as much as genre, with insights that skitter productively across their sites of origin to reflect a larger story and more dynamic argument than previously possible.

Martin and Shaw have prioritised a contextualising and thematic approach in order to bring these writers 'into conversation' with one another, a strategy that recalls for me the function of the New Latin American cinema festivals in Havana in the 1980s. There, films were allowed to escape their national borders, if only momentarily, and come together in a temporary utopia of Martiesque pan-Latin-Americanism. Out of the combustions of that chemistry lab of a film festival, there arose new and bold cinematic approaches, bolstered by a shared vision.

Borrowing Eduardo Coutinho's term 'cinema of conversation', I would argue that this volume has a kindred spirit: it initiates and prolongs a women's conversation that has rarely been recorded in a form suited to that subject. Lucrecia Martel herself has long ascribed her narrative style to a childhood filled with eavesdropping on the conversations of her mother, aunts and grandmother. In that tradition, may this volume inspire a new and renewed recognition of how much women directors and producers have done to create a new expanded Latin American cinema shaped by female experiences – and reconfigured to give as much importance to the home as to the street and as much attention to the subtle signifiers of lives lived under the surface as to the headline-making gestures in the public sphere. With its example, the utopian projects by women across the continent at last have found their critical match.

Notes

1. See my discovery of Martel: Rich (2001).
2. For more on my experiences in Cuba and Latin America, including the fight in 1983 over showing *Word Is Out* in Havana, see Rich (2013). For more on Sara Gómez and Cuba in 1988, see chapter 6 and its prologue in Rich (1998: 85–102).

References

Rich, B. R. (1997). 'An/other view of the New Latin American Cinema', in Michael T. Martin (ed.), *New Latin American Cinema, Vol. 1: Theory, Practices and Transcontinental Articulations*, Detroit: Wayne State University Press, pp. 273-97. Originally published in slightly different form as 'After the revolutions: the second coming of new Latin American cinema', *Village Voice*, 10 February 1987; then revised and published in 1991 as 'An/other view of new Latin American cinema', *Iris*, 13, pp. 5-28.

—— (1998). *Chick Flicks: Theories and Memories of the Feminist Film Movement*, Durham: Duke University Press.

—— (2001). 'Making Argentina matter again: Lucrecia Martel's *La cienaga*', *New York Times*, 30 September.

—— (2013). 'Part IV: Queering a new Latin American cinema', in *New Queer Cinema: The Director's Cut*, Durham: Duke University Press, pp. 139-82.

Introduction

Deborah Martin and Deborah Shaw

Since the early 2000s, Latin American women filmmakers have achieved unprecedented prominence. Films by directors like Lucrecia Martel, Anna Muylaert and Lucía Puenzo have been acclaimed by critics and festival audiences around the world. This volume analyses this phenomenon, while setting it within a context of other – in many cases less celebrated – women working in production and direction across Latin America. Without wishing to arrive at any reductionist characterisation of the politics or poetics of Latin American women's filmmaking, this book recognises the important political impact that women filmmakers have had, and discusses the shift from a public and overt politics to a politics of the personal and the private often found in their work. This shift was identified by B. Ruby Rich in her field-defining essay 'An/other view of the New Latin American Cinema' (1997), a point of reference throughout this introduction and in a number of chapters in the collection. In turn, the volume acknowledges the close relationship between politics and aesthetics which is part of the heritage of Latin American cinema, and discusses ways in which women's filmmaking takes up this aesthetic challenge. Much of the surge in women's filmmaking across the region has been facilitated by new transnational co-production funding landscapes and this is another area of focus for the book.

In a recent book on Mexican women's writing, Nuala Finnegan takes issue with the notion of the 'exhaustion of difference' (Moreiras 2001) in

Latin American cultural studies, arguing that it hints at an 'exhaustion with the "gender question"', and more specifically with women' (2007: 14). Finnegan suggests that the current climate in Latin American cultural studies is not especially conducive to feminist analysis, arguing that:

> one of the reasons why it has become necessary to raise explicitly feminist questions in relation to cultural production in Mexico is that, despite the boom in publishing by women [...] there is a tendency visible in much critical writing on the subject of Latin America to erase [gender] systematically as a separate and distinct category. (Finnegan 2007: 14)

While aware of the dangers of ghettoising women and their work, we believe that – since gender categories are still pervasive in (Latin American) society and culture – there continue to exist important reasons to spotlight the work of women filmmakers. One of these, as the critic Emily Hind puts it in her discussion of Mexican women's writing, is the '*still* unfamiliar landscape that results from eliminating the [...] men' (2010: 7). While not 'eliminating' the men – as, given the collaborative nature of the film industry, women and men generally work alongside each other even in women-led projects – this collection demonstrates that the film historical landscape looks very different when we shift our focus to women's filmmaking.

We are not alone in this endeavour. Focused studies exist on women's filmmaking in individual countries, such as Argentina (Rangil 2005), Mexico (Rashkin 2001; Magallanes-Blanco et al. 2012), Colombia (Goldman 2000; Martin 2012) and Brazil (Marsh 2012; Benamou and Marsh 2013). In addition, an earlier text presents a panorama of exceptional Latin American female filmmakers (Trelles Plazaola 1991), a situation that is fortunately increasingly less exceptional. We build on the work carried out by Gutiérrez-Albilla and Nair (2013) and contributors in their edited collection *Hispanic Lusophone Women Filmmakers: Theory, Practice and Difference*, a book that 'focuses on the aesthetic, theoretical and sociohistorical analyses to question the manifest or latent gender and sexual politics that inform and structure the emerging number of cinematic

Introduction

productions by women filmmakers in Portugal, Spain, Latin America and the US' (back cover). Our volume responds to their view that there remains work to be done within academia and within the industry to address the lack of attention given to women directors (6). In a shift in emphasis, *Latin American Women Filmmakers: Production, Politics, Poetics* has a focus on Latin American cinemas, and provides overviews of different national contexts in Latin America. Our volume also brings together work on more recent and contemporary women's filmmaking, and important emerging currents such as women's documentary filmmaking in Chile.

We will develop throughout this introduction our contribution to this emerging field and our approach, but to summarise here, our aims include telling un(der)told stories and presenting neglected histories of Latin American women's filmmaking. This includes: women's contribution to the Brazilian Retomada; important collaborations between male and female filmmakers; women's contribution to the film cultures of specific countries and communities, such as Argentina, Brazil, Chile, Mexico, Venezuela and US Chicanas; and the legacies and influences on contemporaries and younger generations of key figures in the film cultures under analysis. As our title suggests, in our readings of filmmakers, film texts and film contexts we pay attention to production, politics and poetics.

The introduction presents, broadly chronologically, an alternative history of Latin American cinema: that of women's filmmaking. Through a discussion of key figures, historical milestones, developments and trends in a range of Latin American countries as well as in Chicana film, we establish the context for the chapters that follow. We present an overview of the social, political, economic and technological conditions – both national and transnational – that have enabled filmmaking by these individuals and groups to take place, for example the establishment and development of feminist groups across the region. We then present a discussion of the chapters and their principal themes and approaches, highlighting how they go beyond the idea of the 'exceptional' (director/producer) figure to analyse the broader economic circumstances and aesthetic trends within which the work can be understood. We explain our formulation of political women's filmmaking and locate this within the domestic, in women's engagement with political militancy and in transgressive sexual and gender representations.

An/other history of Latin American cinema

Women have been active in the direction and production of Latin American cinema since the silent era, though their filmmaking has been far from uniformly exhibited and distributed. In the early period, women participated in filmmaking as part of family businesses, making comedies and scenes of everyday life (Benamou 1994: 262), or worked in 'feminine' capacities: in make-up, costume or as 'script-girls'. Women directors or producers in the first decades of the twentieth century were largely limited to the countries where filmmaking was most established: Argentina, Brazil and Mexico. In Argentina, Emilia Saleny directed *La niña del bosque* in 1917 and *El pañuelo de Clarita* in 1919, María V de Celestini directed *Mi derecho* in 1920, and Camila and Hector Quiroga founded Platense Films in 1918. In Mexico, Mimí Derba founded the production company Azteca Films in 1917, and went on to produce several films that year, while the Brazilian Carmen Santos founded the production company Brazil Vita Filme in 1932, and also produced several films.

Saleny, Derba and Santos started their careers as actresses or singers, a career trajectory which has been repeated many times throughout the history of women's participation in Latin American filmmaking. Discussing the Brazilian case, Benamou and Marsh make the (widely applicable) point that: 'film directing in the early industrial era was possible mainly for women who had access to family or conjugal capital, or whose accomplishments as screen actors provided them with the leverage needed to take the helm as producers and directors' (2013: 54).[1] Benamou notes that, of women who took directorial or production roles, 'most were *criollas* or immigrants [...] who, coming from urban bourgeois and aristocratic backgrounds, invested their own capital in the films they produced and directed' (1994: 263).

The progress made on issues of women's rights during the late 1920s, especially the gaining of the right to own property and recognition as autonomous individuals, was 'critical to women's ability to exercise their full powers as producers and partners in the film industry' (Benamou

Introduction

1994: 262). However, as cinema became increasingly industrialised and as the transition to sound was made, the practices and structures of filmmaking shifted, bringing about what Benamou calls the 'masculinization of filmmaking', as organisations became bigger and more hierarchical, and labour more specialised, with greater status attached to the position of director (265). Women now often found themselves excluded from these top positions. With the advent of sound cinema in the 1930s, women's participation was limited to Mexico and Brazil. Mexican actress turned director and producer Adela Sequeyro founded a film cooperative, Carola, in 1937 with her husband, Mario Tenorio. Sequeyro wrote and produced *Más allá de la muerte/Beyond Death* (1935),[2] and produced and directed the melodramas *La mujer de nadie/Nobody's Woman* (1937) and *Diablillos de arrabal/Little Slum Devils* (1938), and also starred in the first two of these. For Elissa Rashkin, Adela Sequeyro's films exist in a complex relationship to femininity, seeking a 'feminine' perspective and film language while at the same time seeking to destroy constructions of femininity that are limiting to women. They 'reflect a fascination with the European cinema and with modes of storytelling reminiscent of the silent screen, infused with an explicitly feminine sensibility' (Rashkin 2001: 34). In Sequeyro's cinematic vision, Rashkin suggests, the nation is absent, even 'a structuring absence' (34). Her work is also read as containing a challenge to gender regimes: *La mujer de nadie* 'stands as a highly singular and unique challenge to the conservative, antimodernist regime of *mexicanidad* that dominated the era' (41). It is 'a film which ridicules the male stereotype and defies feminine gender stereotypes' (42–3).[3]

The other standout female figure of Mexican filmmaking in the mid-twentieth century, whose films continued the feminist challenge to gender representation yet this time within a strongly nationalist cinematic vision, was Matilde Landeta, who made three feature films: *Lola Casanova* (1948), *La negra Angustias* (1949) and *Trotacalles/Streetwalker* (1951). Landeta is a rare example of a woman who managed to work her way up the new hierarchy of filmmaking – over a period of 15 years – starting out as a 'script-girl' and going on to assistant directorial positions before finally directing her first film in 1948 (Benamou 1994: 265). The overriding tendency of Mexican filmmaking in this period is the production of foundational filmic narratives, a well known example of which are the films of

Emilio Fernández. Landeta's work also adheres to foundational themes: as Rashkin writes, it 'is directly and centrally about the construct of national identity and about women's contradictory place [...] within that construct' (Rashkin 2001: 34). As Sequeyros and Landeta show, where women have historically been given the opportunity to make films, their interventions have been effective in disrupting dominant patriarchal national discourses and have helped shape the cultural landscape.

B. Ruby Rich sees *La negra Angustias* as the inception of an alternative history of the New Latin American Cinema. This movement is generally traced to the late 1950s, to Italian neo-realist antecedents and to canonical (male-directed) films 'strongly identified with the reclaiming of the dispossessed and with the portrayal of the sweep of history' (Rich 1997: 281). Alongside these films, Rich's 'revisionist history' of the New Latin American Cinema constructs an alternative canon of films like *La negra Angustias*, the Argentine Fernando Birri's *Los inundados/Flooded Out* (1962) and the Cuban Sara Gómez's *De cierta manera/One Way or Another* (1974, discussed below), films which, unlike the canonical ones, 'share a refusal to attribute "otherness" to subjects formerly marked as such, accompanied by a commitment to the narrative inscription of an "other" selfhood, identity and subjectivity' (280). Rich sees these aspects, along with their turn 'away from the epic toward the chronicle, [... the] shift from "exteriority" to "interiority"' (281), as precursors to the political filmmaking that came later in the century, especially that of women, arguing that with *La negra Angustias*, Landeta 'laid the groundwork for the Latin American women's films of the 1980s, which began to incorporate women's struggles for identity and autonomy as a necessary part of a truly contemporary New Latin American Cinema' (279). This volume traces the shift towards a politics of the interior, the domestic and the everyday lives of women in the more recent work of Latin American women filmmakers.

For Benamou, *La negra Angustias*, as well as Carmen Santos's *A inconfidência Mineira/Rebellion in Minas* (1948), 'represent an attempt by cinematically empowered women to "re-write" the nation from a feminine perspective' (1994: 265).[4] Subsequent to these important incursions in the nation-building discourse, there is an absence of women participating in fiction filmmaking in the 1950s and 1960s (Torres San Martín 2013: 36). Importantly, this is the period in which the new, militant forms of cinema

Introduction

took hold: collectively known as New Latin American Cinema, this was a 'third cinema' (Getino and Solanas 1969), an 'imperfect cinema' (García Espinosa 1976 [1969]), or offered an 'aesthetics of hunger' (Rocha 1982 [1965]). As Rich has noted, it has also been associated primarily with the cinematic outputs of male directors as well as with the writings of male theorists, including those mentioned above. It was also frequently, though not exclusively, a documentary cinema, and although women were active in documentary filmmaking during the 1950s and 1960s (examples include Venezuelan Margot Benacerraf, Colombians Gabriela Samper and Martha Rodríguez, and Cuban Sara Gómez) their films are not usually listed as key texts of the New Latin American Cinema. An exception is Marta Rodríguez's documentary *Chircales/The Brickmakers* (made with husband Jorge Silva, 1965–72) which is understood by critics Zuzana Pick (1993) and Julianne Burton (1986) as integral to that movement. Even so, *Chircales* is not generally cited as one of its major films in the same way as, for example, Getino and Solanas's *La hora de los hornos/The Hour of the Furnaces* (1968), Tomás Gutiérrez Alea's *Memorias del subdesarrollo/Memories of Underdevelopment* (1968) or Patricio Guzmán's *La batalla de Chile/The Battle of Chile* (1975–6).

Chircales' focus on the female members of a brick-making family living in near slavery on the outskirts of Bogotá, and on women's condition and reproductive relations alongside relations of production, suggests a seizing of the contemporary cinematic discourse in order to talk about feminist issues frequently excluded from that discourse. Following Rich's formulation, there is a clear shift in this documentary from the public to the private, exteriority to interiority in terms of its political content and analysis: scenes of elections, combined with social and political analysis of the relations between bosses and workers, give way to the politics of gender as they play out within both the public as well as the domestic setting.[5] If Colombians Rodríguez and Silva worked within the Marxist parameters of the New Latin American Cinema in order to introduce gender debates somewhat covertly, in Brazil, as Benamou and Marsh discuss, women's cinema re-emerged in the 1960s 'in sharp thematic contrast to the first films of the Cinema Nôvo' – instead focusing on 'the doubts and aspirations of young women' (2013: 54–5). Benamou and Marsh argue that, even while they were influenced by the aesthetic of Cinema Novo, women filmmakers in Brazil forged their own political agenda, which often included the undermining of the patriarchal military values of the culture and a focus on the lives of women – albeit mainly urban and well-off ones – and issues of gender (55).

The revolutionary film movement in the 1960s was a predominantly masculine enterprise, but cultural and political changes in the 1970s brought increased activity of women filmmakers, both in documentary and once again in fiction filmmaking. A key figure of women's filmmaking in the period, and one who to an extent bucked the trend of a turn to overtly political and feminist filmmaking among many women filmmakers, was Marcela Fernández Violante, the first Latin American woman with an academic training in cinema (Torres San Martín 2013: 37) and the first Mexican woman to make a feature film since Matilde Landeta's 1951 *Trotacalles*, with her *De todos modos Juan te llamas* (1974; see Niamh Thornton in this volume). Many documentary and fiction filmmakers were, however, now influenced by the growing feminist movement in Latin America (Goldman 2000: 239) and the political charge of the New Latin American Cinema was now being incorporated into feminist filmmaking projects.

In 1974, Cuban director Sara Gómez – who had made several documentaries during the 1960s and early 1970s – made *De cierta manera* (released in 1978 after the director's death), a film which Rich features as part of her alternative history of the New Latin American Cinema (1997: 280–1). It is a film which juxtaposes documentary and fiction sequences in order to expose contradictions based on race, class and gender, as well as to refute 'Revolutionary platitudes' (280). The radical approach of these films, Rich argues, finds its legacy in the far greater participation of women from the late 1970s and into the 1980s – a shift which saw the formation of a number of women's filmmaking collectives and which was also precipitated by the birth of video, as well as by the return to democracy in a number of Latin American countries. In Brazil, Ana Carolina Teixeira Soares made several fiction features during the 1970s and 1980s, each of which showed women challenging the roles they are supposed to occupy in a patriarchal society (Trelles Plazaola 1991: 67) and which critique 'the patriarchal basis of the social formation' (Podalsky 2000: 115). Her films of this period include the documentary *Getúlio Vargas* (1974) and the fiction films *Mar de rosas/Sea of Roses* (1977) and *Das tripas coração/Hearts and Guts* (1982).

Introduction

In 1975 the UN Conference on Women was held in Mexico City and the UN International Decade For Women was inaugurated in 1976. These developments meant that women in Latin America began to take part in discussions at an international level about women's role in society (Goldman 2000: 239). In 1981, Bogotá hosted the Primer Encuentro Feminista Latinoamericano y del Caribe (First Meeting of Latin American and Caribbean Feminists). In the late 1970s and early 1980s several women's filmmaking collectives were formed, the most successful and enduring of these being Cine Mujer, which was founded by Colombians Sara Bright and Eulalia Carrizosa in 1978 with the aim of 'creating counterhegemonic representations of women and of serving the women's movement with audiovisual media' (Goldman 2000: 242). Other groups formed around the same time included Cine Mujer (Mexico), Grupo Miércoles (Venezuela) and Lilith Video (Brazil) but while Cine Mujer Colombia evolved into a successful production and distribution operation and existed until the late 1990s, the others all folded after a few years due to a variety of shifting political and economic circumstances (Goldman 2000: 240).

The growth of these organisations was partly a product of the boom in video in the 1980s and 1990s. As Patricia Aufderheide discusses, the rise in video production by grassroots organisations was a development of the tradition of oppositional media in Latin America (2000: 219). In some Latin American countries, around a third of households owned a video-cassette recorder (VCR) by 1990 (Aufderheide 2000: 219) and there were hundreds of production centres throughout the continent (219). Cine Mujer in Colombia was influenced both by the growing Colombian feminist movement as well as US and European feminism, and avant-garde and political cinema from Europe and Latin America (Goldman 2000: 242). The group produced documentary and fiction, video and film, including health and educational programmes commissioned by the Colombian government, and films featuring interviews with marginal female subjects. Some of the most commented upon include *Carmen Carrascal* (1982) and *La mirada de Myriam* (1986), films which Goldman sees as an effort 'to reclaim and record the lives of ordinary Colombian women whose extraordinary efforts to contribute to their community and to transform their lives demonstrate women's productivity' (2000: 252).[6] This focus on quotidian realities as the key to transforming women's lives is a constant of women's filmmaking in Latin American that is explored in several chapters of this book.

Julia Lesage (1990) examines three modes of production in Latin American women's alternative media in the 1980s. As an example of independently produced women's cinema, Lesage examines a film by the Chilean exile Valeria Sarmiento, *Un hombre cuando es hombre* (1983). This she contrasts with collective forms of production, including feminist media collectives like Cine Mujer, as well as leftist (mixed-sex) production groups like Nicaraguan Taller Popular de Video Timoteo Velásquez, whose videotape *La Dalia* (1982) documents the activity of women revolutionary leaders in Nicaragua. Lesage finds that Cine Mujer's work is marked by the perspective of the middle-class intellectual members of the collective, who facilitate and filter the experiences of working-class women; this she contrasts with the process of the Nicaraguan collective, where she reads the revolutionaries as more successfully representing themselves and, in doing so, challenging the cultural distinctions between the roles of mother and revolutionary leader (1990: 340).

The increase in collective, grassroots and popular filmmaking associated with video and, later, with digital technology has also meant increased participation by indigenous groups in filmmaking. Indeed, indigenous film, video and media have, since the 1980s, been developing all over Latin America as a form of communication, decolonisation and empowerment, and while this is well documented, little scholarship exists on indigenous women who have been involved in film and video production. In the 1980s Teófila Palafox, the first Mexican indigenous woman to be awarded a prestigious grant for work on audiovisual production (Zamorano Villareal 2013: 27), worked with Luis Lupone on two documentary shorts exhibited together, *Tejiendo mar y viento/La vida de una familia Ikood* (1987) which Gabriela Zamorano Villareal argues works to undermine national-hegemonic representations of the Tehuana woman (2013: 27).

Later developments in Mexican indigenous women's filmmaking are documented by Claudia Magallanes-Blanco *et al.* in their work on the video production of Oaxacan indigenous women since 2008 (2012). Itandehui Jansen, who has mixed Dutch and Mixtec parentage, has made films about

Introduction

indigenous villages in Mexico, including *El rebozo de mi madre* (2006), which traces the filmmaker's return to the village in which she was born.

The production of films has remained, though, a largely middle-class activity, disproportionately performed by women of higher social status (which usually means white women), who have often been involved in making films *about* indigenous groups. Two such films which have had some international impact are Priscilla Padilla's *La eterna noche de las doce lunas* (2013),[7] which deals with the Colombian Wayúu people's gendered traditions, and Georgina Barreiro's *Ícaros* (2014), which focuses on the traditional use of Ayahuasca among the Shipibo people of the Peruvian Amazon. Lucrecia Martel's recent fictional short film *Nueva Argirópolis* (2010) turns its lens on indigenous people's resistance to capture and interrogation by the state.[8] While these films are important contributions to Latin American cinema, they do point to issues of under-representation and difficulties faced by indigenous communities, and especially indigenous women, in accessing the means of film production, exhibition and distribution. This middle-class Euro-American take on indigenous female identity can result in accusations of neo-colonial appropriation and exploitation, as has been the case with the Peruvian filmmaking of Claudia Llosa (see Sarah Barrow's chapter in this collection).

To return to a chronological overview of developments in women's filmmaking, in the 1980s there was also an increase in the number of women making commercially successful and internationally recognised fictional feature films. Perhaps the best-known of these is María Luisa Bemberg, another privileged director, but one who used her insider status to critique the upper classes in Argentina. Bemberg's films have been the subject of considerable academic attention.[9] She is among the first women filmmakers in Latin America to achieve sustained directorial activity – making six films between 1981 and 1993. Bemberg's films are known for their transgressive female protagonists, from the eponymous nineteenth-century Argentine socialite in *Camila* (1984)[10] – which received two Oscar nominations – to the seventeenth-century Mexican scholar, poet and nun Sor Juana Inés de la Cruz in *Yo, la peor de todas/I, the Worst of All* (1990). As Patricia White remarks of Bemberg (among others), 'The generation of Latin American women filmmakers who came to international prominence in the 1980s were influenced by second wave feminism in their revisions of national narratives and forms' (2015, 47). In this respect she mentions *Camila*, which uses the true story of Camila O'Gorman's execution by firing squad under nineteenth-century dictator Juan Manuel de Rosas as a means of indicting Argentina's more recent dictatorship. White goes on to argue that 'these directors might be described as deploying what Jean Franco characterises as the "art romance" to connect with popular audiences' (47). Bemberg is also notable for her partnership with the highly successful female Argentine producer Lita Stantic, with whom she made five of her six films. Stantic has had a career spanning over 40 years and can be considered a 'producer-auteur' (Burucúa 2014: 215) who makes socially and politically aware cinema and acts as a trademark or guarantor of quality (215). The all-female partnership of Bemberg and Stantic during the 1970s and 1980s was an outstanding achievement in a male-dominated film industry, and Stantic has more recently become known for her work with notable female directors such as Lucrecia Martel.

Brazilian women's filmmaking in the 1980s was marked by a 'departure from allegorical representation' associated with filmmaking under the dictatorship, and a move 'towards a more explicit discussion of women's positioning in society and politics' (Benamou and Marsh 2013: 61). As in other Southern Cone countries, the return to democracy meant there was an increase in women's filmmaking and this was to an extent supported by the state agency Embrafilme. In 1985, Suzana Amaral, a mother of nine who studied film at New York University, released her first film, the commercially and critically successful *A hora da estrela/The Hour of the Star* – an adaptation of the novel by Clarice Lispector – which went on to win Berlin's Silver Bear in 1987. In Mexico, there were also important developments during this period, not only for Marcela Fernández Violante, who continued making films while production in general was declining, but also in the figure of María Novaro, who, by the end of the 1980s, was making the first of her internationally acclaimed feminist feature films, *Lola* (1989), followed in 1991 by *Danzón*. For Patricia Torres San Martín, Novaro, who participated in the Mexican Cine Mujer, 'belongs to the generation of women filmmakers in the 1970s, who believed in feminism as a political discourse for approaching cinema practice' (2013: 38). *Lola* and Novaro's later *Sin dejar huella/Without a Trace* (2000) both won awards at international film festivals.[11]

Introduction

Meanwhile, in the United States, filmmakers like the Mexican-American Lourdes Portillo were making a significant impact. In 1986 Portillo co-directed, with Susana Muñoz, *Las Madres: The Mothers of the Plaza de Mayo*, which deals with the protests and political resistance of the mothers of those 'disappeared' by the state during Argentina's 1976–82 dictatorship. The film was nominated for an Academy Award for Best Documentary. Portillo went on to make other important films, including, in 2001, *Señorita extraviada/Missing Young Woman*, which deals with the killing of young women of lower socio-economic status in Ciudad Juárez, Mexico. Working across the United States and Latin America, Portillo has been described as having 'a uniquely transnational feminist optic that positions women at the centre of her stories and documents the effects of intersecting regimes of domination and violence on their lives' (Fregoso 2013: 140). Rosa Linda Fregoso, who has published a book on the filmmaker, explicitly links Portillo's work to Rich's redefinition of the New Latin American Cinema discussed above, stating that 'the cinema of Lourdes Portillo challenges our normal assumptions about the nature of political cinema, continually pushing the boundaries of conventional models' (2001: 5). It also challenges us to look past the boundaries of the sub-continent and to include Chicana filmmaking in our discussion, which we do in this collection by including a chapter on the Latina filmmaker Sylvia Morales.

Changing production conditions during the 1990s and 2000s have meant that during this time, and in the second decade of the new millennium, there has been a resurgence of Latin American filmmaking. In Brazilian cinema this was known as the Retomada, and was precipitated in particular by a series of incentives brought in by the administration of Fernando Henrique Cardoso. During the mid-1990s, a number of women directors came onto the Brazilian scene, including Tata Amaral, Daniela Thomas and Sandra Kogut, and there was an increase in the number of films made by women, though, as Benamou and Marsh (2013: 65) note, women remained (and still remain) underrepresented. Throughout Latin America, significant increases in production were precipitated in part by new transnational funding arrangements. In 1997 the Programa Ibermedia was established to foster co-production arrangements between Spain and Ibero-American countries, while organisations connected to film festivals, including the Rotterdam Film Festival's Hubert Bals Fund, the Cannes Film

Festival's Cinéfondation programme and the Berlin Film Festival's World Cinema Fund, have offered new funding streams that have been instrumental in developing filmmaking opportunities across the world, and help to explain the increased visibility of Latin American women filmmakers. In the 2000s and 2010s, prominent female directors who have benefited from international co-production include the Argentines Lucrecia Martel and Lucía Puenzo, the Peruvians Claudia Llosa and Rosario García Montero, the Costa Rican Paz Fábrega, the Paraguayan Paz Encina, the Chilean Dominga Sotomayor, the Colombian Priscilla Padilla and the Mexican Yulene Olaizola, among many others.

Latin American women filmmakers: production, politics, poetics

Following on from the historical background provided above, the 1990s saw the inception of a new period of women's increased participation in Latin American film culture, if not a Golden Age, then a Silver Age, which this volume seeks to capture, thus contributing to its momentum and dissemination. As with all edited volumes, the image we present of this phenomenon corresponds to the specialisms of its contributors. While it covers a wide geographical area, including Argentina, Brazil, Chile, Mexico, Peru, Venezuela and the Hispanic United States, we do not pretend that this is the whole story, and instead hope that others will build on this exploration of Latin American women's filmmaking. Although we are critics of rather than agents for the filmmakers, we conceive of our work as nevertheless existing in tandem with the practitioners by re-centring their work and helping to create a research culture wherein there is serious consideration of their films. As the chapters in this book demonstrate, the landscape is broader than a few key names of award-winning directors suggest. Important though these are, there is a need, also, to go beyond the concept of the exceptional director working against a male-dominated industry.

One aim of this book is, then, to chart the shifting landscape of Latin American cinema through a focus on women filmmakers. While several books have been published that offer a survey of women's filmmaking in Latin America since its inception, or an in-depth study of a particular country or director,[12] this book is the first to offer sustained analysis

Introduction

of the work of Latin American women cineastes which looks at both established figures from the mid- to late twentieth century – including veterans such as Marcela Fernández Violante and producer Bertha Navarro – and directors making films and starting their careers in the 2000s and 2010s. The book is divided into three parts: Industrial Contexts; Representations; and Key Agents. There is, inevitably, some overlap between them, as the contributors to Part I do consider important filmmakers who are part of the national film cultures they are analysing, and industrial context is a consideration in all chapters; the difference is that of emphasis and focus. In Part I, the authors present an overview of the filmmaking cultures in Brazil, Peru and Chile, and present analyses of the conditions that have allowed for the development of women's filmmaking. The chapters in Part II focus on diverse forms of representation illustrated with examples from important female filmmakers. Part III rests on the concept of key agents, and features analyses of pioneering and influential filmmakers who have made a mark on national and transnational circuits.

We have attempted to keep the definition of 'filmmaker' broad, by including a chapter in Part III on renowned and influential producer Bertha Navarro, who has been responsible for so much high-profile Latin American filmmaking. We also consider it important to acknowledge the significant contribution made by Latin American women to the documentary genre throughout its history, and include chapters on the work of Chilean and Chicana documentary filmmakers. We have tended to avoid significant emphasis on established figures who have already received considerable critical attention, such as María Luisa Bemberg, Lourdes Portillo and María Novaro, and instead devote chapters to filmmakers who, like Bertha Navarro, Marcela Fernández Violante and Solveig Hoogesteijn, have achieved sustained activity throughout the late twentieth century and who, each in their own way, are critically neglected pioneers or shapers of the filmmaking scene. There is a strong emphasis in the collection on work which can be read as politically engaged or having transnational reach – for which read low-budget 'art' or 'festival' films – rather than women who are involved in the making of 'mainstream' film. Part of the rationale for this book is the idea that the emergence of a number of high-profile women directors onto the international scene in recent years constitutes a 'moment' (hopefully an ongoing one) in Latin American film which must be both analysed and explored as a new phenomenon, as well as contextualised, where this includes the exploration of antecedents.

The chapters: approaches and arguments

In this section we present an overview of the chapters, however, we have chosen a thematic approach in order to present the story of Latin American women's cinema that has emerged through the writing and editing process, and thus, do not present an overview of each chapter in chronological order. We stage post-script encounters between the authors and aim here to place their chapters in conversation with each other. The concept of the conversation can be applied to the chapter by Lúcia Nagib, 'Beyond Difference: Female Participation in the Brazilian Film Revival of the 1990s', since Nagib's focus is on collaborative working practices between women and men as she considers the cultural factors behind women's increased participation in the Brazilian film industry. Rather than focus on any single director or a few exceptional women, she discusses the phenomenon of shared authorship and highlights directing partnerships between male and female filmmakers. Nagib also considers other female/male partnerships, for instance the relationship between actresses and directors, a (female) director and (male) sound engineer, and (male) directors and (female) producers, and draws attention to the usually neglected female editors in the Retomada. For Nagib, to attempt to isolate and define women's filmmaking is limiting and essentialist when collaboration is intrinsic to the creative processes of feature films, documentaries and television productions. This is part of her project to de-essentialise our understanding of filmmaking and to conceptualise gender and culture in a way that goes 'beyond difference'.

In Chapter 3 Claudia Bossay and María-Paz Peirano also recognise working partnerships between female and male filmmakers, and go beyond the figure of the director in their assessment of the current state of documentary filmmaking in Chile. In their chapter, '"*Parando la olla documental*": Women and Contemporary Chilean Documentary Film', the authors' focus is on women's involvement in Chilean documentaries following the dismantling of Augusto Pinochet's dictatorship and the country's return

Introduction

to democracy from 1989. Their chapter tells the story of professional networks that have developed among documentary filmmakers, and considers their roles not just as directors, but also as producers, technicians and mentors to future generations. This work is seen to bear fruit in the 2000s with a range of new films directed and produced by women in numbers never before seen in the country. The chapter outlines both advances with changes in cultural legislation to promote documentary filmmaking and the precarious nature of the work of women filmmakers due to financial challenges. While women are not working in isolation from their male colleagues, they have led important initiatives that have helped to foster Chilean film culture. This overview from two academics working in Chile maps exciting new developments in women's filmmaking in their country.

In Chapter 2, 'Through Female Eyes: Reframing Peru on Screen', Sarah Barrow writes on a new generation of female filmmakers from Peru, and she, like Nagib, and Bossay and Peirano, avoids the 'exceptional woman' approach. Like their Chilean counterparts, the directors who form the case studies share a number of elements that have allowed them to emerge in a country with scarce resources for filmmakers: they are well-educated, they have effective international links and networks, and they are well-informed about foreign (largely European) funding schemes. Claudia Llosa is the best-known Peruvian filmmaker in international circles following the successes on art cinema circuits of *Madeinusa* (2006) and *La teta asustada/The Milk of Sorrow* (2009). Yet, while acknowledging her influence on Peruvian culture, the chapter does not focus on Llosa exclusively. Instead, Barrow notes the 'Llosa effect': the demonstrating to Peruvian women filmmakers that it is possible to make award-winning festival films that can go on to secure international releases. In addition, she traces the national and transnational factors that have enabled more opportunities for women. Barrow discusses the fiction and documentary filmmaking of Marianne Eyde and her exploration of controversial themes in films set during the period of the Shining Path conflict, and the woman-centred feature films of Rosario García-Montero. Nonetheless, while celebrating the new visibility of filmmakers, she makes the important point that the high-profile women directors to date are from wealthy families and have had opportunities to study in Europe or the United States, a continuation from the early days of filmmaking when only bourgeois or aristocratic women had access to the industry. As Barrow notes, 'it is [...] clear that some kind of strategy needs to be put in place at national level to extend and enhance the range of diversities within and across Peruvian cinema for those who wish to direct' (63).

Deborah Martin takes a similar approach in her analysis of contemporary Argentine women's filmmaking, noting the influence of María Luisa Bemberg on Lucrecia Martel, and then tracing the 'Martel effect' on directors who are influenced by Martel's film language, but also by her success on a global art cinema stage. Like others in this volume, Martin's chapter thus places an individual filmmaker within the context of a wider film culture. This approach is also particularly apparent in Marvin D'Lugo's work on Bertha Navarro, who has contributed enormously to internationalising Mexican film culture throughout her long career. D'Lugo does not attempt to isolate women's filmmaking; rather, he places Navarro at the centre of what was a male-dominated film industry, and demonstrates the ways in which she shaped cultural production through her work with generations of some of the most successful directors. Familiar with the workings of international film festivals and film funding bodies, Navarro guided and mentored important Mexican directors to create a transnational cinema and to take their films to a global stage. Rather than remove auteurist credit from her stable of mainly male directors, D'Lugo extends the concept of auteurism to Navarro herself by applying Walter Benjamin's concept of the producer as author, and by tracing thematic and aesthetic patterns across her corpus. These include border-crossings and 'a borderless visual style' (227) seen in her model of hybrid (commercial/genre/art house) films with transnational appeal.[13]

D'Lugo's contextualisation of Navarro is echoed by Niamh Thornton in her chapter 'Re-framing Mexican Women's Filmmaking: The Case of Marcela Fernández Violante'. Thornton argues that this important filmmaker is an anomaly whose work does not fit within the generation of filmmakers who came to the fore in the 1970s, or that of more mainstream directors working within the studio system. However, for Thornton, neither can she be considered alongside younger emerging feminist filmmakers of the 1980s. As a result of this, Fernández Violante has been neglected in histories of Mexican cinema. Yet she is no lone vixen and is deeply entrenched within this history as an early graduate of the Mexican film

Introduction

school, the Centro Universitario de Estudios Cinematográficos (CUEC), and its director from 1984 to 1988, as well as a director of eight feature films produced between 1976 and 2002. Rather than attempting to shoehorn Fernández Violante into a generation, movement or fixed ideological position, Thornton embraces this in-between status, while highlighting her contribution to Mexican film culture and recuperating her position within it.

Another key concern that recurs through the chapters is the redefinition of the political. As discussed above, a central approach in this project is to rethink the idea of Latin American political filmmaking as a masculine enterprise. Latin American film has been inextricably linked with politics and has been frequently used as a vehicle to share knowledge about turbulent periods of history with audiences around the world. Yet the process of canon formation reveals a male-dominated vision of these historical-political landmarks, with a frequent focus on examples of New Latin American Cinema films directed by men portraying the revolutionary forces sweeping across the region through the 1960s and early 1970s, as well as post-dictatorship films that reflect on repressive regimes, and more contemporary genre-inflected films that address socio-political issues. We share Rich's view that an alternative history of the New Latin American Cinema is required and argue with her that this needs to extend beyond the 1960s and 1970s. We aim to reinsert women into the story of Latin American political filmmaking, with canon reconfiguration understood as a political act. This requires a feminist reconsideration of the political, an approach taken by a number of the contributors to this book. Rich's argument about the shift to an individual and interior focus in Latin American women's cinema is extremely apposite to the work of more recent women filmmakers from Latin America: as Rich puts it, 'In today's New Latin American Cinema the old phrase "the personal is political" can almost be heard murmuring below the surface. Its expression however is not a privatized one at all but very much social, political, public' (1997: 281). She goes on to add that 'interiority is not a retreat from society, but an altered formal engagement' (284).

This politics of interiority is core to the readings of a number of the case studies in this collection. Sarah Barrow writes that *Las malas intenciones/ Bad intentions* (García Montero, 2011), 'renders private citizens as political subjects and centres the political within intimate spaces' (p. X), while Deborah Shaw also follows this line of argument in her chapter 'Intimacy and Distance – Domestic Servants in Latin American Women's Cinema: *La mujer sin cabeza* and *El niño pez*'. For Shaw, an exploration of the servant/employer dynamic as treated in a new genre of recent films across Latin America reveals the political heart of nations and deep structural inequalities. As she argues, 'the domestic server/served pairing is unique for the ways in which it allows for the probing of cross-class and ethnic relations in an intimate setting, and for the way it dramatises personal affective relationships' (128). These films focus on everyday interactions between women of distinct classes, and place the servants who are often invisible or marginal into the centre of the cinematic frame, suggesting that any shift in power structures must begin with them. In a close reading of *La mujer sin cabeza*, Shaw examines the social status quo maintained through an internalised segregation between the classes and illustrated in the treatment of the servant class. Her reading of *El niño pez* focuses on the potential for radical social change through a passionate love story and a utopian fantasy shared between two young women, one a servant and the other the daughter of her employer.

In her chapter 'Young Women at the Margins: Discourses on Exclusion in Two Films by Solveig Hoogesteijn', Constanza Burucúa applies Rich's framework in her reading of Solveig Hoogesteijn's films *Macu, la mujer del policía/Macu, The Policeman's Woman* (1987) and *Maroa, una niña de la calle/Maroa* (2006). Burucúa locates the political in these films' challenge to conservative attitudes in Venezuela and their look inwards to the social dynamics of patriarchal institutions of family and marriage, as well as in their connection of the power relations within these institutions to constructions of Venezuelan national identity. The author reads Hoogesteijn in the context of post-1968 politically committed cinema and compares her work to that of Venezuelan and other prominent Latin American women filmmakers in their commitment to foregrounding women's issues and challenging patriarchal oppression. Her chapter engages strongly with the poetics of feminist filmmaking, specifically with relationships between cinematic devices and female subjectivity.

Introduction

The films considered in this book, thus, produce a more comprehensive meaning of the political than that reserved for public realms of popular protest and state control. In her chapter, 'Beyond the Spitfire: Re-visioning Latinas in Sylvia Morales' *A Crushing Love* (2009)', Catherine Leen documents Latina and Chicana feminist challenges to a male-dominated community politics that has reinforced gender oppression through an exclusive focus on class and ethnic oppression. Leen traces the development of Chicana feminist studies through a focus on theorists such as Cherríe Moraga and Gloria Anzaldúa, and the application of non-Eurocentric theoretical frameworks sensitive to Chicana culture. These and other theorists are engaged in political acts of writing against historical erasure and discrimination, patriarchal Chicano political leadership, and forms of liberal feminism that fail to recognise race and class.

After considering shifting patterns in the stereotyping of Latinas and Chicanas, Leen concentrates her analysis on the documentary *A Crushing Love: Chicanas, Motherhood and Activism* (2009) by Sylvia Morales. This is a film that focuses on motherhood and domestic chores as privileged sites of political feminist debate that are often ignored by masculinist leftist circles. Through interviews with Chicana activists and mothers, and an exploration of the director's own difficulties balancing her work with raising her daughter, *A Crushing Love* examines the way that the public sphere of women's political work comes into conflict with domestic demands, and the tensions between activism and motherhood. Leen, through Morales, highlights the complexities of motherhood for women who rewrite the myth of the sacrificial mother through their activism, but who have real struggles in combining their political work with raising their children, tensions that have wide resonance beyond the specific circumstances addressed by Leen's chapter.

Leen's chapter establishes a dialogue with Claudia Bossay and María-Paz Peirano's exploration of cross-generational tensions between mothers and daughters in Chilean women's filmmaking. They also focus on documentary films that examine what it means to be a militant mother fighting for the rights of the next generation, while not being able to be present for their own children. Both chapters develop sophisticated visions of the political dimensions of motherhood in terms of both militancy and domesticity. Filmmaking that focuses on domestic chores, day-to-day interactions between domestic servants and families, and mothers and daughters raised in political struggles inserts both a new politics and a new realism into Latin American filmmaking in which everyday dramas, past and present, acquire new resonances.

That is not to say that women are not represented as active in more traditional understandings of public and social enactments of political militancy. Leen and Bossay and Peirano's focus is on female agents of political activism in Chicana culture and in Chilean leftist circles respectively. Constanza Burucúa chronicles the ways in which women in Venezuela were also integral to politically committed documentary filmmaking that was becoming a privileged artistic site throughout Latin America. She writes on Cine Urgente, a filmmaking collective active between 1968 to 1973 that was run by three socialist-feminist women, Josefina Acevedo, Franca Donda and Josefina Jordán. Burucúa argues that Solveig Hoogesteijn, while not a member of this collective, was influenced by the political climate of the generation of 1968, and her fictional feature films share Cine Urgente's concern with social justice.

Sarah Barrow also demonstrates the way Peruvian female filmic characters are engaged in the violent political times of the wars between government forces and the Maoist guerrilla organisation group Sendero Luminoso/Shining Path in the 1980s. While Barrow demonstrates the personal and subjective/imaginative effects of these political conflicts on a young girl in her reading of *Las malas intenciones*, she also turns her attention to representations of violence and female participation in that violence. Barrow highlights the controversies generated in Peru by Marianne Eyde's film *La vida es una sola/You Only Live Once* (1993) for featuring a female central character who is a member of Sendero Luminoso. While the conflict in Peru awakened the political identities for Eyde's characters, Barrow demonstrates the limits placed on them by their creator and their contexts, as they, through patriarchal social codes and melodramatic cinematic modes, are punished for their transgressions, whilst their actions fail to achieve their transformative potential.

Such transformations and transgressions are often precipitated by desire, an area explored by Deborah Shaw and Deborah Martin in their chapters. Both Shaw (as seen above) and Martin focus on desire as a force which effects social change, and thus acts as a further site of the political.

Introduction

Martin argues that Lucrecia Martel's films demonstrate 'possibilities of rupture and escape' (246) through her cinematic recreations of rebellious young girls' forbidden desires. She notes that, despite the fact that these films depict in detail structures of social and political oppression, desire acts as an uncontrollable and multiple force which can overcome these structures, and which is echoed by the films' diffuse narrative structures. Martin reads Argentine women's cinema through the ethical framework of third-wave feminism, for which gender cannot be separated from other forms of oppression, including those based around sexuality, ethnicity and disability. She notes the ways that films by a new generation of women, including Julia Solomonoff and Lucía Puenzo, explore structural links between these different forms of oppression. Martin also argues that Martel's aesthetic innovation with sound and haptic aesthetics has led to an emphasis in recent Argentine films by women on aquatic imagery and watery locales, wet, damp or swampy images that emphasise the varied associations of touch and wetness. Martin proposes that – in Martel as well as in films by Albertina Carri and Solomonoff – such images are used to create an embodied response in the spectator, a poetics of film which has strong political relevance in the sense of its destabilisation of the spectator's traditional subjectivity, which is shored up by conventional cinematic languages.

There is, of course, no single approach in the creation of political cinema, and the filmmakers who provide case studies in this book have employed *cinema verité* documentary forms, and the languages of poetic and popular art cinema. In Leslie Marsh's chapter, 'Women's Filmmaking and Comedy in Brazil: Anna Muylaert's *Durval discos* (2002) and *É proibido fumar* (2009)', poetics again come to the fore, as Marsh examines Muylaert's use of dark comedy and reworking of tropes of romantic comedy and argues that these are used to produce a socio-political critique of gender relations in contemporary urban Brazil. Muylaert is a prolific director whose corpus includes short and made-for-television films, and four feature-length films, and she is coming to international prominence following her 2015 award-winning and Oscar-nominated *Que horas ela volta?/The Second Mother*. This chapter also focuses on the politics of the intimate, as Marsh argues that Muylaert casts a critical eye on everyday and domestic spaces and the gender and class relations that occur within them to present her vision. Through her analysis of *Durval discos* and *É proibido fumar*, Marsh demonstrates the use the director makes of dark comedy to deconstruct postfeminist heteronormative romantic idealisations, and also explode the myth that gender equality has been achieved in contemporary Brazil. Marsh writes, 'both films motivate a shift in expectations for contemporary affective relationships and examine the social and economic pressures that shape contemporary forms of masculinity and femininity in Brazil' (150).

In a continued focus on the poetics of filmmaking, and specifically the political import of these, Lúcia Nagib seeks to move beyond difference and beyond representational strategies in her assessment of women's contribution to filmmaking. Nagib applies Rancière's concept of the non-didactic aesthetic regime he terms dissensus, 'which, rather than giving univocal lessons, multiplies the meanings of the referent' (32). Here the political is found paradoxically by refusing to fix single transparent political meanings and identities on women, and by allowing them to speak for themselves and to reveal multiple and complex identities. Nagib provides the example of Eduardo Coutinho's documentary *O fim e o princípio* (2005), which gives voice to poor village women in the Brazilian north-east. Here the women become collective authors through testimonies of their everyday lives, without the director framing these lives within coherent discourses of class or gender oppression, as would be preferred in the representational approach of what Nagib calls 'thesis films'. As seen above, Nagib rejects a segregated approach and separates feminist and political engagement from the gender of the filmmakers in her aim to go 'beyond difference'. She juxtaposes the filmmaking of Eduardo Coutinho with that of Lúcia Murat, recognising equally their political feminist credentials. In her account of the Retomada period of Brazilian filmmaking, Nagib writes, 'I would go as far as asserting that the greatest achievement, by both men and women, in the Retomada utopian days was the move towards blurring the boundaries between genres, classes and ethnic determinants, as much as between genders' (36).

This utopian position outlined by Nagib in the first chapter of this book is a positive note on which to conclude our introduction. Filmmakers create worlds that reflect upon the gendered, class and ethnic borders that separate us. Many of the directors and producers, as well as the characters discussed in this book, are transgressors who have defied these borders. The book itself is also part of this process and seeks to disrupt the story that has been told about Latin American cinema, shifting the lens to women filmmakers to investigate the stories that may be un(der)told in relation to that cinema. We suggest that a highlighting of women's production, such as is undertaken here and throughout the book, changes the critical histories and landscapes of Latin American cinema. There is, then, a need to retell the story of Latin American cinema from a feminine/female perspective, but there is also a pressing need to respond critically to the constellation of contemporary circumstances – changes to the financial and political forces shaping film as well as shifting trends in film aesthetics – which have propelled women forward and which have created a cultural moment that *Latin American Women Filmmakers: Production, Politics, Poetics* aims to capture.

Notes

1. A useful resource on women's participation in early Latin American filmmaking is Joanne Hershfeld and Patricia Torres San Martín's 'Writing the history of Latin American women working in the silent film industry'. Available at https://wfpp.cdrs.columbia.edu/essay/writing-the-history-of-latin-american-women-working-in-the-silent-film-industry (accessed 16 November 2015). The site also deals with some early sound cinema.
2. We have included translations of film titles only where the film received an English language distribution.
3. On Adela Sequeyro, see also Eduardo de la Vega and Patricia Torres San Martín (2000).
4. On Carmen Santos, see also Ana Pessoa (2002).
5. For a fuller elaboration of this argument, see Deborah Martin (2012: 147–61).
6. On Cine Mujer, see also Lesage (1990: 328–35) and Martin (2012: 162–73).
7. On this film, see Randall (2014).
8. On this film, see Martin (2016).
9. See King and Whitaker (2000) and Rufinelli (2002).
10. This film is discussed in Chapter 10.
11. The earlier films of Novaro, as well as other important Mexican women directors of the late twentieth century are analysed by Elissa Rashkin (2001).
12. Surveys of Latin American women filmmakers include those by Trelles Plazaola (1991) and Torres San Martín (2002). Country-based studies include those by Rangil (2005) and Martin (2012).

13. Catherine Grant (2013) also considers the vital role of the producer, in the case of the towering Argentinean figure of Lita Stantic in her presentation for the symposium 'Latin American Women Filmmakers on the Global Stage' in May 2013 at the University of Portsmouth. This symposium was the genesis to this edited collection. Grant has published her paper, 'Lita Stantic: personalidad Destacada/Outstanding Personality'. On the Cultural Salience of an Argentine female film producer', on academia.edu (Grant, 2015), to coincide with the final process of the writing of our book, and allowed us to credit it as a companion piece to the chapters.

References

Aufderheide, Patricia (2000). 'Grassroots video in Latin America', in Chon A. Noriega (ed.), *Visible Nations: Latin American Cinema and Video*, Minneapolis: University of Minnesota Press, pp. 219–38.

Benamou, Catherine (1994). 'Notes towards a memography of Latin American women's cinema', *Symposium: A Quarterly Journal in Modern Literatures*, 48.4, pp. 257–69.

—— and Leslie Marsh (2013). 'Women filmmakers and citizenship in Brazil, from *Bossa Nova* to the *retomada*', in Julián Gutiérrez-Albilla and Parvati Nair (eds), *Hispanic and Lusophone Women Filmmakers: Theory, Practice and Difference*, Manchester: Manchester University Press, pp. 54–71.

Burton, Julianne (1986). 'Jorge Silva and Marta Rodríguez: cine-sociology and social change', in *Cinema and Social Change in Latin America*, Austin: University of Texas Press, pp. 25–34.

Burucúa, Constanza (2014). 'Lita Stantic: auteur producer/producer of auteurs', in Andrew Spicer, Anthony McKenna and Christopher Meir (eds), *Beyond the Bottom Line: The Producer in Film and Television Studies*, New York: Bloomsbury, pp. 215–28.

De la Vega, Eduardo and Patricia Torres San Martín (2000). *Adela Sequeyro*, Guadalajara: Universidad de Guadalajara.

Finnegan, Nuala (2007). *Ambivalence, Modernity, Power: Women and Writing in Mexico Since 1980*, Bern: Peter Lang.

Fregoso, Rosa Linda (2001). *Lourdes Portillo: The Devil Never Sleeps and Other Films*, Austin: University of Texas Press.

—— (2013). 'The "poetics of transformation" in the works of Lourdes Portillo', in Julián Gutiérrez-Albilla and Parvati Nair (eds), *Hispanic and Lusophone Women Filmmakers: Theory, Practice and Difference*, Manchester: Manchester University Press, pp. 140–51.

García Espinosa, Julio (1976) [1969]. *Por un cine imperfecto*, Madrid: Castellote.

Getino, Octavio and Fernando Solanas (1969). 'Hacia un tercer cine', *Tricontinental*, 14, pp.107–32.

Introduction

Grant, Catherine (2015). 'Lita Stantic: personalidad Destacada/Outstanding Personality'. On the Cultural Salience of an Argentine female film producer'. Available at https://www.academia.edu/17510702/_Lita_Stantic_ Personalidad_Destacada_Outstanding_Personality_._On_the_Cultural_ Salience_of_an_Argentine_Female_Film_Producer (accessed 1 June 2016).

Goldman, Ilene S. (2000). 'Latin American women's alternative film and video: the case of Cine Mujer, Colombia', in Chon A. Noriega (ed.), *Visible Nations: Latin American Cinema and Video*, Minneapolis: University of Minnesota Press, pp. 239–62.

Gutiérrez-Albilla, Julián and Parvati Nair (eds) (2013). *Hispanic and Lusophone Women Filmmakers: Theory, Practice and Difference*, Manchester: Manchester University Press.

Hind, Emily (2010). *Femmenism and the Mexican Woman Intellectual from Sor Juana to Poniatowska: Boob Lit*, New York: Palgrave.

King, John and Sheila Whitaker (eds) (2000). *An Argentine Passion: María Luisa Bemberg and Her Films*, London: Verso.

Lesage, Julia (1990). 'Women make media: three modes of production', in Julianne Burton (ed.), *The Social Documentary in Latin America*, Pittsburgh: University of Pittsburgh Press, pp. 315–47.

Magallanes-Blanco, Claudia, *et al.* (2012). 'Mujeres detrás de las cámaras: el proceso de empoderamiento de mujeres indígenas Mixe', in Mario Iván Patiño Rodríguez Malpica, Marcela Ibarra Mateos and Francisco Javier Sentíes Laborde (eds), *Los Rostros de la Pobreza. El debate*, vol. VI, León, Guanajuato: Sistema Universitario Jesuita, pp. 143–64.

Marsh, Leslie L. (2012). *Brazilian Women's Filmmaking: From Dictatorship to Democracy*, Urbana: University of Illinois Press.

Martin, Deborah (2012). *Of Border Guards, Nomads and Women: Painting, Literature and Film in Colombian Feminine Culture, 1940–2005*, Woodbridge: Tamesis.

—— (2016). 'Lucrecia Martel's *Nueva Argirópolis*: Rivers, Rumours and Resistance'. *Journal of Latin American Cultural Studies*, 25.3, pp. 449–65.

Moreiras, Alberto (2001). *The Exhaustion of Difference: The Politics of Latin American Cultural Studies*, Durham: Duke University Press.

Pessoa, Ana (2002). *Carmen Santos: o cinema dos anos 20*, Rio de Janeiro: Aeroplano Editora.

Pick, Zuzana (1993). 'The discovery of self and other: *The Brickmakers*', in *The New Latin American Cinema: A Continental Project*, Austin: University of Texas Press, pp. 41–7.

Podalsky, Laura (2000). 'Fulfilling fantasies, diverting pleasures: Ana Carolina and *Das Tripas Coração*', in Chon A. Noriega (ed.), *Visible Nations: Latin American Cinema and Video*, Minneapolis: University of Minnesota Press, pp. 115–29.

Randall, Rachel (2014). 'Agency, performance and social recognition in Priscilla Padilla's *La eterna noche de las doce lunas*', in Carolina Rocha and Georgia

Seminet (eds), *Screening Minors in Latin American Cinema*, Langham: Lexington Books, pp. 179–94.

Rangil, Viviana (2005). *Otro punto de vista: mujer y cine en la Argentina*, Rosario: Beatriz Viterbo Editora.

Rashkin, Elissa (2001). *Women Filmmakers in Mexico: The Country of Which We Dream*, Austin: University of Texas Press.

Rich, B. Ruby (1997). 'An/other view of the New Latin American Cinema', in Michael T. Martin (ed.), *New Latin American Cinema, Vol. 1: Theory, Practices and Transcontinental Articulations*, Detroit: Wayne State University Press, pp. 273–97.

Rocha, Glauber (1982). 'An esthetic of hunger', in Robert Stam and Randal Johnson (eds), *Brazilian Cinema*, East Brunswick: Associated University Presses, pp. 68–71.

Rufinelli, Jorge (2002). 'María Luisa Bemberg y el principio de la transgresión', *Revista Canadiense de Estudios Hispánicos*, 27.1, pp. 15–44.

Torres San Martín, Patricia (2002). *Mujeres y cine en América latina*, Guadalajara: Universidad de Guadalajara.

—— (2013). 'Lost and invisible: a history of Latin American women filmmakers', in Julián Gutiérrez-Albilla and Parvati Nair (eds), *Hispanic and Lusophone Women Filmmakers: Theory, Practice and Difference*, Manchester: Manchester University Press, pp. 30–41.

Trelles Plazaola, Luis (1991). *Cine y mujer en América latina: Directoras de largometrajes de ficción*, Río Piedras: Editorial de la Universidad de Puerto Rico.

White, Patricia (2015). *Women's Cinema, World Cinema: Projecting Contemporary Feminisms*, Durham: Duke University Press.

Zamorano Villarreal, Gabriela (2013). 'Entre Didjazá y la Zandunga: iconografía y autorrepresentación indígena de las mujeres del Istmo de Tehuantepec, Oaxaca', *Limina R. Estudios sociales y humanísticos*, 3.2, pp. 21–33.

I

Industrial Contexts

1

Beyond Difference: Female Participation in the Brazilian Film Revival of the 1990s

Lúcia Nagib[1]

E. Ann Kaplan once defined the common denominator of writings in feminist film theory as follows:

> A central set of concepts worked and reworked by scholars is that of *difference*: in the early days, it is male/female sexual difference; later on gay/straight difference – that is, the differences *within* female sexuality; still later the difference of 'gender' (as distinct from 'sexuality'); and finally, differences between women produced by race and ethnicity. (Kaplan 2000: v)

What interests me in Kaplan's approach is her acknowledgement that the current task of film theory is to learn 'how to move beyond difference' by imagining 'new modes of being' (vi). Focusing on the female participation in what became known as the Retomada do Cinema Brasileiro, or the Brazilian Film Revival, of the 1990s, I will read Kaplan's suggestion as an invitation to think beyond differences of gender, class, age and ethnicity. To that end, I will first reconsider the Retomada phenomenon against the backdrop of its historical time, so as to evaluate whether the production boom of the period translated into a creative peak and, if so, how much of this has carried on to the present day. I will then look at the female participation in this phenomenon, but not only in terms of the numerical growth in female directors – admittedly impressive – enabled by the new film funding schemes introduced in the country in the mid-1990s. I will argue that the most decisive contribution brought about by the rise of women in Brazilian filmmaking has been the spread of teamwork and shared authorship, as opposed to a mere aspiration to the auteur pantheon, as determined by a notoriously male-oriented tradition. Granted, films focusing on female victimisation, directed by both men and women, were rife during the Retomada period and persist to this day, and they have been, and continue to be, invaluable for the understanding of women's struggles in the country. However, rather than resorting to feminist readings of representational strategies in these films, I will draw attention to the female contribution, behind and in front of the camera, and to other, presentational aesthetic experiments bordering on the documentary and open to the unpredictable real, which, I argue, suspend the pedagogical character of representational narratives. This they do by introducing a dilemma, or 'dissensus' in Rancière's terms (2010), which, rather than giving univocal lessons, multiplies the meanings of the referent.

The Retomada and the rise of shared authorship

As I have explained in detail in two books devoted to the theme (Nagib 2002, 2007), the Retomada *senso strictu* refers to the period between 1995 and 1998, when the flow of film production was re-established in Brazil, after being disrupted by the short-lived Collor government between 1990 and 1992. This was achieved thanks mainly to the Rescue Award (or Prêmio Resgate do Cinema Brasileiro), which redistributed the assets of Embrafilme, the governmental film production company shut down by Collor, creating the impression of a boom thanks to the bottleneck generated in the previous years. This did not, however, detract from the real creative boom which accompanied the cinematic revival, in tune with the atmosphere of political liberation after 20 years of military dictatorship. Its most notable characteristic was the drive to rediscover Brazil, in particular its dry, impoverished backlands in the north-east, the *sertão*, once the iconic political arena of Cinema Novo. The Brazilian *sertão* was insistently revisited by filmmakers, not anymore as a call for rebellion against class injustice, but as a euphoric reunion with the culturally rich heart of the country. This process climaxes with *Central do Brasil/Central Station* (Walter Salles), the 1998 Berlin Festival winner held as the epitome of the Retomada movement. As I have elsewhere described, the ascending utopian curve that characterises this phase experiences a rapid downturn after *Central do Brasil*, with films migrating to the southern urban territories of crime and poverty, the Brazilian favelas of São Paulo and Rio, as exemplified by *O invasor/The Trespasser* (Beto Brant, 2001) and *Cidade de Deus/City of God* (Fernando Meirelles and Kátia Lund, 2002), which in my view bring the Retomada to a close. This creative apex, of course, is now gone, although in many ways the sense of a boom still persists, with Brazil's annual film production ranging between 70 and 100 titles. This is, however, a commercial rather than a creative phenomenon, on a par with Brazil's extraordinary economic growth at that time, which was compounded by the increasing participation of the Globo TV network and the American majors in film production and distribution in the country.

It is to the initial creative boom, symbolised by the short Retomada period, that the rise of women to film directing should be connected, and not to the more recent commercial one. This can be easily proven, in numerical terms, by the fact that among 90 filmmakers active between 1994 and 1998, 17 were female, that is, nearly 19 per cent, a significant rise compared with the less than 4 per cent female presence in the pre-Collor years. However, such an auspicious growth tendency lost its momentum in the following years, showing a slight but steady downturn: in 2010, out of 76 feature films released 14 were directed by women, that is, around 18 per cent, and by 2015 this percentage was down to 16 per cent, when out of 132 films released 21 were directed by women. But this is where we need to posit the question of what the terms 'director' or 'filmmaker' actually mean and whether it would be productive to identify them with the author or *auteur* of a particular film.

Visionary as always, Noël Burch, as early as 1993, had denounced cinephilia, as practised by the young Cahiers du Cinéma critics in their *politique des auteurs*, as an 'essentially masculine passion' (Burch 1993: 8). Ten years later, Angela Martin returned to the theme, stating that ' "auteurism" as we call it in English has nothing to do with women's filmmaking' because 'the *Nouvelle Vague*'s call for a personal self-expression is very different from the later feminist call for the personal to be political rather than ego-centric' (Martin 2008: 128–9). She continued:

> While we used to talk in terms of whether there was a feminist aesthetic or a woman's voice that informed women's filmmaking, such questions are now less productive, and, though necessary and very important at the time, they have, in some ways, become as limiting as the auteur theory. (130)

In support of her argument, Martin points out the collaborative nature of progressive practices, as exemplified by couples of thinkers-cum-filmmakers, such as Laura Mulvey and Peter Wollen, or Danièle Huillet and Jean-Marie Straub. Many other couples could be aligned to this pattern, for example Margarethe von Trotta and Volker Schlöndorff in Germany, Agnès Varda and Jacques Demy in France, Jean-Luc Godard and Anne-Marie Miéville in Switzerland and Kathryn Bigelow and James Cameron in the United States, the last commented on in greater length in Martin's article. It is certainly not an irrelevant detail that these couples were united in their private as well as professional lives, suggesting a democratic role-sharing first put in place in empirical reality, before being transported to the screen. Not surprisingly, all these couples are connected to some kind of experimental or avant-garde or, at the very least, new cinema movements.

This finds a striking parallel with the Retomada, littered with celebrated directorial duos, starting with Walter Salles and Daniela Thomas. Though not united in private life, as were many of their colleagues, Thomas and Salles complemented each other's expertise in many interesting ways. With her theatrical background, set-design experience and admirable scriptwriting skills, Thomas was responsible for grooming Salles into fiction filmmaking, as he emerged from a consistent career of documentarian, alongside his brother João Moreira Salles, and an unsuccessful first adventure in narrative cinema, *A grande arte/Exposure* (1991). The result was *Terra Estrangeira/Foreign Land* (1995), co-directed by Salles and Thomas (see Figure 1.1) and considered by many the foundational film of the Retomada, with its vivid, documentary-like depiction of the gloomy Collor era.

From this milestone onwards, joint directorship became a usual feature in Brazilian cinema, launching couples who were partners in their

Figure 1.1. *Terra estrangeira/Foreign Land* (Walter Salles and Daniela Thomas, 1995).

private and public lives, such as Laís Bodanzky and Luiz Bolognesi, Mirella Martinelli and Eduardo Caron, Bia Lessa and Dany Roland. Collaboration was also rife in other specialisms, as in the case of director Domingos Oliveira and actress Priscilla Rozenbaum; director Toni Venturi and actress Deborah Duboc; director Sandra Werneck and sound engineer Silvio Da-Rin; director Sergio Rezende and producer Mariza Leão; director Alain Fresnot and producer Van Fresnot; director Paulo Thiago and producer Glaucia Camargos; and countless others. Even the most world-renowned contemporary Brazilian film director, Fernando Meirelles, took up solo directorship only once he started to shoot abroad, that is, with *The Constant Gardener* (2005), followed by *Blindness* (2008) and *360* (2011), all produced and shot outside Brazil. In contrast to these, all his Brazilian films boast shared directorship, with Fabrizia Alves Pinto in *Menino maluquinho 2/The Nutty Boy 2* (1998), with Nando Olival in *Domésticas/ Maids* (2000) and with Kátia Lund in *Cidade de Deus/City of God* (2002). In fact, Meirelles and the Salles brothers are active propellers of collaborative filmmaking and joint authorship through their high-profile film production companies, respectively O2 and Videofilmes, which support films by the most distinguished and creative figures in new Brazilian cinema, among them Eduardo Coutinho (sadly deceased in 2014), Tata Amaral and Karim Aïnouz, a fact that inevitably leaves an imprint of the producers (themselves creative artists) alongside a director's signature. An eloquent example is the first O2 blockbuster, *Cidade de Deus*, set in Rio, which triggered the TV series *City of Men*, with different directors assigned to each episode. The experience prompted a feminine counterpart, *Antônia* (Tata Amaral, 2006), set in São Paulo, produced by O2 and equally followed by a TV series of the same name with multiple directors. Indeed, since the Retomada period, cinema has become more and more entrenched with television, a realm where teamwork is the rule, further undermining the auteurist approach.

Because this collaborative tradition has not only continued but expanded in contemporary practices, female presence is felt everywhere, even when a female director's signature is not appended to the film's credits. Women in Brazil have an expressive input in editing – a task curiously excelled at by women worldwide – an example being Idê Lacreta, who collaborated with women directors such as Tata Amaral, Eliane Caffé and Suzana Amaral in many of their landmark films, as well as editing dozens of Retomada films. More impressive still is the number of female film producers in Brazil, a realm normally dominated by men, including the aforementioned Mariza Leão, Glaucia Camargos and Van Fresnot, but also other notable figures, active both in high- and low-budget films, such as Lucy Barreto, Assunção Hernandez, Paula Lavigne, Rita Buzzar, Sara Silveira, Yurika Yamazaki and Zita Carvalhosa.

Authorship, since the Retomada period, is, moreover, diluted and diffused; in the accompanying rise of the documentary genre, authorship is necessarily attenuated to make room for the contingent and unexpected pro-filmic event. I would go as far as asserting that the greatest achievement, by both men and women, in the Retomada utopian days was the move towards blurring the boundaries between genres, classes and ethnic determinants, as much as between genders. The most striking examples of this can be found precisely within those films which attempted to reassess Brazil's territories of poverty through a new look, informed by the euphoria of hybridisation. *Baile perfumado/Perfumed Ball* (1997), directed by the duo Paulo Caldas and Lírio Ferreira, for example, includes documentary footage of the north-eastern outlaws (*cangaceiros*) made by the Lebanese peddler Benjamin Abraão in the 1930s, intercut with fiction. This genre intermingling reverberates with the hybrid portrayal of the backlands themselves, which ceases to be the realm of dispossession as compared with the wealthy seacoast, according to the famous Glauber Rocha formula. On the contrary, the scrubland where the *cangaceiro* Lampião hides out is lush, and water, from rivers or the sea, criss-crosses the *sertão*. Rather than a coarse bandit, Lampião himself is presented as a kind of dandy, given to dancing, dressing up, using perfume, drinking whisky and even going to the movies in town. Backlands and sea, as well as town and country, share the same borderless, 'liquid' modernity, as aptly defined by Zygmunt Bauman, who connects this to the prevalence of the collective over the individual:

> The solids whose turn has come to be thrown into the melting pot and which are in the process of being melted at the present time, the time of fluid modernity, are the bonds which interlock individual choices in collective projects and actions – the patterns of communication and co-ordination between individually conducted life policies on the one hand and political actions of human collectivities on the other. (Bauman 2000: 6)

Baile perfumado thus breaks free from Cinema Novo's insular representation of the north-east to create an atmosphere of globalised confraternisation, in which a Lebanese man is drawn to a Brazilian *cangaceiro* and, vice versa, the *baião* fuses with American pop, and middle-class filmmakers merge with the rustic *sertão* population.

Another telling example of fluid boundaries is *Crede-mi/Believe Me* (1997), again shot in the north-east backlands by another couple in professional and private life, multi-artists Bia Lessa and Dany Roland. The film typically opens with a tracking shot on a large water expanse in a digital revelling in liquid modernity (see Figure 1.2). Directors Lessa and Roland are clearly fascinated with the rediscovery of the arid backlands in the north-east of Brazil, with their colour, popular festivals, music and religion, which provide them with the opportunity to create hybridities at all levels. Lessa and Roland's background in theatre and opera came into play in the series of workshops they coordinated with amateur actors from the interior of Ceará state, in which they reworked excerpts from Thomas Mann's novel *The Holy Sinner*. The actors' improvisations, in a way, restore the origins of the medieval oral tale of Mann's cultivated text, intercut with documentary footage of religious festivals and popular celebrations where there are no oppressors or oppressed, victims or defendants. Needless to say, there are no victims of gender either, in a story of incest between twin siblings, whose offspring, abandoned in the sea, returns as an adult to unwittingly marry his own mother. Rather than being punished for his sin, as in the Oedipus myth, he goes on to become the Pope. Apolitical though it may seem, this tale finds a curious parallel with the story of Luiz Inácio Lula da Silva, born in the same drought-stricken north-east, who went on to become the most popular President in Brazil's history. With its fairy-tale presentationalism, conveyed by a handheld, bedazzled camera, as if unable to differentiate between fact and fiction, *Crede-mi* ends up being more realistic than the crass representation of Lula's ascension in the more recent *Lula, o filho do Brasil/Lula, the Son of Brazil* (Fábio Barreto, 2009), entirely conceived on the basis of melodramatic victimisation.

What fascinates about these films is precisely their refusal to find politics in the realm of representational victimology, that is, in difference. This resonates with Rancière's misgivings about representational art of political intention, which resorts to the mimetic device in order to reveal, in his words, 'the power of the commodity, the reign of the spectacle or the

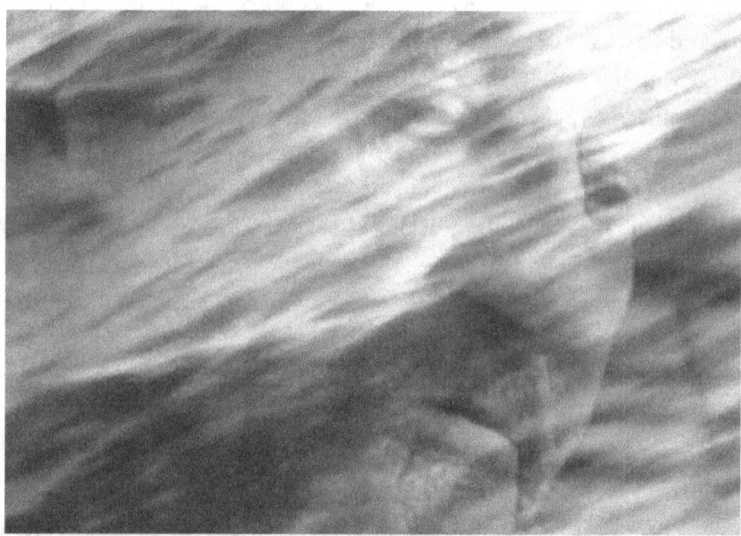

Figure 1.2. *Crede-mi/Believe Me* (Bia Lessa and Dany Roland, 1997): a digital revelling in liquid modernity.

pornography of power'. He says: 'since it is very difficult to find anybody who is actually ignorant of such things, the mechanism ends up spinning around itself', that is, reproducing consensus (2009: 144). Instead, Rancière proposes dissensus, which he explains as follows:

> If there exists a connection between art and politics, it should be cast in terms of dissensus, the very kernel of the aesthetic regime: artworks can produce effects of dissensus precisely because they neither give lessons nor have any destination. (Rancière 2010: 140)

Dissensus is, moreover, for Rancière, the element that separates the aesthetic from the representative regimes in art. In the aesthetic regime, according to Rancière, the function of fiction is not to oppose the imagined to the real, but to re-frame the real, that is, to frame a dissensus. Fiction, in this regime, 'is a way of changing existing modes of sensory presentations and forms of enunciation; of varying frames, scales and rhythms; and of building new relationships between reality and appearance, the individual and the collective' (Rancière 2010: 141). In the consensual representative mode, sensory reality is given as univocal, whereas 'political and artistic fictions introduce dissensus by hollowing out that "real" and multiplying it in a polemical way' (149).

This thought presents the irresistible attraction, as far as the Retomada is concerned, of redefining political art as that which refuses to anticipate its effects and which questions, instead, its own limits and powers: that is to say, an art which accepts its own insufficiency and, even when it infiltrates the world of social relations and power struggles, 'remains content to be mere images', in Rancière's handsome vocabulary (149). Indeed, the Retomada has left a legacy of thought-provoking films, touching on the female question, which, rather than offering univocal views, multiply the possible meanings of the referent. An example is Eduardo Coutinho's film *O fim e o princípio/The End and the Beginning* (2005), a documentary focusing almost exclusively on the poor women of a remote village in Paraíba state, again in the Brazilian north-east, and indeed where former president Lula was born, in which characters are asked to tell their personal, rather than communal or social stories. As a result, their female or class conditions hardly feature in their testimonials, which offer instead an intimate, open-ended reflexion on common lives as the quintessential illustration of a dissensual take on reality.

Beyond representation

Films like Coutinho's *O fim e o princípio* are a far cry from thesis films centred on the assumption of female victimisation in an essentially chauvinistic, male-centred environment. Instead it is left up to their subjects to define themselves to the camera, contradictory though their testimonies might be with regard to the premises at the origin of the film. This is because such works embrace a presentational regime, whose ethical stance is the fidelity to the unpredictable event of truth, in tune with Alain Badiou's thought that 'there can be no ethics in general, but only an ethic of singular truths, and thus an ethic relative to a particular situation' (2002: lvi).

As for the difference between presentational and representational modes in cinema, it goes back a long way and is inextricable from the question of realism, a staple of shared-authorship cinema as developed in Brazil from the Retomada onwards. Noël Burch, in his pioneering assessment of early cinema, famously opposed what he called 'bourgeois representationalism' to a 'popular presentationalism', and drew from this division two very distinct phases of cinema: before and after the emergence of an 'institutional mode of representation', which he located around 1906 (1990: 186ff). Burch's resolute stand in favour of 'presentational' filmmaking was due to the fact that 'representational' cinema was, for him, directed towards producing an 'impression of reality', whereas 'presentational' cinema, examples of which were to be found, for him, in experimental cinema, was quite at ease in acknowledging its own artifice. Along the same lines, Gunning (1997: 56–62) defined as eminently 'presentational' the 'cinema of attractions' which prevailed in early cinema until 1906–07. The distinctive quality of this cinema, according to Gunning, was its ability to 'show' something rather than 'represent' it. 'Contrasted to the voyeuristic aspect of narrative cinema analysed by Christian Metz', says Gunning, 'this is an exhibitionist cinema', in which actors are constantly looking at the spectators – that is to say, 'breaking the theatre's fourth wall', as Brecht would put it some 30 years after such films were made.

In the 1990s, presentational cinema became a privileged object of study for narratologists, such as André Gaudreault, who defined cinematic narrative as a 'dialectical combination of the two basic modes of narrative communication: narration and monstration' (1997: 73). 'To monstrate', a literal translation of the French *montrer*, is another way of signifying 'presentation', for which Gaudreault found a perfect illustration in the figure of the live narrator who used to provide explanation for silent films before the advent of intertitles. They were to be found all over the world and were called, for example, *bonnimenteurs* in French and *benshi* in Japanese.

More recently, presentational modes of address have been connected to the historical contingent, as in Paul Willemen's approach, which formulates the issue in terms of 'representation (one thing standing for another) versus presentation (something manifesting itself even if only in a disguised, distorted or translated manner)', triggering the question: 'how do the dynamics animating historical change "present" in representations?' (Willemen 2010: 252). Rancière replies to this question by defining the film medium itself as inherently presentational. As a mechanical reproduction of the real, he says, cinema 'revokes the old mimetic order, because it resolves the question of *mimesis* at its root': 'At the origin of the cinema, there is a "scrupulously honest" artist that does not cheat, that cannot cheat, because all it does is record' (Rancière 2006: 2).

This suggests that cinema can be used to *resist*, as much as to elicit, simulation, leaving it up to filmmakers to decide whether to privilege presentation or representation. The hypothesis embraced in this chapter also defines itself on the basis of cases in which simulation is averted, even if only to the benefit of the realism of the medium itself, a real which in any case retains a strong claim to the film's very authorship, as the case of *Crime delicado/Delicate Crime* (2006), looked at below, will hopefully demonstrate. In particular, in the Retomada period, the need to reconnect with a historical cinematic past and to retrieve the true image of a country for too long obscured by political censorship and/or commercial interests led filmmakers to instinctively lean towards a presentational regime, favouring natural colours, language accents and the expression of non-professional acting that are so outspoken, for example, in the gallery of faces in the opening of *Central Station*, the film-symbol of the Brazilian Revival of the 1990s. Instances of co-participation of the contingent real in the film's genesis are actually to be found everywhere, for example in the unexpected green that covers the *caatinga*, or the semi-desert area of Brazil's north-east, in the aforementioned *Baile perfumado*, due to a very rare rainy season; in the inventiveness of the peasants that re-enact

Thomas Mann in *Crede-mi*; in the dwindling population of the Paraná coast who see their land increasingly swallowed by the sea in *Terra do mar/Sea Land* (Eduardo Caron and Mirella Martinelli, 1997). Open to what the landscape and its real inhabitants have to offer, the Retomada films, together with the art cinema that developed in its wake, lend themselves naturally to collaboration.

Beyond difference

The widespread collaborative system adopted in Brazilian cinema since the Retomada days leaves us with the question as to whether it would be possible or even productive to identify a specific female contribution to this production. There is no denying the political importance of female filmmakers, such as Tata Amaral, who have consistently addressed the theme of female repression within the Brazilian lower classes in ground-breaking films such as *Um céu de estrelas/Starry Sky* (1996) and the aforementioned *Antônia*, both of which culminate in the murder of the male oppressor by the liberated woman. But do they differ substantially from those by male directors, such as *Contra todos/Up Against Them All* (2003), featuring the same Leona Cavally of *Um céu de estrelas*, and directed by Amaral's close collaborator, Roberto Moreira? The same could be asked of one of our most outspoken feminist filmmakers, Lúcia Murat, director of the celebrated pre-Retomada docudrama *Que bom te ver viva/How Nice to See You Alive* (1989), a courageous attack on the dictatorship crimes against women whose launch coincided with the regime's final demise. Ever since, Murat has consistently returned to the female theme, as in *Maré, nossa história de amor/Another Love Story* (2007), a Bollywood-style musical set in a favela. But are her films in any way more 'feminist' than, say, those by her contemporary Eduardo Coutinho? As much as Murat, Coutinho boasts impeccable political credentials, with his two-decade struggle against the military regime, wonderfully documented in his *Cabra marcado para morrer/Twenty Years Later* (1985). In the post-Retomada years, he repeatedly turned to women, be they inhabitants of the Rio favelas, as in *Santo forte/The Mighty Spirit* (1999); female professional and non-professional performers, as in *Jogo de cena/Playing* (2007); or north-eastern peasants, as in the aforementioned *O fim e o princípio*.

Male–female shared authorship as well as male feminism in fact draws us away from the debate on the specificity of feminine authorship, and this is why, in order to really grasp the achievements of feminist and other political struggles in Brazilian cinema, we must move beyond questions of difference. Processes of 'othering' and the acknowledgement of 'difference' underpin much of cultural studies, drawing mainly on Emmanuel Lévinas' defence of, and respect for, what he calls 'the infinite alterity of the other' (1991: 121), but also on Lévinas' followers, notably Derrida, Irigaray and Spivak. However, as David Rodowick has pointed out, the binary machine, entrenched in Western philosophy, as represented by the male–female opposition, 'always pretends to totality and universality' (Rodowick 2000: 182), making it fit for abstract thinking but necessarily reductive when applied to concrete reality.

There is no questioning the totalising impetus of the male–female dualism in feminist film theory. This is because its foundational premises hinged on a centre–periphery scheme which placed the Hollywood mainstream against the rest of the world, ascribing a male sign to the former so as to characterise avant-garde or experimental cinema, in particular that made by women, as the only possible alternative to it. This scheme made sense and had an extraordinary political impact at its launch, as best represented by Laura Mulvey's ground-breaking essay 'Visual Pleasure and Narrative Cinema', first published in 1975. But its totalising drive ended up leaving middle-level world cinema out of the feminist radar, or at best reducing it to peripheral voices in need of Hollywood's centrifugal power to be activated. Indeed, the clear-cut male–female opposition that determines the active and passive elements in cinematic gaze construction can be understood only on the basis of the paradigms provided by classical Hollywood cinema, leaving no space for the fluid boundaries of gender and sex in modern cinema. Rodowick reminds us that, despite its capital importance, Mulvey's pioneering feminist film theory take fails to find theoretical backing even in Freud's thought itself:

> We are accustomed to say that every human being displays both male and female instinctual impulses, needs and attributes; but though anatomy, it is true, can point out the characteristic of maleness and femaleness, psychology cannot. For psychology the contrast between the sexes fades away into one between

activity and passivity, in which we far too readily identify activity with maleness and passivity with femaleness, a view which is by no means universally confirmed. (Freud in Rodowick 2000: 195)

Evidence that new theoretical tools are needed to understand the gender powers at play in contemporary world cinema is given by the film *Crime delicado*, directed by one of the most creative artists emerging in the Retomada period, Beto Brant. Multiple authorship marks this film from the outset, with a script jointly written by five collaborators: writer Sérgio Sant'Anna (adapting his own novel), writer Marçal Aquino (Brant's regular collaborator), Luiz Fernando Carvalho Filho, Maurício Paroni de Castro and actor Marco Ricca (one of the film's stars). The film also relied on extensive improvisation by the actors, based on their own biographies, most strikingly in the case of the female protagonist, played by Lilian Taublib. From its opening images the film demonstrates an awareness of, and an intention to challenge, the main principles of traditional film theory, including the female position as the passive object of the gaze, but also issues pertaining to the representation of minorities, such as the disabled. The film's engagement with feminist film theory relating to gaze construction is particularly noticeable in the bar scene, in which the male and female protagonists – the theatre critic Antônio and the artists' model Inês – meet for the first time. Inês is first shown sitting at a table with friends, while Antônio, by himself, eats a sandwich at the counter opposite her. Inês's friends leave and Antônio and Inês glance at each other. Antônio moves to Inês's table and the dialogue that follows reveals Inês as the offspring of a feminist, egalitarian era. She is a middle-class, liberated woman, free to do, and achieve, whatever she wants. She is the one who flirts with a man, makes the first physical advances and invites him out with the undisguised intention of sex. In this scene, if there is any victim within the male–female relationship, it is certainly the man. This notwithstanding, the way the audience read this relation may still be inflected by Antônio's male point of view, as he continues to be the film's narrator and thus the 'bearer of the look of the spectator', as Mulvey famously defined gaze construction in Hollywood classical cinema. But the axiom of the passive female is challenged when the object of the gaze is suddenly revealed as a lack. As Inês stands up and grabs her crutches, it becomes clear that her 'plus' is actually a 'minus', a lacking leg. The focus of interest is thus diverted towards an absence which cannot conjure up the stereotype of the passive object of desire, but only its inexistence.

In the story, Inês models for a painter, José Torres Campana – played by real-life Mexican painter Felipe Ehrenberg. Later in the film, in a flashback, we see Inês posing for this picture. The painter and the model are naked and engaged in different embraces during which he draws the sketches which are subsequently transferred to the canvas. Both processes (the drawing of the sketches and the actual painting) are shot while in progress, that is, Ehrenberg produced this painting during the actual shooting of the film. Thus, what we see in this scene is the actors leaping out of representation and into a presentational regime in which the production of an artwork is concomitant with its reproduction, as in André Bazin's favourite example of Clouzot's *The Mystery of Picasso* (Bazin 1997). The fact that this involves full nudity and physical intimacy between painter and model, and that, to that end, the model, who is disabled in real life, had to remove her prosthesis before the camera, indicates the transformative effect the film necessarily had in their actual lives, and how they authored the film itself in the shape of a work in progress.

The resulting picture, 'Pax de deux', has at its centre an erect penis next to a dilated vulva (see Figure 1.3). Most notably, however, the male organ appears as a substitute for the lacking leg, filling up, so to say, the gap in representation that allows for art (and sex) to flourish. The fact that 'Pas de deux' became the unpredictable centrepiece of the film demonstrates cast and crew's fidelity to the event of truth and their ethics of the real. This painting, and the way it is composed, further suggests that Brazilian cinema at its best has moved beyond unified representations of women and placed them, instead, alongside men in a complementary, commingling form. I would go as far as stating that the context of the film and the one from which the film has emerged make up a world post-difference, where notions of normality, against which to define the 'other', have ceased to exist. It is a world in which, as Badiou puts it, 'Infinite alterity is quite simply *what there is*' (Badiou 2002: 25). The disabled woman is different from the able man insofar as all individuals are different from each other and depend on how they are seen in order to make sense. Instead of a victimising attribute, difference becomes the grain of originality essential to artistic creation.

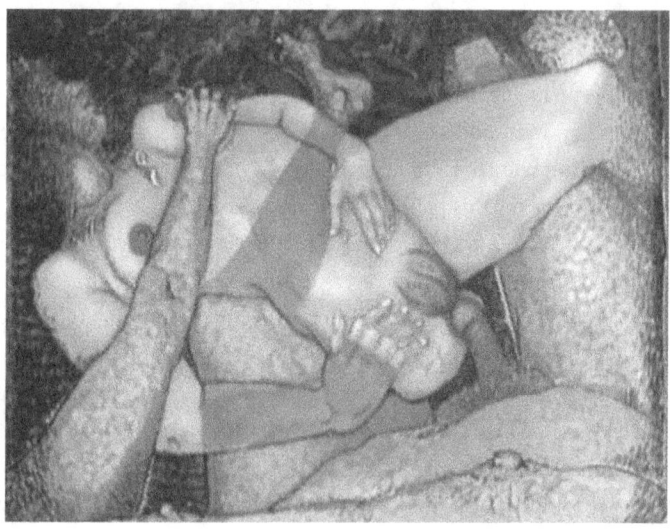

Figure 1.3. The painting 'Pas de deux', which came to existence during the filming of *Crime delicado/Delicate Crime* (Beto Brant, 2006).

Note

1. An earlier version of this chapter was delivered as a keynote speech at the Conference 'Mulheres da Retomada – Women Filmmakers in Contemporary Brazilian Cinema', held at Tulane University, 19 February 2011.

References

Badiou, Alain (2002). *Ethics: An Essay on the Understanding of Evil*, translated by Peter Hallward, London: Verso.
Bauman, Zygmunt (2000). *Liquid Modernity*, Cambridge: Polity.
Bazin, André (1997). *Bazin at Work*, translated by Alain Piette and Bert Cardullo, Bert Cardullo (ed.), New York: Routledge.
Burch, Noël (1990). *To the Distant Observer: Form and Meaning in the Japanese Cinema*, Berkeley: University of California Press.
—— (1993). *Revoir Hollywood: la nouvelle critique anglo-américaine*, Paris: Nathan.
Gaudreault, André (1997). 'Film, narrative, narration: the cinema of the Lumière Brothers', in Thomas Elsaesser (ed), *Early Cinema: Space, Frame, Narrative*, London: BFI, pp. 68–75.

Gunning, Tom (1997). 'The cinema of attractions: early film, its spectator and the avant-garde', in Thomas Elsaesser (ed.), *Early Cinema: Space, Frame, Narrative*, London: BFI, pp. 56–62.

Kaplan, E. Ann (2000). Preface to E. Ann Kaplan (ed.), *Feminism and Film*, Oxford: Oxford University Press, pp. v–vi.

Lévinas, Emmanuel (1991). *Totality and Infinity: An Essay on Exteriority*, translated by Alphonso Lingis. Dordrecth, Boston, London: Kluwer Academic Publishers.

Martin, Angela (2008). 'Refocusing authorship in women's filmmaking (2003)', in Barry Keith Grant (ed.), *Auteurs and Authorship: A Film Reader*, Malden: Blackwell, pp. 127–34.

Mulvey, Laura (1975). 'Visual Pleasure and Narrative Cinema', *Screen* 16. 3, pp. 6–18.

Nagib, Lúcia (2002). *O cinema da retomada: depoimento de 90 cineastas dos anos 90*, São Paulo: Editora 34.

—— (2007). *Brazil on Screen: Cinema Novo, New Cinema, Utopia*, London: I.B.Tauris.

Rancière, Jacques (2006). *Film Fables*, Oxford: Berg.

—— (2009). *The Emancipated Spectator*, London: Verso.

—— (2010). *Dissensus: On Politics and Aesthetics*, New York: Continuum.

Rodowick, David N. (2000). 'The difficulty of difference', in E. Ann Kaplan (ed.), *Feminism & Film*, Oxford: Oxford University Press, pp. 181–202.

Willemen, Paul (2010). 'Fantasy in Action', in Natasa Durovicova and Kathleen Newman (eds), *World Cinemas, Transnational Perspectives*, New York: Routledge, pp. 247–86.

2

Through Female Eyes: Reframing Peru on Screen

Sarah Barrow

Introduction

In July 2011, a roundtable was held at the fifteenth annual Film Festival in Lima on the topic of women in Peruvian cinema, in celebration of the upsurge in the number of female filmmakers emerging from Peru over the previous decade. The event included six women who had produced short and feature films on a diverse range of topics, in documentary and fiction form.[1] Hosted by acclaimed director Josué Méndez, whose own films have included strong roles for women in front of and behind the camera,[2] the occasion acknowledged a significant shift in the demographic landscape of Peruvian cinema in terms of the role of women as filmmakers in Peru since the turn of the century. Compared with the relative paucity of Peruvian women in directorial roles until early in the new millennium, it should be noted that a fifth of the 39 fiction and documentary features scheduled for release during 2014–15 were directed by women (Rojas 2014). Commentators such as Claudia Salazar Jiménez, Peruvian writer and founder of a biennial festival of Peruvian cinema in New York, have also remarked that there seem to be several characteristics – a higher level of skills, more varied experience, and broader, including international, professional networks – that are shared by this so-called 'new' generation of female filmmakers from Peru but less so with their predecessors.[3] Such observers also point out that these directors have benefited from a much higher level of technical training, with access to a more sophisticated set of equipment, benefactors and knowledge about funding schemes, in part because most have studied at postgraduate level overseas.[4] In common with the pioneers, though, they also share an interest in developing their own personal vision and innovative style and focus on female characters from a range of classes, cultures and generations that otherwise tend to be neglected by most Peruvian feature cinema. They have all – much like their male counterparts – also shared the hardships that stem from a lack of adequate and sustainable financial support from government-led initiatives, which has led to them having to raise and invest private resources into the production of their films. Moreover, some of the most celebrated feature films made by women from Peru of recent years, such as Claudia Llosa's *Madeinusa* (2006) and *La teta asustada/Milk of Sorrow* (2009), *Las malas intenciones/Bad Intentions* by Rosario García-Montero (2011) and *Climas* by Enrica Pérez (2014), have been supported by some of the most prestigious transnational funding schemes.[5]

Several questions emerge from such observations. For example, how does the apparently 'new' transnationality of the experience of these women affect their approach to their work and their status as 'national' filmmakers, given that many of the funding schemes mentioned above are linked to European institutions and thereby provide potential new routes for post- or neo-colonialist intervention? To what extent does that experience differ from that of their male counterparts and their female predecessors, and what is specific about this in the contemporary Peruvian context? Moreover, what influence might these women have on the development of film policy, production, criticism, spectatorship and funding avenues in Peru? Do they, as Barbara Koenig Quart foresaw, contribute to 'opening up literally new worlds on screen, women's worlds, to which probably only a woman could provide entry in depth'? (1989: 4). And to what extent do their films align with the processes of resistance, refusal and opposition to 'the conventions and stereotypes not only of Hollywood ... but also of Third Cinema with its adherence to a Marxist ideology that subsumes, and thus erases, the particularities of sexism and racism' (Robin and Jaffe 1999: 27)? In their end-of-millennium text, Robin and Jaffe draw attention to the following common characteristics that make up their anthology of 'woman-centred' films: a focus on ordinary women, brought from the margins to the centre; a foregrounding of the 'specificity of the cultures, nations, local discourses, and critiques, within which these women's lives are enmeshed' (27); a primary concern for the challenges of maternity as opposed to any conventional romantic storyline; and an emphasis on self-discovery as an ongoing process as well as a part of community and family building. These are all themes and structural devices that continue to resonate among the filmmakers mentioned here and which are foregrounded in the specific films chosen for analysis.

In sum, then, this essay probes the extent to which these female-directed films by the likes of Llosa, García-Montero and Pérez serve to disrupt or redirect the gaze of the spectator away from hegemonic assumptions about issues of gender and national identity, and whether this apparently feminist turn represents anything more than yet another sporadic phenomenon in the fragmented history of Peruvian cinema. The response to these questions is developed in two main ways: firstly, through an exploration of the relationship between gender and nation as articulated by contemporary female filmmakers of Peru, with close analysis of some of their work that draws attention to some of the shared concerns; and secondly, through a mapping out of the national and transnational conditions that might have made this particular moment possible and which acknowledges the significance of the work in this area of previous generations.

Landmark women: the 'Llosa' effect

As many critics and academics have recognised, Claudia Llosa was noted and 'celebrated almost immediately as an auteur as much for her style as for her subject matter' (White 2015: 187), garnering transnational funding and critical acclaim from the worldwide festival circuit, alongside accusations of Euro-centrism for exposing the apparent barbarity of indigenous cultural practices. Her commitment to woman-centred issues is clear in her works, even though her portrayal of other cultural themes has been called into question for the tendency to focus on the exotic and the eccentric aspects of rural and urban indigenous communities. Like many of her generation, she grew up amidst the turmoil of the Shining Path conflict (1980–2000) and socio-economic chaos. She studied film both in Lima and overseas, in her case in New York and Madrid, and used her extensive family networks to enhance the potential of her undeniable talent for storytelling.[6] Having grabbed the attention of arts and independent film enthusiasts worldwide with her debut feature *Madeinusa* (2006), she broke new ground cinematically speaking with her surprise win of the Golden Bear award at the Berlin Film Festival 2009 for her second feature, *La teta asustada*. It was this event that created a truly landmark moment in the history of Peruvian cinema generally, topped by an Oscar nomination for the same film later that year. Not only was it the most significant recognition of international scope to have been achieved by a filmmaker from Peru, but it marked Claudia Llosa out as the best-known name in Peruvian cinematographic history to date.

While acknowledging Llosa as one of the most remarkable Peruvian filmmakers and her work as the most scrutinised of recent times, this essay is concerned to take a broader view of the context around her, historically as well as contemporaneously.[7] This approach has the aim of placing Llosa's work within a landscape of women who have defied considerable logistical, ideological, financial and socio-political odds to bring, echoing Patricia White, Peruvian 'women's stories to the transnational public sphere' (2015: 198).[8]

By starting with Marianne Eyde, whose work began in documentary form in the 1980s, at the height of the Shining Path conflict, moved to fiction in the 1990s and 2000s, and back to documentary in 2015, this essay pays tribute to another Euro-Peruvian's commitment to revealing the challenges of cultural diversity, her courage in taking on controversial subject matter at the height of the Shining Path conflict, and her resolute dedication to the art and craft of filmmaking in the face of countless adversities. There then follows a discussion of the more recent woman-centred work of Rosario García-Montero, a contemporary of Llosa, whose short and feature-length fiction films explore the breaks and continuities between past and present. It should be noted that García-Montero took part not only in the event mentioned above in Lima 2011, but also in the first edition of Perufest, the first biennial film festival dedicated exclusively to Peruvian cinema to be held in New York. Her work was included in a DVD project called *8 y ½*, which featured the short films of a group of female Peruvian directors of this same generation who were profiled at this first festival event.[9] In common with several of her contemporaries, García-Montero's work focuses on the figure of the girl, coming of age amidst conflict and thus in many ways emblematic of the experiences of these directors. In the final analysis, I am interested in scrutinising the ways these female filmmakers continue to seek, as Robin and Jaffe suggest they might, 'a retrieval of a history in which women are repositioned in the center of things, as narrative agents of their own lives' (1999: 27).

Cinema, nation, gender and conflict: Marianne Eyde

Peru has an idiosyncratic, inconsistent and intermittent history of film-making, dominated since its humble beginnings by the elite classes, mostly male, Hispanic and based mainly in Lima, and by tensions among cultural creators in Latin America over how – politically and socially – to shape the aesthetics of a nation in search of an identity. Leading Peruvian critic Ricardo Bedoya describes it as a film history marked by 'an obstinate predilection for failure', and he accordingly reflects on the range of initiatives that have been launched and withdrawn at state and grassroots levels, and the apparent inability for any sustainable infrastructure or policy to emerge (Bedoya 1995: 13). Peru is a country composed of and challenged by several ethnicities and languages, and that perspective of cultural diversity has riven its film politics, policies and poetics. The military government that came into power in 1968 subsidised cinema to a certain extent with the aim of projecting a more modern nation to the outside world, and some filmmakers benefited from these interventions, but few of them were based away from the political or economic centre. Then, from 1980 to 1992, the violence between the state and the Shining Path rebel group – purportedly motivated by a desire to fight social injustice – threatened to destroy a society that had struggled to make a successful transition to democracy. During this period, a combination of economic and political crises triggered by the violence had devastating effects on filmmaking generally and yet – paradoxically – those same crises also played a pivotal role in the survival and reconfiguration of film production in Peru. For, as Keith Richards has noted, 'the relative prominence of the Shining Path theme [in national cinema] shows how deeply this episode has affected the nation's psyche' (2011: 85). Indeed, most of the films referenced here include stories which invoke that period of intense civil conflict and female characters for whom that conflict serves as a site of self-discovery and resistance.

Until the late 1990s, one of the few female directors with any significant profile in Peru and overseas was Marianne Eyde, who studied journalism at the University of Lima and from 1980 became a highly regarded filmmaker. Her early documentary works focus on the diverse rituals and everyday customs of ordinary Peruvian communities in various parts of the country.[10] Eyde holds an interesting position as a Peruvian filmmaker – Norwegian-born but with Peruvian citizenship, ostensibly part of Peru's white European elite – which sees her at times marked out for special attention by critics and policy-makers who have not been completely convinced by her sympathetic treatment of the more marginalised groups. Her debut feature film, *La vida es una sola/You Only Live Once* (1993), centred on the coming-of-age dilemma faced by its young female protagonist, Florinda (Milagros Del Carpio), under extreme socio-political and personal circumstances. *La vida es una sola* was released after four years in development, a significant period during which the Shining Path conflict had wreaked havoc in the major cities, the rebel leader had been captured and a hard-line neo-liberal regime had come to power. It is a realist drama which focuses on a traditional Andean community caught between the violence of the Shining Path and an increasingly repressive military response. While Florinda's tragic tale is at the heart of the story and was designed to arouse sympathy for the victims of the conflict, it was the introduction of a second female character, Comrade Meche (Rosa María Olortegui), as the leading member of a rebel group which infiltrates the village, that sparked much of the controversy surrounding this film, which resulted in unprecedented scrutiny on the part of the government and the removal of the writer's name from the credits for fear of persecution.[11]

As Bedoya remarked shortly after the film's release, although it was accused by many critics of being sympathetic to terrorists, 'there was not … a single image, piece of dialogue, situation or character that could justify such a claim' (Bedoya 1977: 308). And yet, it would seem that by giving cinematic space to a female character whose political beliefs were ultra-leftist and who was emblematic of a large number of young women from a range of ethnic backgrounds who became involved, sometimes willingly, in the most brutal aspects of insurgent life, Eyde was committing a different kind of transgression that threatened to undermine hegemonic, Hispanic patriarchal social order. The film drew attention to the potential this conflict gave for women to overcome 'the subordinate role and status historically ascribed to them in Peruvian society' by participating as equals in the Shining Path cause and leading on many of its initiatives (Whittaker 2001:159). With its portrayal of young women committed to revolutionary ideals, it was very much at odds with the way public opinion was being shaped by a state-sponsored discourse regarding the Shining Path movement at the time, which preferred to refer to them as self-serving, debauched drug traffickers and (male) thugs. The film suffered particularly badly in part due to the timing of its release shortly after the capture of the Shining Path leader Abimael Guzmán, that is to say, at just the moment when the government was more determined than ever to restore public order and to quell any discussion at all about the motivations for anyone, let alone young women, to sign up to a revolutionary cause that set out to destroy social structures as established up to that point.

When finally approved by the state, Eyde's film opened at only four cinemas in Lima, with little media attention, while national TV channels rejected it for screening. On the other hand, it is now considered a landmark of contemporary Peruvian cinema and was selected for screening at the International Film Festival of Rotterdam in 1994. It continues to be acclaimed by the global arts cinema circuit and was included as a highlight of Perufest in New York in 2012, which focused on cinema and memory of the internal armed conflict in Peru. Moreover, Eyde's work generally is embraced by socially conscious global film festivals that foreground issues of human rights, such as Tiburon (United States) which in 2006 featured *Coca mama*, her third fiction film to focus on marginalised women caught in the crossfire of armed struggle.[12]

Eyde's approach to her subjects is markedly woman-centred in that her main protagonists are young women struggling to deal with the unwritten rules of patriarchy that restrict their development as they come of age. In the case of each of the main female characters in her debut feature, transgression from expected norms of female behaviour in the form of taking up arms to fight (whether by choice or force) leads to difficulty: Florinda is forced to flee from her village despite escaping from the insurgents; Meche has to resign herself to death, although does so with resolute commitment to her cause. Importantly, Eyde's work serves to critique patriarchal institutions – the military, normative 'family' hierarchies and gender divides – and this led in the first instance to her persecution by Fujimori's regime and in the second to her neglect by (mostly male) national critics and exhibitors. However, Eyde's perspective may not be regarded as a radical vision of a new position for Peruvian women, since although her films represent women as engaged in a process of self-reflection that leads them to attempt to resist the system, they are not able to overcome it. In the mode of classical melodrama, they are punished as a result of their efforts to transform situations. Eyde's heroines of the 1990s failed to achieve their desired freedom and agency because the law of social prohibition exerted its ultimate power to re-establish the symbolic order of patriarchal discourse.[13]

Memory and self-discovery: Rosario García-Montero

García-Montero, who studied film in Lima, New York and Cuba, released her debut feature, *Las malas intenciones/Bad intentions*, in 2011, after much anticipation. This cinematic portrayal of its young female protagonist's coming of age amidst unstable familial circumstances also reflects on the impact of Peru's civil conflict on the nation's urban elite. The production context of this film followed a pattern that has become all too familiar for filmmakers of Latin America: it took six years to come to fruition and required six funding schemes (a mix of the national with the transnational). García-Montero's film was successful first on the arts cinema festival circuit, most notably achieving a nomination for the Crystal Bear award at the Berlin Film Festival, where it had its premiere in 2011, before receiving acclaim from audiences and critics in her home nation.[14]

Thematically and in terms of narrative structure, *Las malas intenciones* adopts a distinctive approach by not foregrounding the Shining Path conflict but ensuring that traces of it are felt from the outset and that explicit references are brought in gradually, in keeping with the perspective of the child. Despite being set in the same decade as Eyde's feature, García-Montero's debut film focuses on an intimate and darkly humorous portrayal of the effect of stultifying privilege on its protagonist, Cayetana de los Heros (played by an impressive nine-year-old newcomer, Fátima Buntinx). The story begins in the mid-1980s and focuses on the domestic difficulties faced by this young girl growing up in the suburbs of Lima; while clearly set during a troubled period for the whole of Peru, those broader social and political troubles are seen largely from a child's perspective, that is to say in terms of how they affect her daily life. Nevertheless, Cayetana's personal situation– defined by illness, entrapment, familial absence and strife – is aligned cinematically with the broader national picture of conflict, difference, political uncertainty and social disconnection through a range of devices, such as the heightening of the garden walls to protect the family house from insurgent attack, which also has the effect of cutting the girl off from the neighbours, who represent the poor and indigenous social strata of Peru.

Left increasingly to her own devices, Cayetana retreats into a fantasy world where she surrounds herself with various historical heroic Peruvian (male) figures whose stories have fascinated her at school, in particular their extraordinary deeds and painful deaths. With images cut out from her history books, she brings to life figures such as Tupac Amaru, the last indigenous monarch of the neo-Inca state, who was executed by the Spanish in 1572, as well as a range of national heroes from the War of the Pacific (1979–1883), including Colonels Francisco Bolognesi and Alfonso Ugarte, who were killed while defending the port town of Arica from a Chilean attack in 1880, Admiral Miguel Grau, whose body was blown to smithereens in 1879 in a naval battle during the same war with Chile, and José Olaya, Afro-Peruvian hero in the Peruvian War of Independence, who acted as secret emissary carrying messages between the government of Callao and Lima patriots, and who suffered torture and execution as a result. These images become more and more realistic in their depiction, transforming from two-dimensional cut-outs which Cayetana manipulates and accompanied by the girl's own voice-over, to animated sequences that bring to life moments of battle, to scenes, when she is at her most desperate, where those heroes appear before her and inspire her with words of bravery. She sets great store by their potential to help save her, and is disappointed when they, like her father, teacher and driver, all fail to live up to her expectations and abandon her.

As the writer-director García-Montero has explained, she drew on her own childhood experience to craft a script 'with an inner voice – an inner gaze – that seems completely detached in its absurd tendencies, but is actually deeply rooted in precise and specific traumas, that are both very local and universal at the same time' (Yi 2012). The Peruvian heroes referenced above mark very specific moments of national history (the War of the Pacific and the War of Independence) and yet what is important to this film, in particular to the young protagonist, is their heroism in the face of suffering and their unerring commitment to a cause despite the mortal consequences. Moreover, the references to the Shining Path, mostly through indirect signifiers which show the fear and chaos generated by the conflict, signal another very specific traumatic moment of Peruvian history, but mainly serve to emphasise how isolated Cayetana has become in physical and psychological terms from real life around her in the present. Not being able to fully understand herself, much less what is going on around her, Cayetana sublimates her feelings into an obsessive and romanticised interest in the historical drama of Peru's colonial origins.

Blurring social realism with fantasy in the way it presents these specific aspects of social, historical and political context, the film is transgressive in form in terms of its refusal to be contained by standard generic conventions. In some ways it is reminiscent of the Mexican/Spanish fantasy/horror *El laberinto del fauno/Pan's Labyrinth* by Guillermo del Toro (2006), which also draws attention to the horrors of conflict through nightmarish projections from the perspective of a young girl at the point of her coming of age. Like del Toro, this filmmaker has made interesting aesthetic choices, eschewing the warm pastels that are often used to portray childhood and offering instead a sense of the ghostly presence of the real horrors of the Shining Path with mist and cold hues that signify death and isolation, also echoing del Toro's colour coding and use of metallic blues to represent the militaristic cruelty of the post-Civil War period in Spain. However, whereas Ofelia in del Toro's drama fully enters into a fantasy dimension, García-Montero's Cayetana retains just enough connection with the real world to suggest that she might recover and transition to womanhood. The non-standard 'heroine' of *Las malas intenciones* is portrayed as being full of contradictions: hard and vulnerable, lonely, sad and confused. While outside her household social conflict is about to erupt as Shining Path attacks edge closer to the capital city and the adults are seen taking practical measures to protect themselves, Cayetana is preoccupied with the way her own world seems to be falling apart with the news that her mother is pregnant by her new partner, which triggers Cayetana to become convinced that she is doomed to die when the baby is born. Since her mother already suffers anxiety and has little room in her life to care for her daughter, Cayetana believes she will be completely cast adrift when her brother arrives, and she becomes more introspective (see Figure 2.1). Feelings of betrayal and jealousy overcome her and she retreats to her imaginary world more and more. Having already begun to imagine herself as a key player in the War of Independence from the Spanish crown, she becomes particularly attached to Simón Bolivar's dramatic challenge to Antonio José de Sucre for the rule of Gran Colombia, that 'two suns cannot exist in the same sky', as a means of expressing her fear of, and resentment towards, her brother, whom she regards as a rival for her mother's affections. As commentator-reviewer Rick Segreda has pointed out: 'she becomes convinced that fate has it that just as a sky cannot accommodate two suns, and Bolivar and Sucre could not jointly rule, that either she or her brother will die upon his birth' (2013).

The film drifts between fantasy and reality in a way that allows its writer-director to present some disturbing images of violence as imagined by the girl, and which allow the spectator to experience the narrative from her disoriented subject position, watching the events unfold through the eyes of this protagonist who is made insecure and fearful through the instability of family life, and takes comfort in the fortitude of her fantasy heroes. Of particular interest here is Cayetana's situation as only child, as abandoned child (in that her family is largely absent from the household) and the extent to which her pre-pubescent 'malleable identity' might be

Figure 2.1. Cayetana contemplates her future in *Las malas intenciones* (Rosario García Montero, 2011).

read as synecdochically linked to the broader crystallisation of national identity at a time of intense change (Driscoll 2002: 2).

The idea for this partially autobiographical debut feature film originated in the director's own childhood experiences and the girl protagonist thus becomes a cipher for the memories of the filmmaker. In various interviews given at the time of the series of festival screenings that announced her work in 2011, the director recounted that she:

> grew up in Peru in the 1980s, a turbulent decade of social transformations and crises, punctuated by the terrorist attacks of the Shining Path. It is a drama that seems quite divorced [from the political context] in its absurdist tendencies, but is actually deeply rooted in precisely that period of my country's history. (2012)[15]

As García-Montero suggests, the film's address to socio-political concerns is hardly explicit, little more than part of the *mise-en-scène* throughout. And yet, echoing Laura Podalsky writing about *La ciénaga/The Swamp* (Martel, 2001), an Argentine film with similar qualities, 'it is *there* in [the] sensorial charge that one finds the politics in this ostensibly apolitical film' about an alienated girl (2011: 111). Indeed, many critics have emphasised the film's affective features in their reviews, which praise the work for encouraging its audience to sympathise with Cayetana even when her behaviour towards those close to her might be regarded as cruel.

In her everyday life, the invisible yet ever-present threat of death, pain and violence transmutes strangely in the mind of this child, who is particularly susceptible to influence from male authority figures, real and imagined. Cayetana seems overwhelmed by guilt from a firebrand Catholic priest; she yearns for attention from her absentee father, who is frequently shown as unreliable and immature; she rejects the potential for paternal commitment from her stepfather, an artist and businessman who, despite his considerable affection and responsible custodianship of her, is somebody she refuses to regard as a parent; and, as outlined above, she is obsessed with the centuries-old historic revolutionary heroes of South America's past, envisioning entire imaginary adventures with them and drawing on their imagined words of reassurance as ways to deal with her own personal struggles. When Cayetana then finds out that her depressive mother is pregnant, her own neuroses converge illogically, but no less potently, into the belief that she will have to die when her mother gives birth to the male child.

The personal/private and the national perspectives are fused through Cayetana's morbid story, in which the fear and fact of death, illness and pain are pervasive; it redefines 'masculine' models of aesthetics and politics by offering a personal, subjective take on national and ideological conflict – placing a girl's experience, imagined and real, at the centre of the frame. For, on the one hand, Cayetana's world (and, she believes, her life) are threatened by the pending arrival of a baby brother and the possibility that her relationship with her mother might become further distorted; on the other hand, Peru's capital city and its inhabitants (including Cayetana and her family) are about to find their lives rocked by the arrival of the civil conflict on their doorstep. As Cayetana is not the daughter of her mother's partner, the arrival of a male baby/heir in the family constitutes a real fear of being displaced by a child shared by the new couple. In Cayetana's mind, the date of the baby's birth will determine her own expiration date; while this turns out not to be the case, on the very day her mother goes into labour, the Shining Path announces its attacks in central Lima through the tactic of hanging dogs' corpses from lampposts across the city. Dates are crucial here: the narrative takes place during the six final months of the pregnancy, coinciding with the period of the Shining Path conflict that saw the campaign of violence move from the remote rural parts of the country to the streets of the capital city. The largely imagined conflict in the eyes of many Peruvians suddenly became very real indeed.

The film opens, closes and is punctuated by scenes that show Cayetana being driven home from her private college, first by the elderly hired driver who serves as a father figure, then by her mother, whose difficulty negotiating the roads draws attention both to her disoriented state of mind and her upper-class disconnection from the city streets, and finally by the new chauffeur, who tries to insist that the newly blacked out and reinforced windows remain firmly closed to protect her from the perceived dangers of the streets. The connection made between the calm, logical approach of the male drivers to the navigation of chaotic space as compared with the anxious mother's difficulty in doing so is underlined by the more fragmented editing style used to present the middle sequence. It is clearly a long journey to school, which Cayetana finds boring, despite the 'excitement' and increasingly horrific signs of conflict and chaos on the streets. She is disconnected from that reality physically and psychologically. Indeed, her parents seem intent on protecting her from reality while at the same time disrupting it with their own 'bad' behaviour, which, in the case of the father, borders on the infantile or adolescent in terms of his apparent inability to understand that his daughter needs his attention. On a separate car journey in the film, Cayetana is with her father and asks for his help to decipher the signs of social disorder outside; she sees something out in the darkness: a fiery hammer and sickle burning on a hillside. When she asks her father what it is, he refers to it as burning trash, nothing important, even though it has been established for the viewer that this is Peru in 1982 and the 'burning trash' is the unambiguous mark of another act of terror by the Shining Path. The girl is abandoned to exist in a fenced-off indecipherable present full of questions that no adult seems able or willing to answer in a way that makes sense to her. In the end, this chaotic gloom-laden world makes sense for her only when she allows into her imaginary world the heroic ghosts of this nation's past.[16] And yet, like her father, even these (male) figments of her imagination let her down. She has to find a way to exert agency, find her own young female voice and save herself; indeed, in the final scenes, Cayetana finally takes control and starts to embrace her future, however uncertain, in a more positive and pro-active fashion. She accepts her baby brother's arrival, leaves the hospital alone and defies her new driver/protector by winding down the darkly tinted and reinforced window of the car, weeping as she does so, in a small but significant moment of resistance.

Thus the film deploys the Shining Path conflict largely as the backdrop for a dark portrait of Cayetana's morbid childhood, and of her abrupt and early transformation to adolescence, in line with so many young people in urban and rural Peru at that time and as portrayed more directly in Eyde's film of the 1990s. The violence and its aftermath are part of the backdrop to the diegesis, helping to link the narrative and its characters with the national experience without explaining those events precisely. For Cayetana, the need for strengthened windows, heightened walls and candles to cope with the electricity blackouts is part of her everyday life: she is annoyed that she can no longer peer over the garden wall to chat with the neighbours who live in far more impoverished circumstances, but she fails to appreciate the broader significance of the social divisions that are thereby indicated. The girl might not seem to be either politically or ideologically engaged as yet, but the director provides a politicised message by demonstrating in her film that the cost of sustaining the privileges of the upper classes is the state of constant fear in which they live. The film thus renders private citizens as political subjects and centres the political within intimate spaces. The core message of the film appears to be, therefore, that active female participation and agency are essential, whether in family life or more broadly; passive spectatorship alone is simply not enough in order to live life to the full. As her grandmother tells Cayetana on the way to visit her newborn brother in the hospital: 'You can't act as if nothing is happening'.

As evidence of its resonance and national status, the film – like Llosa's *La teta asustada* in 2009 – was selected by the Ministry of Culture to be Peru's nomination for the foreign-language award at the Oscars, having already won best-film awards at all the major events in Peru itself. Moreover, its young actress was nominated for a prestigious Young Artist Award 2013 at the Oscars for her powerful performance as the young girl who struggles to come to terms with the reality of the changing world around her. Meanwhile, García-Montero won a special prize at the annual Lima Film Festival, the premiere event for cinema in Peru and a significant date on the broader Latin American festival circuit, for her sympathetic direction of children within this film; more notable still in the context of this essay were the interview opportunities shared by the director with her star at such events as the Berlin Film Festival, where the young girl was given her own voice and agency within the cinematic context when handed the microphone by the adults and invited to speak about her own experiences on set.[17] This could be construed as yet another example of the 'Llosa effect', which sees more women from Latin America, of all ages and from behind as well as in front of the camera, entering onto – literally and figuratively – the transnational stage.

Conclusion

This discussion of some recent advances by female directors in Peru must take account of the relatively homogenous nature of this group of filmmakers and the extent to which the other diversities of a complex nation are concealed. In terms of class and ethnicity, for example, it should be noted that all the female filmmakers highlighted here are quite wealthy and/or well connected, well educated, and linked to Europe and/or the United States in some way, whether through family, training or education. While their stance of speaking for the female subaltern other is important, it is also clear that some kind of strategy needs to be put in place at national level to extend and enhance the range of diversities within and across Peruvian cinema for those who wish to direct.

In any case, drawing on the paradigms set out by Mette Hjort and Susan Hayward on the thematisation and framing of nation, it is possible to claim that, despite their international acclaim, Eyde, García-Montero and even Llosa might be positioned, above all, as national filmmakers.[18] They take topical themes important to the Peruvian nation; they deploy quotidian signifiers pertaining to collective rituals involving food, religion and domesticity to give a sense of the everyday life of Peru. From an economic and ideological point of view, they have all received a degree of funding from the various legislative incentives brought in to support Peruvian cinema since the 1970s, and thus can be regarded as acknowledged, if not always without controversy, as significant national directors with transnational reach and impact. Nevertheless, the situation has become more complicated in part due to the constraints and possibilities of new funding models. These women make films that take the diversity of Peruvian national identity as a theme to explore in itself, and yet part of the reason they continue to be funded is that they have had transnational success, even when (as in the case of Eyde and *La vida es una sola*) they are rejected on a national level.

Significantly, each director confronts and critiques the patriarchal institutions, private and public, that impose their notion of societal convention – such as the military in Eyde's *La vida es una sola* and family in Llosa's *Madeinusa* and García-Montero's *Las malas intenciones*. Indeed, the more recent female-directed films seem to reveal an increasing confidence in portraying the ambiguities and potentiality of female transgression and resistance on screen. Certainly, as noted by that roundtable of 2011 and in subsequent festival programmes domestically and overseas, their works have become more appreciated and recognised on both the home and the international front through awards, critiques and festival acclaim.[19] Finally, it is apparent that some of the most successful contemporary films by Peru's female directors are often about children and/or told from the child or young woman's perspective. In this respect, certain themes remain paramount, such as the ongoing infantilisation of women; the situation of women and children as traditionally excluded from full subjectivity and agency; and the stifling and claustrophobic environment of the bourgeois child as a signifier of the situation of women themselves. As Carolina Rocha and Georgia Seminet have pointed out, such portrayals indicate 'the precariousness of the lives of girls as they come of age during globalization' and the determined concern on the part of the protagonists with agency in the face of tragic adversity is compelling (2014: xiii).

As this chapter has set out to explain, the situation for female directors in Peru is increasingly interesting. While there are more and more women gaining access to the (admittedly limited) nationally based sources of funding, infrastructure and exhibition, two of the directors mentioned here, Llosa and García-Montero, have also gained significant attention on the international circuit, as have the young women (Magaly Solier, star of *Madeinusa* and Buntinx) who have become recognised as talented actors through the central roles they took in these films. In the case of all the works referenced here, we see a focus on young women – Florinda, Meche, Madeinusa, Cayetana – from indigenous, mestizo and Hispanic ethnic backgrounds brought together in their struggle to make sense of their private worlds in the context of violence and conflict on a personal/private as well as a political/public scale. The most interesting and complex relationships they appear to have and which they need to overcome are those with their mothers, aunts, grandmothers, female friends, patrons, employers and compatriots, with whom they share many of the same desires and struggles. They are all ordinary young women placed in extraordinary situations through their specific circumstances; in each case those circumstances are framed to a more or less explicit degree by the very topical/national context of the Shining Path conflict and the inequalities prevalent in that period, exposed most intensively across all the social strata of Peru. Of course, timing is crucial to the mode of production, approach to drama and context of reception: while Eyde's film was made at the height of the conflict, for example, Llosa and García-Montero's works are much more to do with the way the past lingers on into, and affects, the present. The intensive drama of that political framing device is further underscored by the much more personal drama for each of the protagonists who are in effect coming of age before us on screen, battling to decipher their own adolescent awakenings within largely patriarchal contexts. Moreover, we find an emphasis in these stories on the discovery of a more distinctive female voice and agency which privileges the characters' development as active participants in the building of new communities and families over more conventional romantic storylines.

The specific cultures, nations and local discourses which frame such stories are important, as Robin and Jaffe pointed out, but so too are the perennial and more universally translatable discourses of their female protagonists, such as friendship, love, betrayal, if they are to be understood and enjoyed on a global scale, and if they are to continue to be funded and supported by transnational schemes, initiatives and festivals. Finally, while issues of gender and national identity continue to be explored through the works of these filmmakers, as they are by several of their male counterparts,[20] the focus on the troubled, perplexed perspective of their young female protagonists, often blending fiction and fantasy, and the unsettling, unresolved nature of their stories, continues to provoke a disruptive questioning about the situation for women in Peru. It is to be hoped, too, that the female filmmakers themselves continue to develop their own spheres of influence on the national and international scene so that their efforts become much more than another chapter in the history of this nation's cinema.

Notes

1. The speakers at this event were Valeria Ruiz (*Rey de Londres/King of London*), Rosario García-Montero (*Las malas intenciones/Bad Intentions*), Judith Vélez (*Seis con ocho*), Gabriela Yepes (*Danzak*), Marianela Vega (*Payasos*) and Silvana Aguirre (*Ela*).
2. For example, his first feature, *Días de Santiago/Days of Santiago* (2004), included a series of strong female roles against whom the male protagonist tried to define himself. See Barrow (2014) for a fuller discussion of this film. His producer on this film was Enid 'Pinky' Campos, of the company Chullachaki Cine, who also produced *Climas* (2014), directed by Enrica Pérez, referenced in this essay. Both he and Campos were associate producers of the multi-award-winning *Las malas intenciones*, by García-Montero, which features in this chapter.

3. Note also that, in her festival programmes, Salazar has featured films by several of the women who participated in the roundtable, and director Rosario García-Montero's debut feature opened the 2012 edition of the festival, which took as its theme 'Cinema and Memory of the Internal Armed Conflict in Peru'.
4. García-Montero, for example, has studied film in Lima, New York and Cuba.
5. For example, these films have benefited variously from funding from European bodies such as the Dutch Hubert Bals Fund, linked to the Rotterdam Film Festival; the French Cinéfondation programme and Aides aux Cinéma du Monde; the German World Cinema Fund, coordinated through the Berlin Film Festival; and the Spanish-led Hispanic Programa Ibermedia, as well as the Sundance Screenwriters' Lab, among others. Festival-based schemes have proved crucial in this regard. García-Montero's *Las malas intenciones* was in fact registered as a co-production between Peru, Germany and Argentina, was a recipient of a Peruvian state funding award, had significant post-production support from Argentine facilities and expertise, and had funding for its production and distribution from Berlin Festival's Talent Campus and Co-Production Market under the 'Produire au Sud' initiative.
6. Claudia Llosa is the niece of Peruvian writer Mario Vargas Llosa and the US-based film director Luis Llosa.
7. There now exists a relatively large body of academic work that explores the complexities of Llosa's work. Moreover, Deborah Shaw has spoken and written about the topic of European co-production funds, othering and bourgeois cinephilia in Claudia Llosa's work, for example at events at St Andrews and Lincoln Universities in February 2015 and on the blog page of the project MECETES: Mediating Cultural Encounters through European Screens (Shaw 2015).
8. White also focuses on Llosa; indeed, her text does not mention other female directors from Peru. Her approach is a more global/transnational one, eschewing the specific intertwining of the national/regional/local.
9. The directors involved in this project in addition to García-Montero were: Claudia Sparrow, Valeria Ruiz, Silvana Aguirre, Enrica Pérez, Gabriela Yepes, Melina León, Mariaela Vega and Rosana Alalú, some of whom were also part of the roundtable mentioned in note 1. The second edition of Perufest (2012) featured another emerging set of female filmmakers from Peru of the same generation whose work is considered more experimental in form: Ana Balcázar, Milagro Farfán, Malena Martínez, Tilsa Otta, Sofía Velázquez and Maya Watanabe.
10. Eyde's filmography includes: as fiction, *Los ronderos* (1987), *La vida es una sola/You Only Live Once* (1992), *La carnada/The Bait* (1999) and *Coca mama* (2004); and as documentary, *Casire* (1980), *Alpaqueros de chimboya* (1983), *La cuna del bacalao* (2008) and *Dibujando memorias/Drawing Memories* (2015).

11. Respected playwright Alonso Alegría requested that his name be removed, although many online listings of the film still feature his name as the film's screenwriter.
12. For a fuller discussion of the controversy, including a comparison with the fate of a film by Francisco Lombardi that also dealt with Shining Path concerns, see Barrow (2006).
13. In Eyde's other film of the 1990s, *La carnada/The Bait* (1999), protagonist Maria is ultimately forced to accept her husband's continued absence and her new role as mother. Having been labelled as deviant by the fishing community where she has grown up whenever she attempts to break out of her assigned role of dutiful wife and expectant mother, she remains caught between the opposing forces of inner desire and external order.
14. In one of many interviews given by the director at the time of her debut feature film's release, García-Montero describes herself as the 'slowest blossoming new face of independent film' (Caceres 2012).
15. These words also highlight the link between the film and the director's own childhood memories and were captured in the promotional material and cited at events such as Viva! The 18th Spanish and Latin American Film Festival, at Cornerhouse, Manchester, where the film received its UK premiere in March 2012.
16. See Laura Marks (2000: 21) and Laura Mulvey (2006: 31) for a discussion of the 'indecipherable' in the context of cinema.
17. The extensive set of interviews with filmmaker and star at the Berlinale 2011 can be seen on YouTube: '*Las malas intenciones* Berlinale' (2011), http://www.youtube.com/watch?v=SNYsuH3iD_M (accessed 16 July 2015).
18. See Hjort (2000: 103–17) and Hayward (2000: 88–102).
19. The Festival de Lima of 2015 selected Eyde's latest documentary, *Dibujando memorias/Drawing Memories* (2015), on the use of drawing workshops to retrace the horrors of the Shining Path conflict from the point of view of those Andean villagers who suffered, to screen as part of its official competition. Moreover, one of the festival jury members that year was another female director – the globally respected Peruvian/Dutch documentary-maker Heddy Honnigan.
20. The debut feature of Josué Méndez, mentioned in note 2, focuses on the troubled male perspective of his protagonist, blends reality and disturbing fantasy, and has a similar lack of resolution. Both this film and García-Montero's debut of 2011 were produced by the impressive Enid 'Pinky' Campos. While it is beyond the scope of this essay to pursue this further, Campos' role in and influence over many of the developments discussed here should not be underestimated.

References

Barrow, Sarah (2006). 'Political violence, cinematic representation and Peruvian national identity', in Peter Lambert and Will Fowler (eds), *Political Violence and the Construction of National Identity in Latin America*, Basingstoke: Palgrave Macmillan, pp. 131–48.

—— (2014). Out of the shadows: New Peruvian cinema, national identity and political violence. *Modern Languages Open*. Available at http://www.modernlanguagesopen.org/index.php/mlo/article/view/18/56 (accessed 18 July 2015).

Bedoya, Ricardo (1995). *100 Years of Cinema in Peru: A Critical History*, Lima: Universidad de Lima.

—— (1997). *A Cinema Rediscovered: Illustrated Dictionary of Peruvian Films*, Lima: Universidad de Lima.

Caceres, Juan (2012). 'LatinoBuzz: interview with Rosario García-Montero', *Sydney's Buzz*. Available at http://blogs.indiewire.com/sydneylevine/latinobuzz-interview-with-rosario-garcia-montero (accessed 6 July 2015).

Driscoll, Catherine (2002). *Girls: Feminine Adolescence in Popular Culture and Cultural Theory*, New York: Columbia University Press.

Hayward, Susan (2000). 'Framing national cinemas', in Mette Hjort and Scott Mackenzie (eds), *Cinema and Nation*, London: Routledge, pp. 88–102.

Hjort, Mette (2000). 'Themes of nation', in Mette Hjort and Scott Mackenzie (eds), *Cinema and Nation*, London: Routledge, pp. 103–17.

Koenig Quart, Barbara (1989). *Women Directors: The Emergence of a New Cinema*, New York: Praeger.

Marks, Laura (2000). *The Skin of the Film: Intercultural Cinema, Embodiment, and the Senses*, Durham Duke University Press.

Mulvey, Laura (2006). *Death 24x a Second: Stillness and the Moving Image*, London: Reaktion Books.

Podalsky, Laura (2011). *The Politics of Affect and Emotion in the Contemporary Latin American Cinema: Argentina, Brazil, Cuba and Mexico*, Basingstoke: Palgrave Macmillan.

Richards, Keith (2011). *Themes in Latin American Cinema: A Critical Survey*, North Carolina: McFarland.

Rocha, Carolina and Georgia Seminet (eds) (2014). *Screening Minors in Latin American Cinema*, Lanham: Lexington Books.

Robin, Diana and Ira Jaffe (eds) (1999). *Redirecting the Gaze: Gender, Theory and Cinema in the Third World*, Albany: State University of New York Press.

Rojas, Lazlo (2014). 'Conoce las más de 30 películas peruanas que veremos este 2014', 5 January. Available at http://www.cinencuentro.com/2014/01/05/peliculas-peruanas-estrenos-2014/ (accessed 29 July 2015).

Salazar Jiménez, Claudia (2010). 'PERUFEST: Festival de Nuevo Cine Peruano'. Available at https://claudiasalazarjimenez.wordpress.com/ (accessed 7 July 2015).

Segreda, Rick (2013). *'Bad Intentions'*, 4 July. Available at http://southernpacificreview.com/2013/07/04/film-review-bad-intenions-las-malas-intenciones/ (accessed 30 June 2015).

Shaw, Deborah (2015). 'European support for Latin American Cinema'. Available at http://mecetes.co.uk/european-support-latin-american-cinema/ (accessed 6 August 2015).

White, Patricia (2015). *Women's Cinema, World Cinema: Projecting Contemporary Feminisms*, Durham: Duke University Press.

Whittaker, David J. (2001). *The Terrorism Reader*, London: Routledge.

Yi, Esther (2012). 'Five questions with *The Bad Intentions* director Rosario García-Montero', 17 December. Available at http://filmmakermagazine.com/60860-five-questions-with-the-bad-intentions-director-rosario-garcia-monteros/#.VcJOX87bKUk (accessed 16 July 2015).

3

Parando la olla documental: Women and Contemporary Chilean Documentary Film

Claudia Bossay and María-Paz Peirano

During the 1973–89 dictatorship established in Chile by the military forces headed by General Augusto Pinochet, the popular sectors developed various means of solidarity and resistance. Among them were armed groups, the families of the *detenidos desaparecidos* (detained disappeared), mostly women, and various groups of activists, including feminists and human rights advocates. Within this environment, a widespread phenomenon was the *olla común* (common pot), a collective action of communal feeding where everybody pitches in with ingredients and helps with the cooking so that nutritional standards can be sustained at a time of precarious economic conditions. This symbolic act of union (and nutrition) appears during times of shortage, protest, tragedy or celebration. As an act of survival, it creates a culture of solidarity, community and leadership (*la olla común*).

At the time, this form of popular solidarity was mainly led by women: 'the dictatorship forced us to take our homes onto the streets' states one of the interviewees in the documentary *Calles caminadas/ Walked Streets*, directed by feminists Eliana Largo and Verónica Quense (2006), indicating that women had to apply their experience as mothers, teachers and home-makers to the public sphere. The *olla común* is also recalled in the documentary *Calle Sante Fe/Santa Fe Street* (2007), directed by Carmen Castillo. While speaking of the values of the MIR (Movimiento Izquierda Revolucionaria), female interviewees suggest that their role was more than merely feeding the neighbourhood, but also involved caring for and educating the young revolutionaries who risked their lives fighting against the dictatorship. This *olla común* is part of a broader Chilean cultural phenomenon in which women continuously *se hacen cargo* (take charge) of urgent business in order to survive. It expresses a particular habitus that has helped women overcome precariousness by creating new forms of resistance and solidarity in moments of need.

The *olla común*, which symbolises strength in the face of oppression, lends itself as a metaphor to the precariousness that Chilean cinema endured during the 1970s, and the censorship and silence enforced during the 1980s and 1990s. This precariousness reflects a historical condition of Latin American cinema that led to particular filmmaking strategies, modes of production and theoretical approaches, in many ways reminiscent of the cultural logic behind the *olla común*. Production conditions in Chile have changed in recent decades and the documentary field has expanded, despite its precariousness, in many ways thanks to women's leadership. Professionals have *parado la olla* (supported the common pot) of Chilean documentary by developing strategies of solidarity and leadership in filmmaking, distribution and exhibition.

This chapter discusses the nature of documentary cinema made by women in Chile in this context, exploring the extent to which it is adequate to conceptualise films made by women as an extension of certain conventional discourses of femininity, such as those immediately linking women's concerns mainly with motherhood, family ties, intimacy and emotional engagement. The presence of these topics along with more 'subjective' forms in women's documentary filmmaking worldwide seems to reaffirm those discourses. We will show that women filmmakers working today in Chile approach this issue differently. Recent transformations in the documentary field have led to the expansion of women's work, which indeed tends to follow more intimate stories and to explore essayistic forms, affirming filmmakers' subjectivity. However, while their point of view could be interpreted as a typically 'feminine' one, the younger generations working today debate this labelling, as they believe it has been imposed *a posteriori* on their work. We will see that the presence of these topics and forms is a result of filmmakers' shared habitus and filmmaking practices, which filmmakers often understand as 'neutral' in terms of gender.

Despite the above, we still identify in women filmmakers' practices other attitudes that are related to a particular cultural construction of gender roles in Chile. We argue that women's documentary cinema is influenced by the gendered position of the filmmakers in the field, only not in the straightforward way that it might seem to be at first sight. We will see that traditional gender roles related to collective practices in the face of precariousness, like the *olla común*, are the ones that have an impact on the production practices, the presence in the field and the films of these women filmmakers.

To do this, we first give an account of the precarious configuration of the Chilean field of documentary production, and explain the way women have used a habitus of traditional collaborative strategies to overcome these conditions. We then give an overview of current Chilean documentary films made by women, and present three generations that coexist in the field. We go on to analyse the impact of women's habitus on their films, with a focus on those dealing with political trauma and those belonging to a less political 'subjective turn' in local documentary filmmaking.

A diagnosis of the field: between precarious conditions and international success

Over the last decade, the production and circulation of Chilean documentary films has noticeably increased, a process accompanied by wide international recognition. While Chilean documentary filmmaking is well known for its strong tradition, rooted in the Nuevo cine chileno movement of the 1960s, it suffered a significant downturn after the military coup in 1973. The state abandoned support for local cinema, only a few productions were made and exhibited in Chile, and documentary films were transformed into a form of urgent, underground cinema, willing to denounce the abuses of Pinochet's regime although the production of such films could lead to detention, torture and death, which in turn created an atmosphere of censorship and self-censorship (Villarroel 2005: 28). During this time, Chilean cinema was able to continue only in exile. After the return to democracy in 1990, Chilean cinema started a slow process of recovery. By 2010, an average of 30 documentaries a year were being premiered, three times as many as just a decade earlier (ChileDoc 2014: 13).

We can understand the Chilean 'field' of documentary film production as a space of social positions and position-takings that constitute a set of objective relations that enable the creation and circulation of cultural products (Bourdieu 1993: 30). From Pierre Bourdieu's perspective, the field relies on the social practices and habitus of the agents involved in film production – that is to say, their particular values, dispositions and expectations acquired through the experiences of everyday life. The Chilean documentary field is thus a structured set of manifestations of the social agents involved, whose practices, particularly those of women, have constituted and transformed the cultural field.

The Chilean documentary field has expanded due to its professionalisation, linked to factors such as the increasing sponsorship of film production by the Chilean state (Mouesca 2005; Trejo 2009), the strengthening of national and international professional networks among documentary filmmakers, the emergence of the figure of the documentary film producer and the re-emergence of national film schools in the mid-1990s. The appearance of an increasing number of female agents (i.e., directors, producers and technicians) since the mid-1990s has been key for this development. As in other professions, women have increasingly entered the public space and have taken leading positions in the Chilean documentary field,[1] where they have influenced many of the collaborative strategies described in the next section.

State sponsorship of cinema has resulted from various changes in Chilean legislation, thanks to the collective struggle of documentary film professionals during the 1990s to create favourable cultural policies.[2] Their endeavour led to the creation of new institutions and funding resources for a growing number of independent documentary films, mainly thanks to the (National) Council of Audio-visual Art and Industry (Consejo del Arte y la Industria Audiovisual, CAIA) which has increasingly sponsored their distribution, exhibition and promotion, including their participation in international film festivals and markets (Peirano 2015). Nevertheless, the conditions for documentary production in Chile are still precarious. Documentary films are not normally distributed outside the specialised film festival circuit and are rarely released in commercial showcases and art house cinemas. Chilean television rarely funds and broadcasts local productions – only an average of five Chilean documentaries per year, according to ChileDoc (2014: 37) – or has done so in very poor conditions, particularly in the case of political or more 'creative' documentary films.[3] In terms of production conditions, Chilean documentary filmmakers normally work 'by project', without fixed contracts, similarly to other 'creative professionals' worldwide (Boltanski and Chiapello 2005: 166–7).[4] This practice simultaneously encourages and limits their creative work, and generates stressful working conditions. The lack of secure funding to complete film projects makes it extremely hard to make a living solely from working in film, and professionals depend on alternative sources of income, which may become their main source of regular income.

These precarious conditions are not exclusive to contemporary Chilean cinema but have deep historical roots. The rhetoric in the late 1960s and early 1970s of Latin American cinema and its manifestos can shed some light on this persistence. In *Aesthetics of Hunger* (1982 [1965]), Glauber Rocha describes the shortage of technicians, lack of technical means and scarcity of freedom of Latin American cinema. According to Ignacio Del Valle, 'hunger' means 'in literal terms – precariousness, malnutrition and poverty – and in metaphorical terms – a search for acknowledgement, an anxiety to create and the impossibility of development' (Del Valle 2014: 231, our translation). Yet, despite these difficulties, hunger was, and still is, Latin American cinema's biggest creative asset. 'Perfection' – as understood in Julio García Espinosa's *For an Imperfect Cinema* (1976 [1969]) – was not possible within the budgetary and political constraints, and would even imply a lack of content and commitment. Both manifestos agree that material poverty does not stop but rather feeds the creative process, encouraging resourceful solutions manifest in examples of 'imperfect cinema', Cinema Novo, and other examples of low budget socially conscious filmmaking. The acknowledgement and embrace of precariousness partly explain the ways in which women filmmakers developed documentary film in the past, frequently as part of a collective effort and new forms of collaboration (Lesage 1990: 316). These modes of production, embedded in the tradition of social documentary in the region, can still be recognised in recent filmmaking and networking practices among Chilean filmmakers.

Collaborative production strategies and the professionalisation of the field

The way in which filmmakers face the precarious conditions in Chile, drawing from their traditional collaborative practices, has changed the documentary scene in recent decades. Filmmakers have aimed to develop production strategies based on strong cooperative networks, which have helped to position documentary film in both the Chilean and the international mediascape. Their new practices have resulted in an increase in both the production of Chilean documentaries and their recognition on the international film festival circuit. For example, films like *La once/Tea Time*, by Maite Alberdi (2014), and *La última estación/The Last Station*, directed by Catalina Vergara and Cristián Soto (2012), were consistently selected for some of the most respected festivals and received multiple awards. Both films also represent the expansion of the themes and subjects of contemporary Chilean documentary, as they portray the private lives of elderly people who had previously been under-represented in Chilean cinema.

The success of Chilean documentary is directly linked to the advocacy of women film directors and film producers, who have led the creation of stable professional networks (ChileDoc), active political organisations (ADOC; Asociación de Documentalistas de Chile), novel distribution platforms (Miradoc) and diverse exhibition initiatives, particularly specialised local film festivals such as FIDOCS (Festival Internacional de Documentales de Santiago). The ChileDoc network in particular, created in 2010 by producers Paola Castillo and Flor Rubina with public funding from the CAIA (2010 and 2013), has played a pivotal role in the promotion of Chilean documentary. This organisation has aimed to establish a transnational professional network that brings together a whole 'community of documentary filmmakers and producers' (ChileDoc 2015), and helps internationalise, professionalise and expand documentary film. The organisation makes international connections with festivals and markets that increase the participation of local filmmakers in those settings, and it also promotes the exhibition of national documentary in Chile through the Miradoc project, which releases the most recent local documentaries simultaneously in various Chilean towns (ChileDoc 2015). In addition,

ChileDoc encourages professional development by organising workshops, open talks and lectures for Chilean directors and producers.

These women-led initiatives have been facilitated by their habitus of cooperative work and social responsibility, which is, in turn, sustained by their close relationships with each other and their common filmmaking practices. Leading figures in the field have shared political struggles, and studied and worked together on numerous projects. The generation of filmmakers who started to work in the late 1980s and early 1990s (a second generation who coexist today in the film mediascape) participated in the struggles for the state's protection and sponsorship of national cinema mentioned above, and they currently teach together in the same film schools. As they cannot be full-time filmmakers due to the precariousness of the job market, professionals often share multiple working spaces, both producing and teaching in practice-based research modes. As a result, women filmmakers have not only strengthened their social ties with other professionals but have also had an important impact on documentary education and research, building a community of documentary professionals. The learning process of younger generations has been reinforced by these communitarian ties, which are maintained in further work relationships.

In accordance with the ethos behind the *olla común*, working together and learning from each other have encouraged various reciprocal forms of collaboration within academic institutions and among individuals, helping to build strong friendships. For example, award-winning filmmaker Maite Alberdi was the student and teaching assistant of producer and director Paola Castillo. Later, Castillo would become Alberdi's producer on *El salvavidas/The Lifeguard* (2011). Reflecting on their relationship, Castillo states, 'Maybe there was a time when my role was that of mentor, but today I learn a lot from her' (in Jurado 2015: 26), showing a work ethic in which horizontality and reciprocity reinforce communitarian bonds.

The emergence of documentary producers and their involvement in creative work also express this collaborative dimension. Women producers have led most of the aforementioned initiatives of networking and professionalisation, and producers such as Viviana Erpel, Claudia Barril, Paola Castillo, Flor Rubina, Catalina Vergara and Clara Taricco have been actively and intimately involved in the creative process of recent Chilean films. Similar to other cases in the region (Burucúa 2014), they have been active supporters of new Chilean 'author' documentaries, promoting them both in Chile and abroad. Beyond their financial role, which includes securing multiple sources of funding, managing project finances and promoting their films, they are directly involved in the projects they believe in and 'love' (ChileDoc 2014: 45).

Cooperative social practices are hence linked to specific production strategies. Similar to what happens in other small film industries (see Mathieu 2011), films often share similar crews, and professionals exchange positions on different film projects in order to overcome the difficulties of the job market. These strategies have supported the maintenance and enhancement of a cooperative artistic community, since filmmakers take overlapping positions that intensify their collaborative ties. Film directors, producers and scriptwriters tend to work on several projects together, exchange roles and create cooperative networks. There are strong and often recurrent collaborations between certain directors and producers (*La once/ Tea Time*, Alberdi, produced by Clara Taricco, 2014) and directors and editors (*El otro día/The Other Day*, directed by Ignacio Agüero and edited by Sophie França, 2012). In these terms, much as Lúcia Nagib comments in her focus on Brazil in Chapter 1 of this book, in Chile the collaborative nature of filmmaking can be found both between women (from the same or different generation) and between women and men. Stable filmmaking partnerships normally include at least one woman, for example that of Bettina Perut and Ivan Osnovikoff, who have worked together on six documentaries, including *El astuto mono Pinochet contra La Moneda de los cerdos* (2004) and *La muerte de Pinochet/The Death of Pinochet* (2011).[5]

Local filmmakers, producers and technicians have an impact on each other's work, influencing and guiding projects, and developing production strategies that involve continuous social exchanges among documentary professionals. As director and academic Tiziana Panizza states:

> I think there's something historical, generational there [...] Many of us met in those years [the 1990s]. We were learning, and between all of us, it's like we encouraged each other [...] probably because of how close documentary is to politics. Thus, there was a kind of resistance, a complicity [...] So there's still something in common that makes us collaborate with each other [...] I'm not sure if it's the same in fiction film,

but documentaries involve crews of just three or four people, there is not much hierarchy, and relationships are a bit more horizontal. Also, besides those formal collaborations, what happens is that we show each other's work a lot, that's to say, you often make a first cut and then you screen it to other filmmakers. There's a kind of trust; it's not so competitive, although the field actually is.[6]

As Panizza suggests, collaboration is particularly noticeable in documentary film production, probably because it depends on smaller crews and more horizontal work relationships. Arguably, this is also one of the reasons why women have entered the field and position themselves more as makers of documentaries than of fiction films. Documentary film production seems to be an extension of other forms of women's work, in which they have held leadership positions that do not depend on (or aim for) individual success, but privilege collaborative teamwork. Women filmmakers' social positions and practices coincide with their historical roles as communitarian leaders, expanding from their family lives to their public performances, independently of the different social classes they belong to.

This women's habitus has enhanced the development of the Chilean field. Production strategies and professional networks such as ChileDoc are grounded in filmmakers' close social bonds and *modus operandi*, which have facilitated the expansion of Chilean cinema. Against all the odds, female cinema workers have created unions, worked in partnerships and constructed communities. They have been 'feeders', teachers, mentors and leaders, and have thus repositioned Chilean documentary cinema abroad as well as on local screens. They have *parado la olla* (supported the common pot) of Chilean documentary.

Women's cinema? Themes and strategies in Chilean documentaries by women

The recent transformation of Chilean cinema has also had an impact on the type of documentaries being made. Three generations of women filmmakers coexist in the field: one that started filming before and during the dictatorship (1970s–1980s), one that started in the transition to democracy (late 1980s and early 1990s) and one that came out of film schools in the 2000s–2010s, whose films have increasingly diversified. Since the mid-2000s there has been an expansion in 'creative documentaries' that express the personal vision of the filmmaker, for whom documentary is an art form.

This has meant a proliferation of documentaries that challenge previous aesthetic boundaries in documentary filmmaking, moving away from the dominant forms of linear narrative and television news conventions. In the Chilean case, this has meant expanding the thematic scope of documentary filmmaking, from militant and social films to more intimate stories, exploring essayistic, aestheticised and experimental forms, even when they refer to the Chilean dictatorship, frequently the focal point of political documentaries. Films are often first-person and/or performative, revealing the subjective gaze of the filmmaker rather than trying to express an objective 'reality' or macro-historical and political processes. Some scholars have interpreted this subjective turn as an intrinsic characteristic of women's filmmaking (Espinosa 2010; Petrolle and Wexman 2005), although it is important to note that there is a subjective turn also in documentaries directed by men and in fiction films.[7] Moreover, the films by women highlight other social and political issues, as well as the poetics of the documentary form, alongside gender.

As we discuss in the following pages, while it is possible to identify some trends easily associated with 'women's themes' in the growing corpus of documentaries made by women, these films do not deal with gender issues *a priori*, and hence filmmakers consider that to analyse these films exclusively through a gender framework is limiting. Most women filmmakers, especially the younger generations, are reluctant to be labelled as 'women filmmakers' and try to avoid gender markers, even when their films have themes that are conventionally identified with the 'feminine', such as autobiography and intimate portraits of family matters. For them, exploring private and public memory and their families is not a gender quest, but rather one that society as a whole should undergo. Indeed, the two younger generations making documentary films have tended to move on from the more common feminist approaches of the 1970s and 1980s. These filmmakers position themselves more in line with a certain 'post-feminist' consciousness (McRobbie 2004) that has both 'incorporated the fruits of the earlier ("second wave") feminist movement and rejected the idea of, or the necessity for, continuing to pursue feminist goals' (Ortner 2014). The younger generations seem to agree with Angela Martin, insofar as for them the debate about a 'feminist aesthetic or a woman's voice' in their films is limiting (2008: 130).

Director Lorena Giachino, for example, suggests that she thought of interviewing only women for *Reinalda del Carmen, mi mamá y yo/Reinalda del Carmen, My Mum and Me* (2006), but she let this notion go, as she considered it capricious. For her, making the film a 'gender study' would have distorted the aim, which was not about 'womanhood'. Reflecting on this labelling of women's films, she proposes that women's work may be constructed as gendered both *a priori*, from an openly militant gender standpoint, and *a posteriori*, from a later analysis of the director's gender and the theme of the film (Giachino 2010: 141–3). Chilean documentaries have often become gendered after the production process, that is, *a posteriori*. Pamela Pequeño, for example, suggests that her film *La hija de O'Higgins/ O'Higgins' Daughter* (2001) 'unconsciously became something feminine' (Pequeño 2010: 135) because of the family matters that it deals with.

Taking this standpoint into account, we consider that while many documentary films engage in the subjective turn of local filmmaking, moving towards the domains of intimacy, family relationships and emotions, an assumption that these topics are a natural result of filmmakers' gendered experiences only reinforces a reified distinction between women's private sphere and men's public world. By immediately associating the presence of gender issues in women's work as the main expression of a totalising female experience, these distinctions remain uncontested, and in fact obscure some of the more important creative drives of Chilean female filmmakers, discussed in the following sections.

Having said this, it is still necessary to explain some of the recurrent themes in the work of women filmmakers. Women's documentary films from the 2000s in Chile reflect sometimes unconsciously and sometimes unintentionally female themes and sensibilities. However, it is more accurate to note that they render visible queer issues, the elderly, immigrants and unrepresented members of society, all of which are presented in the cutting-edge language of contemporary world documentary, including first-person narration, mixed media and performative or other experimental forms. Films show Chilean filmmakers' aim to reflect on Chilean society by moving beyond a woman-centred focus and engaging with other forms of political critique. In line with 'third wave feminism' (see Martin's Chapter 10 in this volume), filmmakers reflect on issues of identity that could be previously understood as women's issues, but in conjunction with the political struggles of other groups traditionally excluded from a subject position. Filmmakers' cultural drive goes beyond an essentialist 'feminine' tag, and these films express in indirect ways the new social position of their makers as women in the precarious field. The specific ways these filmmakers approach filmmaking practices and documentary narratives offer new interpretations of Chilean women's traditional social and political roles. The analysis of the following cases will shed some light on this.

Women filmmakers, family and political trauma

The first generation of women filmmakers, who lived through the consequences of the dictatorship at first hand, in forced exile or self-censorship, deal with Chile's 'bigger history' and engage primarily with the social and personal consequences of the dictatorship. Although their films include a personal point of view, the broad historical process is still foregrounded. After the coup, women represented their experience in documentaries and contributed significantly to the portrayal of trauma from a female perspective. For decades, Angelina Vázquez and Marilú Mallet, together with Valeria Sarmiento, were some of the only women dealing with trauma in film.[8] Both Vásquez and Mallet approached their experience of living in exile from an *a priori* feminist perspective, and made experimental films that reflected on Chilean history through their private lives, by blurring the boundaries between fact and fiction. Besides these exiled filmmakers, during the 1980s female video artists residing in Chile, such as Gloria Camiruaga and Lotty Rosenfeld, also opposed the dictatorship by making video essays of everyday life from a feminist perspective. By the mid-1990s, other filmmakers of this generation, such as Carmen Castillo, were also working on traumatic history from a female standpoint.[9] For example, in *La Flaca Alejandra* (1994) Alejandra Merino, an ex-member of the MIR (Movimiento Izquierda Revolucionaria), is confronted with her former comrades, who feel betrayed by her collaboration with the military in order to survive. Later films, such as Caminuarga's *La venda/The Blindfold*

(2000), Mallet's *La cueca sola/The Lonely Cueca* (2003) and Castillo's *Calle Santa Fe*, represent a continuing desire to create a feminist visual exploration of trauma.

These directors deal openly with both militant and feminist issues such as political oppression, sexual and gender violence, relationships with partners, lovers, husbands and family, and bring to light the inequality and human rights violations undergone by the women who '*pararon la olla*' during the dictatorship. This first generation often combines autobiographical narration, experimental filmmaking and feminist issues as an essential part of their work exploring exile, torture and gender solidarity. In this sense, their films coincide with Janet Walker's proposal about other filmic explorations of trauma, such as Holocaust and incest films; she states that 'probing the limits of the filmic – and videographic – representation of traumatic past events has been for several decades a fully articulated project of feminist experimental autobiographical documentary theory and practice' (Walker 2005: 21).

However, despite these common autobiographical explorations, not all women's films use this strategy, and most of them do not focus on specific feminist topics. The aforementioned *Calles caminadas* is an exception that explores the history of political feminism in Chile, and even this documentary has a more journalistic and educational approach than a subjective or experimental one. Luis Valenzuela (2010) suggests that most of the themes of the documentaries directed (or co-directed) by women from the first and second generations present male subjects, such as public idols like anti-poet Nicanor Parra, politician Clotario Blest, musician Victor Jara, boxer Martín Vargas, as well as non-public male figures. On the other hand, most documentaries about female subjects were directed by men, with the exception of *La hija del General/The General's Daughter* (María Elena Wood, 2006).

Some films by the second generation of woman filmmakers deal with the 'big history' –the country's grand narrative, its public history as opposed to the private stories of its citizens – from women's points of view, using a journalistic approach. For example, Carmen Luz Parot's *Estadio Nacional/National Stadium* (2002) has specific, rather small sections on women remembering their pasts as detainees, nurses, mothers and wives. However, this film does not follow an auteurist approach. Added to this, the director's gender is hidden from viewers. On the other hand, Marcela Said's *I Love Pinochet* (2001) focuses on groups of female Pinochet supporters and their blind love for the dictator. However, although the director's gender is more explicitly presented, beyond the inclusion of women's perspectives the film does not deal with feminism or autobiographical issues. Hence, if the first generation had a militant and feminist approach, the issues dealt with in second-generation documentaries continued the focus on subjects such as 'big history'. However, this was combined with a more subjective turn and a shift towards a non *a priori* feminist approach.

Among the second generation of women filmmakers, who *pararon la olla* of documentary since the mid-1990s, we also find films dealing with the traumatic past, in this case from a subjective perspective. These documentaries could be understood as what Marianne Hirsch has described as post-memory, or the memory of the second generation, who may have experienced the traumatic events as children, so they cannot remember without the aid of their relatives and imagination. As Hirsch suggests, post-memory is 'a very particular form of memory precisely because its connection to its object or source is mediated not through recollection but through an imaginative investment and creation' (2012: 22). Macarena Aguiló and Susana Foxley's *El edificio de los chilenos/The Chilean Building* (2012), for example, focuses on Aguiló's experience in Proyecto Hogares, an institution in which 20 foster parents took care of the 60 children of militants who had clandestinely returned to Chile to fight Pinochet's dictatorship through Operación retorno ('Operation Return'). The children became 'social siblings', who, together with their foster parents, created a 'social home'. This 'traveling memory' film (Ramírez 2015) examines the experiences of Aguiló and her siblings and friends, and explores why their parents, particularly their mothers, sent their children to these social homes.

El edificio de los chilenos also demonstrates some of the Chilean women's habitus linked to solidarity and collaboration. Aguiló and Foxley worked together on both script and direction, and used their resourcefulness to secure funding from Chile (CNCA and CORFO) and abroad (Jan Vrijman Fund). Aguiló, who lived in Cuba herself, talks to her foster father, as well as her biological mother. The film includes archival footage and animation to explore the more emotional and ethereal aspect of Aguiló's memories and experiences of exile and those of other children from Proyecto Hogares, and required expert editing (see Figure 3.1). Hence, the recalling exercise is mediated by the stories of the adults who experienced the trauma of the coup and exile, as well as the trauma they unwittingly developed in their children. As a visual exercise in memory and its limits, it is forced to be creative to fill the silences and interpret the first-hand experiences.[10]

El edificio de los chilenos dialogues with issues that had already been explored in other female-directed documentaries, such as Castillo's *Calle Santa Fe*. In this film, Castillo and Margarita Marchi (a fellow MIR militant and Aguiló's mother) reflect on the costs of their militant and feminist lifestyles. In the late 1970s, the MIR called for the aforementioned Operación retorno, and militant parents had to decide whether it would be the father or the mother who would return. Through these evaluations, the MIR women decided that they should not be forced to stay in exile just because they were mothers, and instead developed Proyecto Hogares. Both Castillo and Marchi made sacrifices as mothers by sending their daughters to Cuba so that they could continue their militant work in defence of Chile's freedom. While *Calle Santa Fe* deals with exile, the return to the country, the history of the MIR and the identity of being a militant mother, *El edificio de los chilenos* explores Proyecto Hogares from the perspective of the children who question their parents' decisions and speak out on the emotional consequences, which had remained invisible.

In *Calle Santa Fe*, Aguiló is shown editing her documentary and presenting it to Castillo (Figure 3.1 and 3.2), and together, as affected parties, colleagues and women, they reflect on Chile, its history, the nature of memory and gender. The film includes footage of other trauma documentaries to explore how memory is affected by trauma, and how a dialogue is created between different images and testimonies, scattered over time and space. Thus, the film becomes a collaboration between two generations, revealing some of the aforementioned 'common pot' strategies of filmmaking practices among Chilean women filmmakers in every generation.

The second generation of female filmmakers has dealt many times with the memory of growing up in exile. Other cases are Paula Rodríguez's *Volver a vernos/Pinochet's Children* (2002) and Alejandra Carmona's *En algún lugar del cielo/Somewhere in Heaven* (2003). While these postmemory explorations deal with gender issues, such as being a militant mother or her daughter, they are mainly concerned with politics, traumatic

Figure 3.1 Macarena Aguiló editing *El edificio de los chilenos* (Macarena Aguiló and Susana Foxley, 2012).

Figure 3.2 Castillo and Aguiló watching footage from *Calle Santa Fe* (Carmen Castillo, 2007).

memory and the psychological aftermath left by the dictatorship, beyond gender-specific experiences.

In the 2000s, family and memory are not themes exclusive to female directors. Centred on the relationship with their parents and grandparents, films by male directors such as Germán Berger-Hertz (*Mi vida con Carlos/My Life with Carlos*, 2009), René Ballesteros (*La quemadura/The*

Burn, 2009) and Sebastián Moreno (*La ciudad de los fotógrafos*, 2006) also explore the nature of intimate family relationships and the aftermath of the dictatorship. For them, families and personal relations also become metaphors for the country and the collective. Like those produced by women filmmakers, in most of their films the political stand is not an openly militant approach like that of previous generations, but a more personal reflection.

The expansion of the field: new themes and strategies

Besides the work on historical trauma, the younger generations of documentary filmmakers have increasingly touched on a variety of topics, from transgender issues (and transvestism) and male homosexuality (*El gran circo pobre de Timoteo/Timoteo's Great Poor Circus*, by Giachino, 2013) or *Naomi Campbel* (a film by Camila José Donoso and Nicolás Videla, 2013) to Chilean popular culture and everyday stories apparently marginalised from the broader political and historical context (*El salvavidas*), and contemporary social issues, including poverty, elderly people, migration and ethnicity (*74m2*, by Panizza and Castillo 2012; the aforementioned *La última estación*; *Palestina al sur/Palestine in the South*, by Hurtado, 2011; *Dungún, la lengua/Dungun, the Language*, by Pequeño, 2012; *Surire*, by Perut and Osnovikoff, 2015). Since the return of democracy, women filmmakers, in partnerships or by themselves, have explored pressing social and economic issues that have expanded the politics of documentary filmmaking in Chile.

As previously mentioned, despite this diversity, we can identify some recurring themes in women's work, particularly in relation to the portrayal of strong female characters and the treatment of family relationships. Portrayals of women tend to evidence the filmmakers' gender roles discussed above. We have seen how films such as *Calle Santa Fe* and *El edificio de los chilenos* narrate complex relationships among women, their identity and their life stories; these films portray women whose political, family and social duties often overlap. In these and others, women tend to be the ones who take care of people and show accountability in difficult situations, as this has been the familial role of those behind the cameras. Female characters also take on caring roles and reveal questionable family relationships, as in these films they instigate truth telling.

For example, Marcia Tambutti's *Allende mi abuelo Allende/Beyond My Grandfather Allende* (2015) narrates the ex-President's family history. This family portrait, which includes the testimonies of male characters, is mostly narrated by different women, as Allende's life was marked by his relationships with his wife, his three daughters and his lovers. The film opens up the family's unspoken relationship with suicide. As with the cases of Castillo and Aguiló, it is a younger generation (Allende's granddaughter, protagonist and director) who reopen old wounds in an attempt to repair the damage. Even when the male family members are more willing to talk openly about the trauma, it is the female director who aims to bring peace to a broken family by initiating a communal conversation, once again taking care of her family, her community.

Much of the female directors' work refers to these family matters, and particularly matrilineal lineage. Similarly to *El edificio de los chilenos*, films have mother and grandmother figures as their main characters, such as *Hija/Daughter* (González, 2011), *La once/Dear Nonna* (Panizza, 2005), *Genoveva* (Castillo, 2014) and the aforementioned *La hija de O'Higgins*, *Volver a vernos* and *En algún lugar del cielo*. This choice certainly makes visible worlds that are mostly absent from masculine-centred films. The stories of mothers and grandmothers often facilitate the narration of other broader social and cultural issues. While acknowledging the importance of female characters and increasing the visibility of women through their focus, in most cases filmmakers seem far more concerned with other political issues overlapping gender (such as ethnicity or social exclusion), as well as with the poetics and politics of less conventional narrative forms.

González's *Hija*, for example, focuses on the director's relationship with her mother, but rather than emphasising gender constructions it reflects on the broader nature of identity, myth and storytelling. The film works as a road movie in which the director and her mother drive across Chile from south to north in a Volkswagen Beetle, searching for their two lost fathers. González's mother, who raised her alone, had invented a suitable – and dead – father whom the director never knew. In addition, the mother had always waited for her own missing father, a figure made up from fragmented stories she overheard during her childhood. Both stories overlap in a film that reflects on the nature of memory, rediscovery and loss.

The film evidences women's social position by touching on a world of fictional fathers. The absence of male figures who have left women to take care of their families by themselves is one of the main cultural traits of Chilean society (see Montecino 1993) and presumably a fundamental drive behind women's attitude towards accountability and solidarity. In this sense, the film shows the historical disposition of women to solve problems when facing adversity. Moreover, *Hija* shows again the role of a female filmmaker who uses a documentary apparatus to reveal a secret past and then rebuild family ties. In addition to gendered themes, the film focuses on developing this topic in depth, and on discussing the nature of documentary filmmaking and storytelling. It presents both the characters' journey and the documenting of their quest, portraying the production process by incorporating not only the director but also the film's producer and technicians into the diegesis. By revealing behind-the-scenes conversations, decision-making processes and filmic devices, it also shows the closeness and solidarity among the filmmaking team which characterise Chilean production strategies, as described above.

Panizza's trilogy of film letters (*Dear Nonna: A Film Letter*, 2004; *Remitente, una carta visual/Postage: A Visual Letter*, 2008; *Al final: La última carta/In the End: The Final Letter*, 2012) is another example, from a more experimental stance. The trilogy explores the intimate spaces of memory and forgetting. The films, which started as a visual letter to the director's grandmother, collect visual memories linked to traces of emotions, experiences and sensations. Shot on Super 8, they use found footage and collage editing to reflect on both the nature of memories and the mysteries of forgetting, while moving away from these themes to explore 'big' political memories. The trilogy highlights the subjective dimension of memory, embodied in fragments of everyday life: images of words and objects from personal recollections, at home, in the streets, in Chile and abroad. Emotional imaginaries are not detached from 'reality' but constitute it as the only possible truth.

While this approach seems to cover a 'feminine' territory *par excellence*, the trilogy emphasises personal exploration, memory and identity formation, beyond gender frameworks. Above all, the trilogy is concerned with documentary language and the possibilities of documenting 'the real', and thus it reflects broader concerns about documentary filmmaking and the limits of representation. In addition, the films' materiality expresses the local context of production and hints at the careful exploitation of the limited resources available. The trilogy's collages are made of visual fragments, remains which seem to recycle old pieces of memory woven together. Thus, they convey their handmade condition, and denote the paths of artistic creativity in a precarious context of production and reaffirming personal work in the interstices of the broader dominant forms of film production.

Films such as *Hija* and Panizza's trilogy could be inscribed in broader categories of creative documentary film, which correspond to a 'subjective turn' not only in contemporary Latin American film but also globally (Navarro and Rodríguez 2014: 47; see also Renov 2004). As Stella Bruzzi has pointed out, films are 'performative' by acknowledging the construction and artificiality of even non-fiction film, as a result of the filmmaker's intrusion into the situation being filmed, and the challenge to persistent ideas of truth emerging directly from any 'reality' outside the filmmaking experience (2000: 8). Documentary filmmakers from around the world persistently highlight subjectivity, problematise narrative structures and explore new visual forms that clash with conventional expository storytelling. These more 'poetic' or 'reflexive' forms (Nichols 2010: 127) enact knowledge through the unfolding of concrete, embodied and affective experiences of the documentation process, where the distinction between fact and fiction becomes blurred. In Chile, they also reflect on the conditions for image-making and film production, integrating films' narratives and materialities within local filmmaking practices.

One could argue, as indeed many have (see Petrolle and Wexman 2005; Martínez-Collado and Navarrete 2011), that the fact that women are leading these more 'experimental' forms of filmmaking is due to their disadvantaged position in the field. Innovation and alternative forms of narration are precisely the ways in which women have historically contested the hegemonic forms of a field dominated by men, while at the same time contesting the (gendered) conventions of documentary film. Petrolle and Wexman, analysing the explosion of women's experimental film in the 1980s and 1990s, have suggested, for example, that 'women who direct experimental films respond to a patriarchal context fraught with voices and images that describe the world from a male-centred perspective', revising 'the very paradigms within which this cinema has traditionally been considered' (2005: 1). From this perspective, their work does not have to be driven by any feminist agenda (and many have not been comfortable with being categorised as 'feminist' filmmakers) but is inspired by an 'auteur desire' (2005: 2), which has been facilitated by the artisanal conventions of the experimental mode. Women have positioned themselves as active agents, whatever political or aesthetic agenda they may have and whatever their relationship to feminism.

However, these new documentary forms in Chile have emerged alongside the expansion of the documentary field, and not only in relation to 'women's' filmmaking. In a field where women have been increasingly included as directors, and have taken a prominent position as producers, creators and advocates, it comes as no surprise that these new forms of documentary filmmaking are also led by women.[11] New documentaries are grounded in the social practices that enable their existence, in most cases promoted, constructed and 'fed' by women.

The recent predominance of experimental documentaries and small stories in Chile could be understood indirectly, then, as part of women filmmakers' habitus. We have seen that these films employ documentary filmmaking as a form of contestation to conventional filmmaking narratives. They also reflect Chilean cinema's particular conditions of production and the ways in which directors and producers have used their resources creatively in a difficult context. More experimental forms have emerged in the interstices of dominant film practices. The fact that women feel more comfortable making documentary films in horizontal, collaborative and relatively inexpensive ways, expresses their position in the field, but does not naturalise their films as 'feminine'. Their cultural learning processes reflect the broader forms of problem-solving that have traditionally been ascribed to Chilean women, and that are set in motion by the need for a professionalised 'common pot'. Women, once again, tend to fulfil a proactive social role, assessing and using the available resources to create and consolidate something new.

Conclusions

We have seen how women have played a pivotal role in the creation and promotion of Chilean documentary film, *parando la olla* for documentary production and creating adequate conditions for the development of Chilean film. We have shown how the flourishing documentary field of production in Chile, understood as a social practice, evinces broader cultural practices of solidarity, collaboration and resistance led by women, and how their films show the positions and habitus of women filmmakers in Chile.

Different generations of female directors, producers and collaborators are currently involved in the creation of an expanding and diverse field. They have produced documentary films exploring new narratives and aesthetic forms, notably more subjective, intimate and experimental constructions exploring identity, memory and political trauma. The films coincide in certain topics that have been conventionally related to 'women's themes', such as intimate and family relationships, yet it could be argued that this is a contextual response rather than solely a gender motivation. These topics still reveal, however, the social position of Chilean women and their collaborative working practices. Their films touch upon broader social issues, Chilean popular culture and everyday stories, all of which follow contemporary trends in international documentary film, responding to local ways of thinking and doing cinema, but that often have a global resonance, as can be seen in the international reception of many of these films at festivals.

Thus, the specificity of 'women's' filmmaking in Chile seems to be more related to social practices, collaborative networks and particular modes of production than to the narration of certain imaginaries and discourses of femininity. Current documentary filmmaking in Chile echoes historical women's practices responding to precariousness, and the films (small and modest, often personal, but internationally appealing) reflect the ways in which women have learnt to maximise cultural and social capital, contributing to a 'common pot' of documentary filmmaking. This *olla común* involves women being resourceful, acting collectively in the face of challenges, creating safety nets and networks, teaching values and 'feeding' those in need of a more professional documentary field, both men and women. In this collaborative and creative practice, the pot is enriched by constant effort, with no gender discrimination. Both the literal hunger – 'precariousness, malnutrition and poverty' – and the metaphorical one, incarnated in the hunger to narrate the silenced, the past, the trauma, the unjust, the invisible and the personal perceptions of family and society, come together in these female directors, producers and technicians who have changed the landscape of contemporary Chilean documentary.

Notes

1. Statistical information from 2008 suggests that 17 per cent of the documentary directors in Chile, 25 per cent of the producers and 50 per cent of the executive producers are women (Marchi 2010: 145). Due to the changes discussed in this chapter, these numbers have possibly increased since this last survey.
2. For example, Plataforma Audiovisual (Audio-visual Platform) supported the development of the Audio-visual Promotion Act, which was drafted in 1994, and fought for it until it was finally passed in 2004. It successfully included the audio-visual sector in the trade treaty agreed with the European Union in the late 1990s. Most importantly, it managed to eliminate the censorship law in operation since the dictatorship (Villarroel 2005: 30–1).
3. There is ongoing censorship by television of cinema that explores the historical-political trauma. For example, Bettina Perut and Iván Osnovikoff's *El astuto mono Pinochet contra La Moneda de los cerdos/Clever Monkey Pinochet* (2004) was part of the 30-year commemoration of the coup d'état, funded by Televisión Nacional de Chile Channel (TVN); however, when the channel saw the reels it withdrew its support. Years later, in 2013, Patricio Guzmán's *Nostalgia de la luz/Nostalgia for the Light* was shown by TVN but was severely cut.
4. According to the latest reports on the Chilean audio-visual sector, more than 40 per cent of workers have independent jobs and, apart from television and advertising employment, there is a high degree of informality (CNCA 2013: 8; Aspillaga 2014: 96).
5. Other examples of partnerships include Susana Foxley and Cristián Leighton's *Nema problema/No Problem* (2001); Macarena Aguiló and Foxley, who together researched, directed and scripted *El edificio de los chilenos/The Chilean Building* (2010); Claudia Barril, who was the assistant director on *La ciudad de los fotógrafos/City of Photographers* (2006) by Sebastían Moreno (produced by Viviana Erpel) and later became her co-director on *Habeas Corpus* (2014); Marcela Said and Jean de Certeau, who worked together on *I love Pinochet* (2006), *Opus Dei, una cruzada silenciosa/Opus Dei, a Silent Crusade* (2006) and *El Mocito* (2010); and Carolina Adriazola and José Luis Sepúlveda, who co-directed their first documentary *Crónica de un comité* (2014) after their collaboration on *Mitómana* (2009) and *El pejesapo* (2007). Similarly, there has been an emergence of film collectives, in which both women and men participate, such as Colectivo Viridiana Audiovisual, led by Pachi Bustos and Jorge Leiva, and five more documentary makers; in 2004

they created *Actores secundarios*. The leading partnership also co-directed *Ángeles Negros* (2006).
6. Personal interview, 19 May 2015, our translation.
7. Chilean critics have described the fiction films from the late 2000s with terms such as *desencantado* (disenchanted) and *centrífugo* (centrifugal) (Saavedra 2013; Urrutia 2013). By this they are referring to films that are more introspective and that reject grand narratives.
8. Further information in Ramírez and Donoso (2016).
9. Further information in Ramírez (2011).
10. Like many of other documentaries from this generation, it was widely recognised both in Chile and abroad, winning prizes at the Festival Internacional de Documentales de Santiago (FIDOCS), the Festival de Documentales de Chillán (CHILEREALITY) and the Festival de Documentales de La Pintana (PINTACANES), as well as at DOK Leipzig, 2º Coral Documental, Festival Internacional de Cine de La Habana and the New York Latino Film Festival, among others.
11. *Sueños de hielo* (Agüero, 1993), *Señales de ruta* (Díaz, 2000), *Tierra de agua* (Klein, 2004) and José Luis Torres Leiva's filmography are examples of this subjective turn in films made by leading men.

References

Aspillaga, Alejandra (2014). *Mapeo de las industrias creativas en Chile: caracterización y dimensionamiento*. Santiago: CNCA.
Boltanski, Luc and Eve Chiapello (2005). 'The new spirit of capitalism', *International Journal of Politics, Culture, and Society*, 18.3, pp. 161–88.
Bourdieu, Pierre (1993). *The Field of Cultural Production: Essays on Art and Literature*, New York: Columbia University Press.
Bruzzi, Stella (2000). *New Documentary: A Critical Introduction*, London: Routledge.
Burucúa, Constanza (2014). 'Lita Stantic: auteur producer/producer of auteurs', in Andrew Spicer, Anthony McKenna and Christopher Meir (eds), *Beyond the Bottom Line: The Producer in Film and Television Studies*, New York: Bloomsbury, pp. 215–28.
ChileDoc (2014). *Comienzo del despegue: estado de la distribución y comercialización de documentales en Chile entre 2000–2010*, Santiago: ChileDoc.
—— (2015). ChileDoc (online). Available at http://www.chiledoc.cl/ (accessed 15 June 2015).
CNCA (Consejo Nacional de la Cultura y de las Artes) (2013). *Resumen ejecutivo: estimación de posibles impactos económicos y sociales de una política de estímulos tributarios directos a la producción audiovisual en Chile*, Valparaíso: Escuela de Ingeniería Industrial, Pontificia Universidad Católico de Valparaíso.

Del Valle, Ignacio (2014). *Cámaras en trance. El nuevo cine latinoamericano, un proyecto cinematográfico subcontinental*, Santiago: Cuarto Propio.

Espinosa, Patricia (2010). 'El documental político realizado por mujeres', in Mónica Ríos, Patricia Espinosa and Luis Valenzuela (eds), *Cine de mujeres en postdictadura*, Santiago: CNCA, pp. 61–77.

García Espinosa, Julio (1976) [1969]. *Por un cine imperfecto*, Madrid: Castellote.

Giachino, Lorena (2010). 'La tela del género', in Mónica Ríos, Patricia Espinosa and Luis Valenzuela (eds), *Cine de mujeres en postdictadura*, Santiago: CNCA, pp. 141–3.

Hirsch, Marianne (2012). *The Generation of Postmemory: Writing and Visual Culture After the Holocaust*, New York: Columbia University Press.

Jurado, María Cristina (2015). 'Mi mentora y yo', in *Revista Ya, El Mercurio*, 28 July, p. 26.

'La olla común' (Online). Available at http://www.laollacomun.net/pedroaguirrecerda/inicio.html (accessed 15 July 2015).

Lesage, Julia (1990). 'Women make media: three modes of production', in Julianne Burton (ed.), *The Social Documentary in Latin America*, Pittsburgh: University of Pittsburgh Press, pp. 315–47.

Marchi, Margarita (2010). 'Las mujeres y sus opciones para trabajar en el medio cinematográfico-audiovisual en Chile', in Mónica Ríos, Patricia Espinosa and Luis Valenzuela (eds), *Cine de mujeres en postdictadura*, Santiago: CNCA, pp. 145–6.

Martin, Angela (2008). 'Refocusing authorship in women's filmmaking (2003)', in Barry Keith Grant (ed.), *Auteurs and Authorship: A Film Reader*, Malden: Blackwell.

Martínez-Collado, Ana and Ana Navarrete (2011). 'Mujeres e (industria) audiovisual hoy: involución, experimentación y nuevos modelos narrativos', *TESI*, 12.1, pp. 8–23.

Mathieu, Chris (2011). 'The cultural of production and career in the Danish film industry: the ideological symbiosis of "auteur" and "craftsperson"', *Creative Encounters* no. 68, Frederiksberg: Department of Organization, Copenhagen Business School, pp. 1–17.

McRobbie, Angela (2004). 'Post-feminism and popular culture', *Feminist Media Studies*, 4.3, pp. 255–64.

Montecino, Sonia (1993). *Madres y huachos: alegorías del mestizaje chileno*, Santiago: Cuarto Propio.

Mouesca, Jacqueline (2005). *El documental, la otra cara del cine*, Santiago: LOM.

Navarro, Vinicius and Juan Carlos Rodríguez (2014). *New Documentaries in Latin America*, New York: Palgrave Macmillan.

Nichols, Bill (2010). *Introduction to Documentary*, Bloomington: Indiana University Press.

Ortner, Sherry (2014). 'Too soon for post-feminism: the ongoing life of patriarchy in neoliberal America', *History and Anthropology*, 25.4, pp. 530–54.

Peirano, María Paz (2015). 'Connecting and sharing experiences: Chilean documentary film professionals at the film festival circuit', in Aida Vallejo (ed.), *Documentary Film Festivals*, New York: Wallflower Columbia University Press, pp. 158–69.

Pequeño, Pamela (2010). 'La memoria privada en *La hija de O'Higgins*: provocaciones a la historia oficial y personal', in Mónica Ríos, Patricia Espinosa and Luis Valenzuela (eds), *Cine de mujeres en postdictadura*, Santiago: CNCA, pp. 133–5.

Petrolle, Jean, and Virginia Wright Wexman (2005). *Women and Experimental Filmmaking*, Champaign: University of Illinois Press.

Ramírez, Elizabeth (2011). 'Memoria y desobediencia. Una aproximación a los documentales de Carmen Castillo', *La Fuga*, 12 (online). Available at http://2016.lafuga.cl/memoria-y-desobediencia/450 (accessed 25 September 2015).

―――― (2015). 'Traveling memories: women's reminiscences of displaced childhood in Chilean postdictatorship documentary', in Christine Gledhill and Julia Knight (eds), *Doing Women's Films: History Reframing Cinemas, Past and Future*, Champaign: University of Illinois Press, pp. 139–50.

―――― and Catalina Donoso (eds) (2016). *Nomadías: el cine de Marilú Mallet, Valeria Sarmiento y Angelina Vázquez*, Santiago: Metales Pesados.

Renov, Michael (2004). *The Subject of Documentary*, Minneapolis: University of Minnesota Press.

Rocha, Glauber (1982, orig. published in 1965). 'An esthetic of hunger', in Robert Stam and Randal Johnson (eds), *Brazilian Cinema*, East Brunswick: Associated University Presses, pp. 68–71.

Saavedra, Carlos (2013). *Intimidades desencantadas: la poética cinematográfica del dos mil*, Santiago: Cuarto Propio.

Trejo, Roberto (2009). *Cine, neoliberalismo y cultura: crítica a la economía política del cine chileno contemporáneo*, Santiago: ARCIS.

Urrutia, Carolina (2013). *Un cine centrífugo: ficciones chilenas 2005–2010*, Santiago: Cuarto Propio.

Valenzuela, Luis (2010). 'El lugar de la heroicidad', in Mónica Ríos, Patricia Espinosa and Luis Valenzuela (eds), *Cine de mujeres en postdictadura*, Santiago: CNCA, pp. 47–59.

Villarroel, Mónica (2005). *La voz de los cineastas: cine e identidad chilena en el umbral del milenio*, Santiago: Cuarto Propio.

Walker, Janet (2005). *Trauma Cinema: Documenting Incest and the Holocaust*, Berkeley: University of California Press.

II

Representations

4

Beyond the Spitfire: Re-visioning Latinas in Sylvia Morales' *A Crushing Love* (2009)

Catherine Leen

From Dolores del Río to Salma Hayek and from Lupe Vélez to Eva Longoria, the portrayal of Latinas in the United States has provoked debate, criticism and controversy. Since the era of silent movies, Hollywood's depiction of the Latina has been rigidly prescribed and reductive, while Latinos and Latinas themselves have contested these problematic portrayals in more nuanced and multifaceted visions of their communities. Sylvia Morales's documentary *A Crushing Love: Chicanas, Motherhood and Activism* (2009) presents a vision of activists and mothers that is radically at odds with the stereotypes of Latinas in Hollywood film and in the US media more generally.[1] This chapter examines the film against the context of persistently problematic representation of Latinas in the media and the ways in which Morales' film counters demeaning images of Chicanas through a multi-layered examination of different experiences of motherhood by politically radical women.

Twenty-first century foxes: Latinas on and behind the screen

The well known sexualised images of Latinas in mainstream US media are perhaps most troubling because of their endurance and the paucity of other images to counterbalance them. As recently as 1995, Chicana theorist and writer Ana Castillo noted that: 'We almost never see women reflective of ourselves (except usually in stereotypes) on television, in Hollywood productions, popular U.S. literature, or anywhere in mass media' (Castillo 1995: 191). Latinas have been relegated to an extremely limited range of roles that overwhelmingly present them as exotic, erotic others whose excessive sexuality is matched only by their irascible and irrational temperaments. The other typical representations of Latinas, which may also include elements of the prevalent highly sexualised characterisation, are as criminals or maids. Films such as Edward James Olmos' *American Me* (1992) and Allison Anders' *Mi vida loca/My Crazy Life* (1993) depict Chicanas as gang members, while a multitude of films, such as Amy Heckerling's *Clueless* (1995), James L. Brooks' *Spanglish* (2004) and Alejandro González Iñárritu's *Babel* (2006), portray Latinas as maids. In Wayne Wang's *Maid in Manhattan* (2002), Jennifer López's character combines all three stereotypes of the Latina – despite being sacked from her job as a maid for stealing, her allure is such that she wins the heart of a rich white man. As Ana M. López reminds us, these persistent images are not merely hackneyed tropes in entertainments that can be dismissed as inaccurate and unrealistic but are indicative of the power of the media to shape beliefs about ethnic groups and their difference:

> Hollywood does not represent ethnics and minorities: it creates them and provides an audience with an experience of them. Rather than an investigation of mimetic relationships, then, a critical reading of Hollywood's ethnographic discourse requires the analysis of the historical-political construction of self–'other' relations – the articulation of forms of difference, sexual and ethnic – as an inscription of, among other factors, Hollywood's power as ethnographer, creator and translator of 'otherness'. (López 1993: 68)

The fortunes of two stars of the silent era whose careers survived the advent of sound are indicative of the power of Hollywood to shape perceptions of the Latina as other. Joanne Hershfield, in her study of the career and screen image of Dolores del Río, comments that the early years of Hollywood saw what she terms 'racial cross dressing', whereby white actors represented various ethnicities, Asian actors could be cast as American

Indians and Mexicans could play 'half-breed Indians and Polynesian princesses' (Hershfield 2000: 3). As del Río herself noted, however, within this racialised casting only light-skinned actors could play any nationality, and she herself was often described as Spanish, to the point where she yearned to play the role of a Mexican woman that would reflect the richness of her culture (Rodríguez 2004: 61). She managed to do so only after returning to Mexico and starring in numerous acclaimed films, including Emilio Fernández's *María Candelaria* (1943) and *Flor silvestre/Wild Flower* (1944) (Mora 2005: 61). Her compatriot and contemporary Lupe Vélez was, on the other hand, unambiguously portrayed as Mexican and thus relegated to roles such as 'the vamp, the wildcat, the vixen' (Rodríguez 2004: 69). Known as the 'Mexican Spitfire' in reference to a series of films of the same name, very little differentiation was made between her on-screen roles and her off-screen life in magazines, newspapers, interviews and other publicity materials. As a consequence, she did not enjoy the same freedom as del Río to reinvent her persona and her enduring image remains that of the tempestuous Mexican troublemaker (Rodríquez-Estrada 1997: 475–93).

Over eight decades later, Latinas in Hollywood today are subject to the same relentless stereotyping and typecasting as del Río and Vélez, although they have taken on roles behind the screen that seem to offer some hope that this scenario may change. In a pattern that reverses del Río's move from achieving stardom in Hollywood and returning to Mexico to play a decisive role in its nascent film industry, Salma Hayek had a very successful career in Mexico, first as a soap opera star and then in serious dramatic roles in films such as Jorge Fons' *El callejón de los milagros/The Street of Miracles* (1995). This success in Mexico did not ease her way to Hollywood stardom, however, and she was initially cast in very small parts, such as a minor supporting role in *Mi vida loca* (Rodríguez 2004: 217). Her roles in mainstream films such as Barry Sonenfeld's *Wild Wild West* (1999) have centred on her erotic exoticism, much in the same way as Vélez's did. She has starred in less mainstream films, however, such as Kevin Smith's *Dogma* (1999), and established her own production company, Ventanarosa, which has produced films such as *In the Time of the Butterflies* (2001), an adaptation of Dominican author Julia Alvarez's novel about feminist revolutionaries (Molina Guzmán 2007: 122). Her collaboration on the biopic *Frida* (2002), about the iconic Mexican artist, best illustrates the ways in which the Latina body in Hollywood continues to be a contested site. The Frida Kahlo film was celebrated by some critics, such as Carl J. Mora, who commended it for bringing a Mexican story to Hollywood and showcasing the acting and producing talents of a Mexican woman (Mora 2005: 187). Criticisms of the film abounded, however, some of which took objection to the fact that the decision to have the characters speak English was inauthentic. There were also many concerns that Kahlo's significance as an artist and a political figure was elided in a character that was as relentlessly sexualised as the traditional Latina screen vamp.[2]

More recently, Eva Longoria's foray into producing the *Desperate Housewives* spinoff *Devious Maids* has also been roundly criticised, both for the sexualised portrayal of the lead characters and the fact that all four of the female protagonists play domestic servants. Longoria had herself played a stereotypically vampish character in *Desperate Housewives* and received negative coverage for this (Merskin 2007). It might have been expected, therefore, that she would distance herself from such a role when she came to produce her own show. Longoria did, but instead resurrected the other most common stereotype about Latinas – that they work only as domestic servants. *Devious Maids* centres on the attempts of four Latina maids to discover the truth about the murder of their friend Flora Hernández, who was working as a maid in Beverly Hills at the time of her death. Even the protagonist, who is not a maid but a college professor – Marisol Suárez, played by Ana Ortiz – prefers to pose as a maid, for reasons that remain obscure, than to take the obvious step of hiring a professional detective to solve the crime. When the killer is found, Marisol does not return to academia but instead marries a wealthy man in Season 2 and sets up a maid service business in Season 3. While again the reasons for this change of career are never given, it may well reflect the fact that Latinas are perceived to be believable on-screen only if they play maids or trophy housewives like Longoria's character in *Desperate Housewives*. This plot development could, in the absence of any explanations for it in the series, be seen either as stereotypical or as subtly subversive, as Marisol, despite seeming to revert to type, is an independent, resourceful character who remains true to her Latina heritage despite her privileged position in society.

The misgivings about the work of Hayek and Longoria in depicting Latinas as either sirens or maids are well founded, but they also speak to the dearth of representations of Latinas in Hollywood and the intense pressure brought to bear on Latinas who act as producers and directors. Morales considers the criticism of Longoria's show excessive, and points out that Latino directors are not subject to the same censure for using stereotypes in their work. While Morales acknowledges that the series' presentation of Latinas working as maids as an entertaining plot is problematic, she considers it to be a starting point: 'I think we need to set the bar high but not crush anything that's coming up that we feel is not political enough. Eva […] is trying to do something. She's in there, so she could start an infrastructure' (Morales 2014). Morales also contrasts the response to Longoria's series with the reception of the work of Chicano director Robert Rodriguez:

> Let's look at Robert Rodriguez. Have you seen his movies? They're not political […] he's not being critiqued but Eva is. There's a double standard. […] he had a big success with […] *El mariachi*. To me, it was well done but it was very stereotypical – the man saves the woman who was raped and he's going to kill everybody. […] it was very accepted because it's the normative – man saves woman, protects and will kill for her but she's got to die in order for him to be a man, and I don't like those movies – but he was not put down for it because that's the normative. We don't like the normative of the maids, I understand that, but it's still a double standard. (Morales 2014)

It is also worth noting that Rodriguez directed Hayek in a number of stereotypically sexualised roles in films such as *Desperado* (1995) and *From Dusk Till Dawn* (1996).[3] In the latter film, Hayek plays Santanico Pandemonium, a dancer in a Mexican bar called the Titty Twister. Amid raucous rock music and a myriad of topless or bikini-clad dancers, she appears on-stage in a feathered headdress, miniscule bikini and a flowing red cloak. The cloak is cast off to reveal an enormous snake, which slithers around her body as she begins a sensual dance. Her performance is constantly intercut with shots of the male spectators' lascivious gaze. She leaves the stage and sashays across the bar's tables to face audience member Richard Gecko (Quentin Tarantino), who pours whisky down her leg and then drinks it from her outstretched foot. As a violent brawl erupts, she remains motionless until, at the sight of the blood dripping from Gecko's injured hand, she transforms into a lizard-headed vampire. This disturbing transformation prompts all of the Mexicans in the bar to turn into vampires, with the women leading an orgy of macabre attacks on men. Film critic Charles Ramírez Berg asked Rodriguez to address criticisms of Hayek's role, pointing out that the portrayal of the Mexican women in the film as vampires was problematic and could be conflated with the traditional one of Mexican women as vamps. Rodriguez first holds Tarantino's script responsible for the role, but then argues that the roots of the character lay in Aztec mythology:

> I based Salma's character (Santanico Pandemonium) on a figure out of Aztec mythology, a goddess with a skull head and snakes. There was a vampire cult that believed that they had to kill to keep the sun shining. We found, you could say, vampires in Mexican history with this cult. [...] I added the snake dance because the image of that goddess was full of snakes and she was the queen of that cult. (Ramírez Berg 2002: 250)

Rodriguez cites Aztec mythology here in a decidedly self-interested manner that recalls Cherrie Moraga's indictment of the leaders of the male-dominated 1970s Chicano Movement for using 'a kind of "selective memory," drawing exclusively from those aspects of Mexican and Native cultures that served the interests of male heterosexuals' (Moraga 2009: 230). Rodriguez justifies his presentation of Hayek's character in an intensely sexual and violent manner by linking it to the figure of the goddess Coatlicue, who is recognisable in his account only from the reference to the skull. He refers to this goddess in an attempt to make Hayek's character more complex and culturally embedded but refuses to engage with the complexity of Coatlicue, who, as Gloria Anzaldúa explains, is a contradictory and multifaceted deity:

> In her figure, all the symbols important to the religion and philosophy of the Aztecs are integrated. Like Medusa, the Gorgon, she is a symbol of the fusion of opposites: the eagle and serpent, heaven and the underworld, life and death, mobility and immobility, beauty and horror. (Anzaldúa 2007: 69)

Far from being criticised for presenting Latinos and Latinas in a stereotypical manner, Rodriguez has been commended by Frederick Luis

Aldama for using Latinidad 'in ways that playfully foreground or overturn the stereotypes', with no reference whatsoever to gender politics (Aldama 2015: 5). Later in the same volume, there is some discussion of possible sexism in *From Dusk Till Dawn*, although this is explained in terms of the film's genre and contextualised with regard to Rodriguez's work as a whole (Aldama 2015: 197–225). Elsewhere, Aldama interprets Hayek's hyper-sexualised role in the film as 'carnivalesque' (2015: 59). Latinas, on the other hand, as we see from the critiques of Longoria and other Latinas, are offered no such latitude. Their representations of women in fictional, comedic series are taken as seriously as any documentary and given no credit for the inventiveness or playfulness credited to Rodriguez.

A case in point is an article from the *New York Times* that criticised both Longoria's *Devious Maids* and the comedy series *Modern Family*, which stars Colombian actress Sofia Vergara as a sexy trophy wife, and that noted that both series failed to appeal to Latina/o viewers. The article cited Mexican-American documentary filmmaker Liz Colunga, who lamented the theme of *Devious Maids* as stereotypical and saw Vergara's role as 'the clueless Latina' (Vega and Carter 2012). Colunga's reservations are understandable, yet the burden of responsibility is placed squarely on Latinas here, while, as we have seen, Latinos have also presented Latinas in stereotypical ways in their work without attracting negative comment. Moreover, *Devious Maids*, despite its less than revolutionary form, does weave some social critique into its melodramatic narrative. In Episode 1 of Season 3, for instance, protagonist Marisol Suárez attends a party to celebrate the publication of her book *Coming Clean: My Year Undercover as a Beverly Hills Maid*. She soon leaves in disgust, however, having upbraided a group of wealthy Anglo housewives for their condemnations of their maids as lazy, stupid and thieving. Vergara's character in *Modern Family*, meanwhile, is much more complex than the stereotype of the sexy siren – she is a savvy, witty woman who supported her son Manny by working as a hair stylist by day and a taxi driver by night before meeting her wealthy husband. A more recent example of a mainstream show that subverts the stereotypes of Latinas from within the confines of the soap opera genre is *Jane the Virgin*. This series follows the eponymous virgin protagonist as she attempts to deal with an unexpected pregnancy, which occurred when a distracted doctor mistakenly artificially inseminated her instead of another patient.

The show's conflation of IVF with the Immaculate Conception is a provocative concept that challenges the neat categories into which screen Latinas are relegated. Younger Latinas may well look more to Gina Rodríguez, the star of *Jane the Virgin*, and América Ferrera, who played the titular role in *Ugly Betty*, as role models, rather than the previous generation represented by Hayek or Longoria. Rodríguez and Ferrera have yet to take on roles outside acting, however, so that although their projects and representations of Latinas may be flawed, the work of Hayek and Longoria remains an important advance in self-representation that mirrors the lesser-known work of Chicana producers and directors such as Sylvia Morales, as we shall see in the next section.

Latinas, feminism and motherhood

Chicana theorists, writers and artists have had a varied and complex relationship with what they often term mainstream or white feminism. As well as confronting gender oppression and sexism, Chicanas have had to overcome racial prejudice and difficulties related to their often straitened circumstances. In her foundational text *Borderlands/ La Frontera: The New Mestiza*, Anzaldúa outlines the challenges facing Chicanas who, through education, can aspire to roles other than nun, prostitute or mother. She cautions that this is an option open to very few Chicanas because of financial constraints, however, and that 'educated or not, the onus is still on woman to be a wife/mother' (Anzaldúa 2007: 39). The Chicano Movement, which did much to address the class and racial oppression endured by Mexican Americans, has been widely criticised for considering the issue of gender to be unimportant or even a potential threat to its goals:

> The Chicano Movement built a group identity for the Mexican American working class in the 1960s that derived its impetus from antiracist politics and from a recuperation of cultural traditions based on an ethos of group solidarity and cultural distinctiveness. This ethos appealed to 'tradition' for culturally specific images of solidarity, such as the family or carnalismo, both of which, in the vision offered by male activists (and often agreed to by women), reproduced gender hierarchies and heterosexual identities. For Chicanas who had begun to move away

from 'tradition,' or at least had been engaged in a process of transformation, this vision stood in contrast to the complexities of family life in the barrio and U.S. society. (Espinoza 2003: 99)

As the above comment suggests, the Chicano Movement was not only divided along gender lines but women responded in various ways to the challenges that faced them. Citing Anna NietoGomez and other Chicana scholars, Maylei Blackwell makes the important observation that there was a marked difference between '"Feministas" and those movement women who, although they were "strong women" and good organisers, were "Loyalists" to the nationalist party line' (2003: 77). Despite attempts to relegate them to secondary roles in the Movement and even opposition from some women to the unmasking of such conflicts within Chicana/o culture, Chicanas spoke out strongly against gender oppression. Writers such as Cherríe Moraga have written extensively on the problematic nature of the rigidly gendered roles traditionally ascribed to both men and women. Noting the refusal to acknowledge the divisions and problems within Chicana/o families, she suggests that until such issues are addressed there can be no unity on a wider scale and so true solidarity remains elusive:

> We believe the more severely we protect the sex roles within the family, the stronger we will be as a unit in opposition to the Anglo threat. And yet, our refusal to examine all the roots of the lovelessness in our families is our weakest link and softest spot. Our resistance as a people to looking at the relationships within our families – between husband and wife, lovers, sister and brother, father, son, and daughter, etc. – leads me to believe that the Chicano male does not hold fast to the family unit merely to safeguard it from the death-dealings of the Anglo. Living under Capitalist Patriarchy, what is true for 'the man' in terms of misogyny is, to a great extent, true for the Chicano. (Moraga 1983: 110)

In response to the lack of support and understanding from many in their community, Chicanas organised to create spaces in which they could produce creative work. Anzaldúa, Moraga and other writers and theorists such as Norma Alarcón were at the forefront of a generation of women whose poetry, essays and fiction gave voice to the experiences of Chicanas in the 1970s and 1980s. Ellen McCracken reminds us, in her account of the continuing importance of this early work to contemporary Chicana writers, that Chicanas even founded their own printing presses and journals in order to publish the work of women writers, who were often dismissed as less political than their male peers (2014: 11–15). Latina and Chicana writers, therefore, redefined community 'as a sisterhood and non-familial solidarity' within which mothering became 'a form of pedagogy, inside and outside the home' (Santos and Crowe Morey 2013: 90). One way in which Chicanas formed their own canon was to collaborate with other women of colour to produce ground-breaking collections of feminist writing such as *This Bridge Called My Back* (1984) edited by Anzaldúa and Moraga, and *Making Face, Making Soul: Creative and Critical Perspectives by Feminists of Color* (1990), edited by Anzaldúa. Such projects were not always straightforward, however. Moraga has noted that in producing the former volume she was disappointed to discover that women of colour could be homophobic and that she encountered 'racism among us cross-culturally' (Saldívar-Hull 2000: 51).

Another strategy that would seem to offer some respite from the chasm between men and women in the Chicano Movement was working with white feminists. Ana Castillo, who coined the term Xicanista to describe an identity 'not just Chicana, not activista for La raza, not only a feminist but a Chicana feminist', has written that many Chicanas could not relate to the white women's movement, which, in turn, did not recognise them (1995: 94–5). Teresa Córdova sums up the situation of Chicanas who experienced gender discrimination from their male activist peers in the Movement, yet could not embrace mainstream feminism:

> Chicanas write in opposition to the symbolic representations of the Chicano movement that did not include them. Chicanas write in opposition to a hegemonic feminist discourse that places gender as a variable separate from that of race and class. Chicanas write in opposition to academics, whether mainstream or postmodern, who have never fully recognised them as subjects, as active agents. (Córdova 2003: 1)

In her account of the development of Chicana Studies, Edén E. Torres goes further, asserting that there is clear racism in the valuation of the work of US or French feminist theorists as superior to that of female Native American, Latina or African American scholars. She adds that the assumption that all college students should be familiar with these theories is in itself a reflection of 'a Eurocentric bias as it presumes everyone should or would want to understand the world through these particular lenses' (Torres 2003: 65). Another factor that played a role for many Chicanas in their development of a unique identity was religion or spirituality. While Moraga describes herself as Marxist though constantly engaging with her pre-Columbian heritage, Castillo suggests that Marxist theories about the oppression of working-class people are incompatible with Chicana spirituality, a view espoused also by Anzaldúa.[4] A final obstacle to Chicanas' embracing of white feminism was the conflation of the term with lesbianism by traditionalists within Chicana/o culture, as Gaspar de Alba signals:

> One of the accusations launched at the *feministas*, apart from calling them *agringadas*, Malinches, and FBI spies, was the term *lesbian*. Because they were believed to be anti-*familia*, they could be nothing but lesbians, according to the *machista* logic, and the term *lesbians*, of course, was a bad word, a dirty name. (Gaspar de Alba 2014: 74)

This is not to say that all Chicanas rejected mainstream feminism out of hand. Moraga has commented on the irony that Chicano theorists cite Marx and Engels without fear of criticism, while the referencing of the work of white feminists by Chicana feminists is seen to be problematic (1983: 106). Gaspar de Alba, meanwhile, references mainstream feminist theory in her work while reminding us that there have been many Latina precursors to Chicana feminism, including Sor Juana Inés de la Cruz (Gaspar de Alba 2014).

All of this brings us back to the issue of motherhood. If there are few works by Chicana theorists that deal directly with motherhood, there is an abundance of work, both textual and visual, about the key figure of the Virgen de Guadalupe. The Virgen de Guadalupe is revered both by men and women in the Chicano Movement as a symbol of solidarity and as the patron of the poor and oppressed. While this veneration, like that of the worship of other virgins in Catholic iconography, has been interpreted by women in contemporary society as repressive and presenting an impossible ideal that women cannot emulate, Chicana writers and activists have re-imagined the figure of the Virgen as a modern, feminist and sometimes queer icon. In an essay published in *Ms* entitled 'Guadalupe the sex goddess', Sandra Cisneros relates the virgin to pre-Columbian goddesses such as Coatlicue and reflects on her importance to the sexual development of Latinas (1996: 43–6). So many Chicana artists have reinterpreted her figure in their work that it has become a distinct genre, which has been analysed by Gaspar de Alba and artist Alma López in their volume *Our Lady of Controversy* (Gaspar de Alba and López 2011). While these reinterpretations of the Virgin are extremely diverse, they share a vision of her as a symbol of solidarity and empowerment, rather than oppressive patriarchy. Just as the figure of the Virgin is multivalent and even ambivalent, so too the representation of motherhood in cinema is something of a contested site for Chicanas, as we shall discuss in the following section.

Motherhood in Chicana/o films: from mamís to mamás

If the preponderance of Hollywood images of Latinas remains mired in the stereotype of the sexy seductress, alternative visions of women in films made by Chicano filmmakers often fall into the trap of desexualising women entirely. No other cinematic trope could accomplish this as completely as the Latina mother. In spite of the efforts by women to carve a space for themselves within the Chicano Movement, as we have seen, its male-centred politics was undoubtedly reflected in the early years of Chicana/o filmmaking. The first Chicano film, Luis Valdez's *I Am Joaquin* (1969), which I will return to when discussing the career of Sylvia Morales, represented Chicano history almost entirely from the point of view of men. Mothers and, predictably, the traditional image of the Virgen de Guadalupe, were the only women featured. Moreover, the four Chicano films made in the late 1980s that led to media speculation about a 'Hispanic Hollywood' – *La Bamba* (1987), *Born in East L.A.* (1987), *Stand and Deliver* (1988) and *The Milagro Beanfield War* (1988) – were all directed by men and focused on male protagonists (Goldman 1987: 82). While these films are laudable for their exposure of the myriad ways in which institutionalised racism affected the lives of Latinos in areas as diverse as socio-economic mobility, citizenship, land and education, they are notably lacking in central roles for women, other than as mothers who are important only in relation to their sons or husbands (Fregoso 1993: 130–47).

Even Chicano films that granted women larger roles in their narratives tended to portray women as paragons of self-sacrificing motherhood. In Gregory Nava's *El norte* (1983), the matriarch of the Xuncax family rarely leaves the kitchen and is remembered fondly by her daughter for her cooking. In Nava's *My Family* (1995), Jennifer López, in her first major screen role, plays the self-sacrificing matriarch María in a multigenerational saga about a Chicano family. María is entirely defined as the interlocutor between her husband and sons throughout the film, so that, despite her central role, 'the absence of her narrative agency reinforced gender inequality within the family structure as much as it freezes her in time, within the biologically inscribed role of motherhood' (Fregoso 2003: 77–8). The work of Morales and other Latina directors provided much-needed alternatives to this paternalistic, one-dimensional view of motherhood.

A Crushing Love: new visions of motherhood

In recognition of her contribution to Latina/o film and media, Morales received the Latino Committee Pioneer Award from the Directors Guild of America in 2013. From 1981 to 1985, she led the Latino Consortium at KCET in Los Angeles. She has directed episodes for Showtime's series *Resurrection Blvd*, PBS's *Chicano! The Mexican Civil Rights Movement* and the ACE and Emmy-nominated series *A Century of Women* (Loglines 2013). She is currently a professor at Loyola Marymount University's School of Film and Television in Los Angeles. In her study of Lupe Vélez's Hollywood career, Carmen Huaco-Nuzum cites Morales as a filmmaker who has reclaimed 'chicana, mestiza, representation from centuries of racial patriarchal containment' (Huaco-Nuzum 1996: 261). Chon A. Noriega also recognises Morales as one of the outstanding female filmmakers whose work was crucial to the development of Chicana/o cinema:

> Although Chicanas such as Susan Racho, Sylvia Morales, Esperanza Vásquez, and Lourdes Portillo were instrumental in

the first decade of Chicano cinema, their work has not received the same critical attention as male-produced films [...] and yet, it is the Chicana-produced work that has consistently challenged and redirected the cultural paradigms of Chicano cinema. (Noriega 1993: 86)

Her first film, *Chicana* (1979), has been interpreted as 'the feminist counterpart to the first Chicano film, *I Am Joaquín*' (Fregoso 1993: 39). Morales observes that she found Valdez's film inspiring, but she was struck by the absence of women in his account of Chicano history and so made her film to reinscribe Chicanas into Mexican–American history (Morales 2014). Throughout her career, Morales has focused on issues of women, family and Chicana feminism (Hidalgo de la Riva 2006: 53). The documentary *A Crushing Love* pays tribute to five ground-breaking Chicana activists, all of whom are mothers who have redefined the roles of Chicanas in society. Morales' examination of the achievements of these women is interwoven with scenes of her own struggle to make the film while looking after her teenage daughter, Michelle. Her exploration of the different ways in which her subjects reconcile motherhood with their work challenges the stereotypical and reductive representations of Latinas in the mainstream media, and stands in sharp contrast to the way in which Latina mothers have been portrayed in Latino films.

The film begins in medias res, with Morales editing her film at home as Michelle asks her to make her something to eat (see Figure 4.1). As an interview with United Farm Workers' co-founder Dolores Huerta plays in the background, Morales insists that she is busy and that Michelle should make herself something to eat. Michelle responds in a rather sulky manner, leaving Morales distracted and under pressure to return to work.

This mother–daughter argument, interspersed with an interview with Huerta, sets the scene for the film to follow, as Morales' own experience of the frustrations of trying to make her film while caring for her daughter is interwoven with the stories of the Chicana activists she interviews – the aforementioned Huerta; Elizabeth 'Betita' Martínez, educator and author of *500 Years of Chicana History*; Alicia Escalante, Civil Rights activist and founder and director of the East LA Welfare Rights Organization; Martha Cotera, entrepreneur and author of *Diosa y hembra*; and Cherríe Moraga, theorist and writer. The interviews with these pioneering women are

Figure 4.1. Michelle interrupts Sylvia editing the documentary *A Crushing Love*. (Sylvia Morales, 2009)

combined with archival photographs and footage, inter-titles, interviews with their children, and scenes from Morales' everyday life. Following the establishing sequence, she reflects on her motivations for making *A Crushing Love*:

> I was in the last stretch of completing my documentary on activist women, who grappled with the dual roles of motherhood and justice and social change. As a single mother of two working full time, I wanted to know, how in the world did they do it? [...] When did they find the time to wash and dry the clothes and then fold them? Shop for food, put it away and later cook it? Help the kids with homework and care for them when they were sick. [...] Did they ever find time for themselves? How did they do it all?

Morales explains that her independent film, which is distributed by Women Make Movies, was initially intended to record the achievements of an older generation of Chicana activists, among them Betita Martínez, who was 84 and had recently had a stroke. While preparing for the interview, Morales discovered, to her surprise, that Martínez had a daughter she had never heard her mention and so she decided to ask her how she combined motherhood and activism (Morales 2014). Martínez's response is characteristically forthright about her shortcomings as a mother:

> Looking back then [...] I was so involved in the other work and I thought, well, I'm doing all this work for humanity, and I didn't pay enough attention to the human life that was right in my own hands. I also, you know, I worried about this a lot, and I thought, am I just some kind of weird freak or whatever? I think that it wasn't that I didn't see my daughter as a human being who needed love and attention and everything, but I just didn't define myself as a, quote, mother.

This admission is so contrary to the traditional expectations of Latina mothers and the idealisation of motherhood so prevalent in Latina/o culture that it spurred Morales to organise her documentary around interviews with Chicana activists who are also mothers. Huerta (Figure 4.2), whose interview is juxtaposed with that of Martínez and Huerta's daughter, Alicia, is similarly pragmatic and unsentimental when she discusses childcare arrangements that involved her children living away from her for extended periods:

> We really didn't have any full-time babysitters once we started the union, so it made it difficult. [...] But then I had help [...] César's wife, Helen Chávez, two of my kids lived with her. My brother Marshall, who lived up in Oregon, in Washington, a couple of my kids went to live with them for a while. So they kind of shifted around, lived with different people, and then I would take them with me. [...] So they were kind of travelling migrant farmworker movement children, you know.

If these interviews are extraordinary in their departure from the expectations of the 'ideal' Latina mother, they are also notable in that a documentary about male activists would never feature such questions. In their study of the Cuban Revolution, Lois M. Smith and Alfred Padula could be referring to the Chicano Movement when they observe that: 'A fundamental problem with male-directed social movements is that their leaders rarely think about who is going to do the dishes' (Smith and Padula

Figure 4.2. Dolores Huerta and her children at a meeting of the United Farm Workers (still taken from *A Crushing Love*).

1996: 131). In the same volume, Fidel Castro, in a rare interview where he discusses his family life, appears to congratulate himself for knowing how many children he has: 'Castro himself told a reporter in 1994 that, as far as he knew, he had fewer than a dozen children: "Well, I don't have a tribe," he said' (Smith and Padula 1996: 155). Childcare would not appear to be an issue to which the leader of the Revolution paid much thought. Domestic work and childcare remain the primary concern of women, however, and the revolutionaries in Morales' film constantly juggled these responsibilities in order to achieve social change. If Martínez judges herself harshly as an inadequate mother, Huerta observes that it was her children, rather than herself, who made sacrifices that allowed her to pursue the work she loved.

The influence of their own mothers looms large in the lives of all five of the subjects in different ways – Huerta was inspired by her mother's decision to treat her brothers and herself equally, so that she did not have to serve them or do more chores than they did. Martínez notes that although her mother was Anglo, she was a Spanish teacher and loved Mexico and this helped her to have a strong sense of her identity despite growing up in a predominantly African-American city where she attended an all-white school. Cotera recalls being inspired by her grandmother's and mother's tales of the female soldiers in the Mexican Revolution: 'I swore to myself that I would be the female Pancho Villa'. Cotera and Escalante remark on the profound influence that their mothers' strength in supporting their families as single parents had on their lives. Moraga, meanwhile, speaks of her loneliness at not being able to confide in her mother about her sexuality and her astonishment that her 'fiercely judgemental' mother was completely supportive of her when she did come out to her.

The interviews with the activists' children also create a powerful testimony of the influence of their mothers on their lives, without glossing over the difficulties that they faced as a result of their mothers' commitment to their work. Alicia Huerta comments movingly on the economic hardship she and her siblings faced because her mother did not take on the typical domestic role of a Chicana mother, but she is unstinting in her praise of her mother's singular achievements: 'She was not the role model or the expectation that they wanted her to be, but now, it took a while for us to recognise, that's a hero, a person that speaks out and cares about others. That's important.' Tess Koning-Martínez, the daughter of Betita Martínez, speaks openly about the pain of feeling, when she was growing up, that her problems were not as important as the global issues that her mother was dealing with. She too reflects on how her mother's unconventional life affected her, but with rather more ambivalence. While she acknowledges that her mother defied expectations of what a Chicana mother should be and thus became an inspiration to Latinas, she has found it difficult to reconcile her expectations of motherhood with her personal experience:

> I would say in terms of a not so much stereotypical but archetypal quality about a mother is the idea of the mother dedicating herself to the child and the nurturing of the child and I have struggled with that, because I do feel that that is an important quality of a mother and I don't feel that I've gotten enough or I had my share of that.

Before the film's conclusion, Morales includes the only piece of archival footage that does not depict the women at the heart of her film. This clip depicts a model US family seated beneath a Christmas tree, as the beautifully dressed, softly spoken mother tells her children the story of another ideal and idealised mother, 'a kind young lady, whose name was Mary'. This footage is juxtaposed with an interview with Cotera's daughter, María Eugenia Cotera, who, like Koning-Martínez, addresses stereotypes about motherhood:

> Here's what I would call the stereotypical vision of motherhood – it would be like a mother who is so self-sacrificing and so self-abnegating that she loses her goals, her dreams, herself in her children, dedicates herself entirely to them, focuses on them, makes their lives as pleasant as possible, something I've talked to other children of activists about. What visions did we hold of childhood and how it should be and how do we feel like we weren't given that? To have a mother that bakes for you, to have a mother that's always there for you in a frilly apron, these are all visions that I don't know of anyone, outside of someone on TV, that has ever experienced that. The thing about stereotypes like that, or these sorts of false visions, is that they make us feel cheated.

Morales' film continues the work of Latina and Chicana feminists in complicating the vision of Latina motherhood. The variety of stories told and the diverse ways in which the activists interviewed reconciled their work with motherhood, to a greater or lesser degree, re-inscribes a hidden history of feminist activism into Chicana/o history. It also points to how much mothers and their children sacrifice in an attempt to achieve societal change and justice. Morales concludes by drawing her own inspiration from the stories of the other mothers in the film as she works to complete her film: 'I press on with faith, humour and a little grit'.

A Crushing Love: Latina and Latin American activism on screen

Chon A. Noriega, in his study of early decades of Chicana/o filmmaking, observed that because of the strong connection with Mexico and the contemporary reality of living and working in the United States, Chicana/o filmmakers have had to find a space between Latin America and Hollywood: 'From the start [...] Chicano cinema has had to mark out a space for itself between a weapon and a formula; between the political weapon of New Latin American Cinema and the economic formula of Hollywood' (Noriega 1993: 86). Chicana directors initially produced activist films in the mould of the new Latin American documentary, where the situations portrayed were represented as objective truths barely mediated by their creators. Lourdes Portillo's first film, *Las madres: The Mothers of the Plaza de Mayo* (1986), is a pan-American exploration of the activism of the Madres de Plaza de Mayo. These mothers, like those in *A Crushing Love*, were activists who brought about social change through their quest for justice. Paradoxically, the Madres de Plaza de Mayo were successful precisely because they organised as mothers, subverting the patriarchal, pro-family rhetoric of repressive military dictatorship in Argentina in the 1970s and 1980s. The Junta initially attempted to discredit their activism by dismissing them as 'las locas de la Plaza de Mayo', a term that is recalled by Alicia Huerta's comment that her mother's family thought that her mother, Dolores Huerta, was 'crazy' to move her family to Delano in attempt to improve farm workers' lives. This example underlines the struggle that women face more generally to be taken seriously as activists and organisers in cultures that do not accept that women can be political leaders. The use of extensive interviews with the mothers in Portillo's film, which often deal with memory, has close parallels with *A Crushing Love*. The memory of the early days of the Chicano Movement looms large in the film, as does the influence of previous generations of women and the recollections of activists' children.

Morales' interweaving of her own story with those of her subjects also makes the film, like Portillo's later documentaries about her own family, intensely personal. Morales did not initially intend to appear in the film herself, as she was wary of seeming to draw comparisons between her work and that of the activists. With much humour, she also comments on how terrible she felt seeing herself appearing less than glamorous. She ultimately decided that the scenes where Michelle films her in unguarded moments added a great deal of levity to the film (Morales 2014). Her decision to include the scenes of her journey towards making the film achieves much more than adding some humour, however, as it opens up a story that may be mistakenly seen as relevant only to Chicana/os to a wider audience interested in the struggles of women to reconcile motherhood with their work, an issue that has been debated since the early days of the women's movement. Morales' personal account of her own motherhood draws the viewer into the story as she and Michelle, who becomes the cinematographer, negotiate boundaries and learn from each other. A powerful unstated message in these scenes is how Michelle, like the children of the activists, continues her mother's legacy. This is turn underlines how Latinas and Chicanas have not only successfully contested the limitations of their culture in their political and creative work but have fashioned their own legacies. Morales' film, to borrow Adrienne Rich's term, re-visions Chicana activism by 'seeing difference differently' and confronting the difficulties of departing from the expectations of motherhood (De Lauretis 2000: 325). In so doing, it expands the meanings of motherhood to embrace mentoring, mutual understanding and true solidarity. Morales' film reflects the way in which Chicana filmmakers are creating their own feminist activism, following Anzaldúa's idea of creating a new *mestiza* consciousness, by integrating their personal stories of the difficulties and rewards of motherhood into Chicana history.

Notes

1. The term 'Chicana/o' is used throughout this chapter to refer to people of Mexican-American descent in the United States, while the term 'Latina/o,' which will often encompass Chicana/os, is used to refer to people of Latin American descent in the United States. Latino/a is also used in the North American sense, that is, to refer both to Latin Americans, such as the Mexican Salma Hayek, and to people of Latin American descent born in the United States.
2. See, for instance, Deborah Shaw (2010: 299–313) and Sofia Ruiz-Alfaro (2012: 1131–44).
3. See also Deborah Shaw's critique of Rodríguez's use of Latina/o stereotypes in *Once Upon A Time in Mexico* (2007).
4. See Castillo (1995: 89–92), Moraga (2011) and Anzaldúa (2007).

References

Aldama, Frederick Luis (2015). 'Rodriguez's cinema of possibilities: an introduction', in Frederick Luis Aldama (ed.), *Critical Approaches to the Cinema of Robert Rodríguez*, Austin: University of Texas Press, pp. 1–14.

Anzaldúa, Gloria (2007). *Borderlands/La Frontera: The New Mestiza*, San Francisco: Aunt Lute Books.

Blackwell, Maylei (2003). 'Contested histories: *Las hijas de Cuauhtémoc*', in Gabriella Arredondo, Aida Hurtado, Norma Klahn, Olga Nájera-Ramírez and Patricia Zavella (eds), *Chicana Feminisms: A Critical Reader*, Durham: Duke University Press, pp. 59–90.

Castillo, Ana (1995). *Massacre of the Dreamers: Essays on Xicanisma*, New York: Plume.

Cisneros, Sandra (1996). 'Guadalupe the sex goddess', *Ms*, 7/8, pp. 43–6.

Córdova, Teresa (2003). 'Introduction', in Arredondo *et al.* (eds), *Chicana Feminisms: A Critical Reader*, pp. 1–18.

De Lauretis, Teresa (2000). 'Rethinking women's cinema: aesthetics and feminist theory', in Robert Stam and Toby Miller (eds), *Film and Theory: An Anthology*, Malden: Blackwell, pp. 318–36.

Espinoza, Dionne (2003). '"Tanto tiempo disfrutamos…". Revisiting the gender and sexual politics of Chicana/o youth culture in East Los Angeles in the 1960s', in Alicia Gaspar de Alba (ed.), *Velvet Barrios: Popular Culture and Chicana/o Sexualities*, New York: Palgrave Macmillan, pp. 89–107.

Fregoso, Rosa Linda (1992). 'Chicana film practices: confronting the "many-headed demon of oppression"', in Chon A. Noriega (ed.), *Chicanos and Film: Representation and Resistance*, Minneapolis: University of Minnesota Press, pp. 168–82.

—— (1993). *The Bronze Screen: Chicana and Chicano Film Culture*, Minneapolis: University of Minnesota Press.

—— (2003). *MeXicana Encounters: The Making of Social Identities on the Borderlands*, Berkeley: University of California Press.

Gaspar de Alba, Alicia and Alma López (eds) (2011). *Our Lady of Controversy: Alma López's Irreverent Apparition*, Austin: University of Texas Press.

Gaspar de Alba, Alicia (2014). *[Un]framing the "Bad Woman" Sor Juana, Malinche, Coyoloxauhqui and Other Rebels with a Cause*, Austin: University of Texas Press.

Goldman, Ilene S. (1996). 'Crossing invisible borders: Ramón Menéndez's *Stand and Deliver* (1987)', in Chon A. Noriega and Ana M López (eds), *The Ethnic Eye: Latino Media Arts*, Minneapolis: University of Minnesota Press, pp. 81–95.

Hershfield, Joanne (2000). *The Invention of Dolores del Río*, Minneapolis: University of Minnesota Press.

Hidalgo de la Riva, Osa (2006). 'Sylvia Morales', *Spectator*, 26.1, pp. 49–54.

Huaco-Nuzum, Carmen, (1991). '(Re)constructing Chicana, Mestiza representation: Frances Salomé España's *Spitfire*', in Chon A. Noriega and Ana M. López (eds), *The Ethnic Eye: Latino Media Arts*, Minneapolis: University of Minnesota Press, pp. 260–75.

Loglines (2013). 'Associate Professor Sylvia Morales honored by DGA', 18 October. Retrieved from http://loglines.lmu.edu/news/associate-professor-sylvia-morales-honored-by-dga (accessed 5 June 2015).

López, Ana M. (1993). 'Are all Latins from Manhattan?', in John King, Ana M. López and Manuel Alvarado (eds), *Mediating Two Worlds: Cinematic Encounters in the Americas*, London: British Film Institute, pp. 67–81.

McCracken, Ellen (2014). 'From chapbooks to Chica lit: U.S. Latina writers and the new literary identity', in Catherine Leen and Niamh Thornton (eds), *International Perspectives on Chicana/o Studies: 'This World Is My Place'*, New York: Routledge, pp. 11–24.

Merskin, Debra (2007). 'Three faces of Eva: perpetuation of the hot-Latina stereotype in *Desperate Housewives*', *Howard Journal of Communications*, 18.2, pp. 133–51.

Molina Guzmán, Isabel (2007). 'Salma Hayek's Frida: transnational Latina bodies in popular culture', in Mayra Mendible (ed.), *From Bananas to Buttocks: The Latina Body in Popular Film and Culture*, Texas: University of Texas Press, pp. 117–29.

Mora, Carl J. (2005). *Mexican Cinema: Reflections of a Society, 1896–2004*, North Carolina: McFarland & Company.

Moraga, Cherrie (1983). *Loving in the War Years: Lo que nunca pasó por sus labios*, Boston: South End Press.

——— (2009). 'Queer Aztlán: the reformation of Chicano tribe', in Francisco Vázquez (ed.), *Latino/a Thought: Culture, Politics and Society*, Maryland: Rowman & Littlefield, pp. 223–43.

——— (2011) *A Xicana Code of Changing Consciousness: Writings, 2000–2010*, Durham: Duke University Press.

Morales, Sylvia (2014). Interview with the author, Venice Beach, California, 18 July.

Noriega, Chon A. (1993). *Chicano Cinema: Between a Weapon and a Formula, Chicano Cinema and its Contexts*, San Sebastian: Festival Internacional de Cine de Donostia.

Ramírez Berg, Charles (2002). *Latino Images in Film: Stereotypes, Subversion and Resistance*, Austin: University of Texas Press.

Rodríguez, Clara E. (2004). *Heroes, Lovers and Others: The Story of Latinos in Hollywood*, New York: Oxford University Press.

Rodríquez-Estrada, Alicia I. (1997). 'Dolores Del Río and Lupe Vélez: images on and off the screen, 1925–1944', in Elizabeth Jameson and Susan Armitage (eds), *Writing the Range: Race, Class and Culture in the Women's West*, Oklahoma: University of Oklahoma Press, pp. 475–93.

Ruiz-Alfaro, Sofia (2012). 'From Chavela to Frida: loving from the margins', *Journal of Homosexuality*, 59.8, pp. 1131–44.

Saldívar-Hull, Sonia (2000). *Feminism on the Border: Chicana Gender Politics and Literature*, Berkeley: University of California Press.

Santos, Cristina, and Crowe Morey, Tracy (2013). '(M)othering the borderlands: testimony and the Latina feminist group', *Motherhood in a Global Context*, 4.2, pp. 89–105.

Shaw, Deborah (2007). 'Robert Rodriguez's Mexicans in *Once Upon A Time in Mexico*', *Reconstruction*, 7.3. Retrieved from http://reconstruction.eserver.org/Issues/074/shaw.shtml (accessed 20 August 2015).

—— (2010). 'Transforming the national body: Salma Hayek and Frida', *Quarterly Review of Film and Video*, 27, pp. 299–313

Smith, Lois M. and Alfred Padula (1996). *Sex and Revolution: Women in Socialist Cuba*, New York: Oxford University Press.

Torres, Eden E. (2003). *Chicana Without Apology/Chicana sin vergüenza: The New Chicana Cultural Studies*, New York: Routledge.

Vega, Tanzina and Bill Carter, (2012). 'Networks struggle to appeal to Hispanics without using stereotypes', *New York Times*. Available at http://latinocollaborative.com/wp-content/uploads/2012/12/Networks-Struggle-to-Appeal-to-Hispanics-New-York-Times-Aug-15-2012.pdf (accessed 1 May 2015).

5

Intimacy and Distance – Domestic Servants in Latin American Women's Cinema: *La mujer sin cabeza* and *El niño pez*/*The Fish Child*

Deborah Shaw

There have been a number of Latin American feature films that have travelled through the transnational circuits of film exhibition and distribution with the relationship between mistresses, masters and servants at their centre. This focus allows cinephiles around the world a voyeuristic insight into the private spaces and fictional homes of far-away protagonists (if viewed from foreign metropolises, as the films often are). Both male and female Latin American directors are making films that comment on the power relations between the ruling and servant classes, and use this relationship to share their observations on wider social/national class paradigms. Nonetheless, this subject matter has been of particular interest to female directors, and it is significant that this has coincided with the rise in women filmmakers on the global stage, the focus of this collection.

This relationship is central to Latin American social and class relations, and Shireen Ally draws attention to the discomforting presence of the maid for many feminists (2015), as the liberation of one social group is often conditional on the subjugation of another. This is particularly pertinent in a region (Latin America and the Caribbean) 'with the largest proportion of domestic workers' in the world (Higman 2015: 33). Patricia White also draws attention to the rise in transnational women filmmakers and notes the focus on domestic servants in Latin American women's cinema; she suggests that, for a number of directors, 'private dramas are as significant, and as deeply imbricated with, public ones' (2015: 54). The private dramas exposed through a focus on the mistress/servant power dynamic mark the daily lives of many women in Latin America, a relationship that rests on a 'dialectic of intimacy and distance', as will be discussed (Ally 2015: 51).

The chapter begins by setting the contextual framework through a discussion of domestic service in Latin America from a sociological perspective in order to examine the specific circumstances in Latin America that the films are responding to. This will be followed by what I argue is a new thematic genre of filmmaking, Latin American films featuring maids, and I discuss recent films that fit within this genre and consider the ways in which new social, aesthetic and political visions are emerging with the films' explorations of the class-riven private spaces of the home.[1] The overview of films will be provided, as this is a little-studied, yet increasingly significant, area of film production that reconstitutes the key focus points for a new cultural politics. I then analyse two complementary yet distinct visions of the relationship between servants and employers: Lucrecia Martel's pessimistic realist *La mujer sin cabeza/The Headless Woman* (2008) and Lucía Puenzo's utopian queer *El niño pez/The Fish Child* (2009).

Domestic servants and maids in Latin America: a brief contextual overview

Latin America and the Caribbean have very large numbers of domestic workers, and this is the result of societal divisions that are the consequence of a colonial past. In the words of Barry Higman, 'the world region with the largest proportion of domestic workers – Latin America and the Caribbean – bears the marks of deep and comprehensive colonization, slavery and the plantation' (2015: 33). The class and ethnic model that continues today was established in colonial times. Unsurprisingly, most domestic servants were indigenous women, and they were less than any other category of servant; they were also 'virtually enslaved' and prevented from leaving the homes in which they were employed, or marrying (Kuznesof 1989: 20).

Following the colonial legacy, Higman estimates that 93 per cent of domestic workers in Latin America and the Caribbean are women (2015: 32).

The fact that 'states derived from former colonies have roughly twice as many domestic workers per capita as states that were not part of the former imperial project' (Higman 2015: 58) has resulted in many more middle-class women in Latin America having servants than their counterparts in the United States or Europe. This reliance by middle- and upper-class women on the labour of poor women clearly has implications for a feminist project, as has been recognised. A number of theorists have referred to the figure of the domestic servant as intrinsic to class and ethnic divisions, and as symbolising the unfinished or incomplete feminist revolution (Ally 2015: 48; Tronto 2002: 47). Joan Tronto, writing specifically on nannies in the US context, frequently originating from Latin America, encapsulates this anxiety for feminists when she notes that 'the use of nannies allows upper middle-class women and men to benefit from feminist changes without having to surrender the privilege of the traditional patriarchal family' (47).

The labour of female domestic servants, consisting of traditionally female-gendered tasks, such as childcare, housework and cooking, has meant that theirs is often not considered proper work, which, in turn, has devalued the position of servants/maids. Their activities are seen as an extension of a 'natural' social order of poor female identity (Ally 2015: 49).[2] This form of naturalising labour and not seeing it as proper work results in the invisibility of domestic servants and means that their position is open to abuse, as it is an occupation rarely governed by employment or union laws, which are enacted for more traditionally male forms of employment.[3] Lucrecia Martel, in an interview with Amy Taubin, responding to the focus on servants in her films, notes the failure of families to recognise domestic servants as employees like others:

> In the upper middle class, they see people who work in their homes as servants, they don't see them as employees who have a job to do. They expect these people not just to do their job efficiently but also to be affectionate toward them and have an emotional connection. (Taubin 2009)

This failure to see domestic service as a respectable profession and the privatisation of labour mean that social boundaries are often porous, confused and result in anxieties in determining the nature of the relationship.

Shireen Ally discusses the unique, often uncomfortable social dynamic between employer and employee that results from the way that these boundaries are inevitably breached within the confines of the home:

> Domestic workers' work within the emotion-laden spaces makes their work intimate. Such abiding intimacies are deeply disquieting for their employers who attempt to manage the contaminating effects of familiarity through the cultivation of social and physical distance, often through degradation and dehumanization. The dialectic of intimacy and distance this structures in domestic service is a unique species of relations in which closeness, familiarity, and intimacy coexist with distancing, estrangement, and dehumanization. (Ally 2015: 51)

New politics in Latin American films featuring maids

This chapter argues that a new genre of films has appeared that marks a collective moment in which there is recognition from filmmakers that to understand the deep, often hidden manifestations of national and social inequalities, the focus needs to shift to daily interactions inside the home. The generic conventions are largely thematic, in that each film will apply diverse stylistic approaches to the subject matter, as will be seen more clearly in the discussion of *La mujer sin cabeza* and *El niño pez*. Films with such a focus include the Brazilian *Maids/Domésticas* (Meirelles and Olival, 2001), Puenzo's *El niño pez*, Sebastián Silva's Chilean film *La nana/The Maid*, Claudia Llosa's Peruvian *La teta asustada/The Milk of Sorrow* (2009), Juan Carlos Valdivia's Bolivian-set *Zona sur/Southern District* (2009), Gabriel Mascaro's Brazilian documentary *Doméstica/Housemaids* (2012), the Mexican *Hilda* (2014) by Andrés Clariond, *Réimon* (2014) by the Argentinean director Rodrigo Moreno, the Brazilian *Que horas ela volta/The Second Mother* (2015) by Anna Muylaert, and Teresa Suárez's Mexican musical comedy *¿Qué le dijiste a Dios?* (2014).[4] The films of Lucrecia Martel, *La ciénaga* (2001), *La niña santa* (2004) and *La mujer sin cabeza* do not have the same intense focus on servants as the other films, because they are concerned with presenting an anatomy of Argentine, bourgeois female identity. Yet, Martel understands that the figure of the servant is central to understanding this identity and thus her films paradoxically highlight their presence by ensuring they are a constant if marginalised feature in her backgrounds.

In this section I argue that there is a new socio-political vision in these films revealed through their focus on intimate, interior, private and domestic spaces, and I present an overview of the films as an introduction to the genre in Latin American film. Filmmaking has been an extremely effective art form in imagining and recreating the dialectic that Ally describes, and it can be argued that the way in which intimacy and distance are enacted is the common feature in all of the Latin American films discussed below that feature maids and employers, and will be a focus of the analysis of the case studies.[5] It is significant that a number of recent films are challenging the inequalities and invisibility faced by domestic servants, and that several draw attention to the contradictions that arise when so called progressive leftist bourgeois characters employ them – see the discussion below of *Hilda* and *Réimon*.

Laura Podalsky's ideas in her book *The Politics of Affect and Emotion in Contemporary Latin American Cinema* can help provide a useful theoretical framework to take forward ideas relating to a new way of evaluating politics in Latin American film. Podalsky presents an alternative view to a critical field that locates progessive politics primarily in the militant, Marxist New Latin American cinema of the 1960s and 1970s (2011: 3). She notes that more commercial, globally successful films such as *Central do Brasil/Central Station* (Salles, 1998), and the best-known Mexican films by Alfonso Cuarón and Alejandro Iñárritu, *Y tu mamá también* (2001) and *Amores perros* (2000), despite their social concerns, are frequently regarded as 'willing participant(s) in the depoliticized, pro-market atmosphere that emerged in the region in the late 1980s and early 1990s as neoliberal administrations took power across the region' (3). Podalsky argues that the relationship between politics and aesthetics is more complex than critics have suggested, and she considers the creation of new 'affective alliances' (3) established in films that employ more commercial strategies than examples of New Latin American Cinema. Her 'goal is to offer a richer understanding of how films "touch us" and to suggest the political potential of certain films regarded as apolitical and sensationalistic by the majority of critics' (7). In her project, Podalsky considers stories of youthful alienation, popular coming-of-age films, and thrillers. While she does not focus on films featuring maids or servants, with the exception of *La ciénaga*, she does highlight the ways in which films, particularly those with a focus on youth, concern themselves with 'the rhythms and textures of the everyday experiences of their young protagonists' (19).

Podalsky takes issue with cultural theorists such as Nelly Richard (2004) and Jean Franco (2002) who argue that radical politics and responsible representations of dictatorship-inflicted trauma are limited to specific cultural forms, in particular avant-garde aesthetics. A thread running throughout *The Politics of Affect and Emotion in Contemporary Latin American Cinema* is that directors can engage viewers more directly through appeals to sensory and emotional responses, and she draws her examples from a broad spectrum of Latin American cinema, including minimalist art films, Mexican New Wave and New Argentine cinema, and genre films (popular thrillers, road movies and Brazilian crime films).

This way of conceptualising the political and emotional charge of films that are not explicitly militant in ways associated with New Latin American cinema of the 1960s and 1970s is particularly apposite for an analysis of Latin American films featuring maids. It can be argued that the domestic server/served pairing is unique for the ways in which it allows for the probing of cross-class and ethnic relations in an intimate setting, and for the way it dramatises personal affective relationships. While the focus is on these private relationships established behind closed doors, the films reveal structural economic and social inequalities in a highly effective way. The depictions of everyday interactions between women of different classes and ethnic groups makes these films, to varying degrees, part of a new feminist project. This project serves to correct liberal bourgeois feminists' neglect of the poor women who sustain their work and the masculinist priorities of earlier New Latin American Cinema. It is significant that women filmmakers have figured strongly in this genre, and in this way are following Teresa de Lauretis' 'project of Women's cinema' in her seminal book *Technologies of Gender*, that is, 'to effect a new vision: to construct other subjects and objects of vision and to formulate the conditions of visibility of another social subject' (de Lauretis 1987: 26; cited in White 2015: 10).

Podalsky's redefinition of politics in popular culture is a position shared by Fernanda Solórzano (2015). Writing on three films – *Cama adentro* (Gaggero, 2004), *La nana* and *Hilda* – that focus on maids, and a photographic exhibition of maids and their female employers in Cartagena de Indias, Colombia, in 2014 entitled 'Lugar común' ('common place' or 'shared space'), she notes the power of the exhibition and films, and rejects criticisms that they somehow diminish political structural problems:

> Many will say that these films, as with the photos of *Shared space*, soften the structural problems: the lack of rights protecting domestic workers, the double-edged sword of being considered 'part of the family', and the belief that affection provides compensation for everything else. I would say, that, on the contrary, these imbalances are the most troubling elements of their stories.[6] (Author's translation) (Solórzano 2015)

The films

The most obvious films to mention when presenting an overview are those that have the terms 'maids' or 'domestic servants' in their title. The co-directed *Domésticas/Maids* by Meirelles and Olival (2001) is perhaps the work that initiated the spate of films in the genre. It is a social comedy that focuses entirely on the stories of five maids in São Paulo, and it is significant that we see only this usually marginalised group and not their employers. The film presents social commentary in a comic format, and viewers witness their hopes, dreams, frustrations and anger. Despite the presence of Meirelles, this was a small film with limited film festival release. A film that follows in the tradition with a near identical title is Gabriel Mascaro's *Doméstica/Housemaids* (2012), a Brazilian documentary made from the work of seven adolescents who were asked to film their maids over seven days. *Doméstica* presents the ways in which the maids illustrate the 'dialectic of intimacy and distance' described by Ally (2015: 51), as they are both subordinate to and part of the family unit.[7]

This dialectic also conditions the relationships in Sebastián Silva's *La nana/The Maid* (2009), the most commercially successful and widely distributed of these films. It considers the complexities in the power relations between servants and the served and the hierarchies within the servant classes. *La nana* focuses on Raquel (Catalina Saavedra), who has worked as a domestic servant for an upper-class Chilean family for 20 years, and explores her confused status as servant and 'one of the family', and the power base she has established from an ostensibly subservient position. This is interrogated through Raquel's hostile reactions towards the domestic workers the family employs to help her when she appears to be suffering from ill health, with the intra-class conflicts highlighting Raquel's emotional insecurity and ultimately precarious position within the family.

Two other recent films deal with the way class, individual politics and personal identities interact to condition the relationship between employers and their maids. The Mexican *Hilda* by Andrés Clariond examines a crisis experienced by wealthy employer Susana LeMarchand (Verónica Langer) that arises due to tensions between her condition as bourgeois housewife and her Marxist past. The irreconcilability of the two positions results in mental health problems. These are manifested in her obsessive relationship with her maid, Hilda (Adriana Paz) and desire that they be friends, which results in a form of incarceration as Susana paradoxically attempts to impose equality while denying Hilda her freedom.[8] A film that deals with an inverse power dynamic is told in comic form by the little-known Panamanian *Chance* (Benaim, 2009), which secured limited festival release. This tells the story of two domestic servants who, fed up with ill treatment and lack of pay, take control of the mansion where they work and take their employers hostage.

The previously mentioned contradiction between Marxist politics and everyday power relations is also explored in Rodrigo Moreno's *Réimon* (2014). This film explores class contradictions through its focus on a Marxist bourgeois family's relationship with their maid. These unacknowledged hypocrisies are described in the plot summary for the film at the International Film Festival Rotterdam (the film's production was supported by the Hubert Bals Fund):

> As she dusts and toils, the yuppies and their friends read endless passages out loud from *Das Kapital – Kritik der politischen Ökonomie*, Karl Marx's treatise on work, money, working conditions, slavery, sleeping, eating and relaxing. While they philosophise, they barely notice Réimon; theory is more interesting and certainly less confrontational than practice.[9]

Another of the better-known films in this genre is Llosa's *La teta asustada*, which presents a less nuanced vision of the mistress/servant relationship through a focus on the relationship of Fausta (Magaly Solier) and her wealthy employer, composer and concert pianist Aída (Susi Sánchez).[10] This film represents an exploiter/exploited dynamic and conceptualises the relationship in neo-colonial terms. Fausta, an indigenous woman of Andean origin, is represented as a victim of the class and ethnic system of Peru and is exploited by her white *criolla* employer.[11] Fausta's only purpose as far as Aída is concerned is to serve her and act as source material for songs that she can appropriate with no acknowledgment. These power relations are highlighted by the fact that Aída pays Fausta in pearls (in a nod to early colonial transactions), with a promise of one pearl for each song, a contract she ultimately reneges on, and Fausta's freedom can be attained only after her position is terminated. Thus, despite criticisms of the representation of the poor Andean protagonist (Barrow 2013; D'Argenio 2013; Shaw 2014), in common with the other films that focus on the marginal figure of the maid the film presents a critique of the class system and exposes the divisions among women from distinct class and ethnic groupings.

The most recent film, at the time of writing, that is attracting media attention is *Que horas ela volta?/The Second Mother* (2015) by the Brazilian Anna Muylaert, a director who is the subject of Chapter 6, by Leslie Marsh, in this collection. This film also seeks to depict the grey areas that characterise the position of the maid/nanny in the (upper) middle-class home and engages with the shifts in class relations following the left-wing President Lula da Silva's term in office (from 2003 to 2011) (Saito 2015).[12] Through the divergences between the maid/nanny and her daughter, a modern aspirational teenager planning to study architecture, the film disrupts traditional hierarchies and denaturalises the order established by the wealthy classes. It also asks important questions about the figure of the mother when women take on this role for other people's offspring, leaving them unable to bring up their biological children, a theme also explored by Walter Salles and Daniela Thomas in their contribution (*Loin du 16e*) to the portmanteau film *Paris Je t'aime* (2006). Interestingly, from the perspective of the new politics in films in this genre, Muylaert refers to the camera's view from behind the refrigerator in the kitchen into the dining room as a 'political shot' (Saito 2015). For Muylaert, the camera takes on an embodied presence, that of the maid: 'When I found that [particular] place [in the house], I had the strange feeling for the first time in my life understanding what it is to be in the perspective of the kitchen because I was born in the living room' (Saito 2015). The political here is thus very clearly seen in placing the maid, Val (Regina Casé) centre-stage and reconfiguring spaces to place the marginal at the centre: in feminist fashion, the domestic and the personal are deeply political.[13]

A final point to make in this overview of recent Latin American films featuring maids is that this character figures in a number of recent films even where she is not the main focus. This reinforces the fact that filmmakers have come to understand that maids/servants can reveal important emotional and social insights. Below I give a few examples of some standout scenes from a selection of the best-known films from a Mexican transnational context to highlight the growing importance given to this figure within Latin American filmic culture. Carlos Reygadas, the internationally fêted film festival auteur, places a dynamic of servitude at the centre of *Japón/Japan* (2002) through the relationship between a middle-class, intellectual, unnamed man (Alejandro Ferretis) who escapes to an isolated rural village, Ayacatzintla, in the state of Hidalgo, to commit suicide, and a poor local elderly woman, Ascen (Magdalena Flores), who assumes a servant role despite her frailty. While she is not by profession a maid, her class, gender and ethnicity determine that this is the role she will take. The concept of servicing him is taken to an extreme in the most controversial scene of the film, when she acquiesces to engaging in a sexual encounter with him, despite her age and evident lack of desire, demonstrating that a white, bourgeois man who is at the lowest point of his existence is still able to manipulate a subaltern.

The fact that the director expected this sexual activity in a non-simulated form from his elderly actress also speaks to the exploitative dynamic between Euro-Mexican bourgeois director and his poor *mestiza* (non-professional) actress, despite the apparent symbolic function of the characters, with Ascen representing the land.[14] To (rather indulgently) cite myself, 'The sexual act [...] is seen as a symbiotic relationship between man and nature, but viewers cannot forget that a real old woman is being asked by a director to have sex on screen' (2011: 129).[15] Thus, while ripe for a critical feminist reading, and ethically questionable, *Japón* highlights the master/servant dynamic between characters and between director and characters in a highly effective way.

Intimacy and Distance

Y tu mamá también, one of the hits of the Mexican New Wave, is another high-profile film that in a number of scenes focuses on the figure of the female servant. While the film eschews a radical leftist political position (Shaw 2013: 190–5), there is nonetheless a critique of the ruling classes (marked as corrupt) and the exploitation of the servant classes whom the film makes a point of noticing. For instance, the straying camera (a technique adopted by the filmmakers throughout) follows the servants when it would be expected to linger on the glamorous guests at a wedding. Two scenes stand out in this film that best illustrate the film's socio-political vision supported by this camera-work, which while not revolutionary is denunciatory. These hinge on the relationship of Tenoch (Diego Luna) with his nana/family maid, Leo.

In one scene the camera lingers on Leo and follows her as she climbs the stairs to answer the telephone ringing for Tenoch, which is located right next to him (and she brings him a sandwich). It is for the viewer to register the ridiculous nature of this servitude as the elderly servant hands him the phone, so naturalised is this social dynamic. In another scene, viewers access Tenoch's private thoughts via the film's omniscient narrator as they pass through Tepelmeme, Leo's birthplace. He thinks about how she came to Mexico City from the age of 13 and worked in the house, and how he called her 'mamá' until the age of four. In this scene it is suggested that for the first time Tenoch registers that she has an identity independent to that of his nanny/servant and a life she sacrificed due to economic need. The personal journey that Tenoch and Julio (Gael García Bernal) experience on their road trip provides a momentary interruption in privileged machista identity that has the potential to create a shift in Mexican culture. The scene where Tenoch is taken to a location that causes him to reflect on Leo's birthplace has more potential to effect this change through the personal affective strategies involved than the more evident political moments in the film. The brief scenes of students demonstrating against the government and calling for free state education, or Julio's sister's support for the Zapatista revolutionaries, rather reduce radical politics to national cultural signifiers empty of emotional significance within the diegesis, as neither has any immediate, direct personal bearing for either Tenoch or Julio.

La mujer sin cabeza

In this section, I pay closer attention to two films by Argentine directors, Lucrecia Martel and Lucía Puenzo, *La mujer sin cabeza* and *El niño pez*, for the ways in which they highlight the new social and political visions discussed. They do this through affective strategies of engagement/disengagement between the bourgeois and servant classes, and explorations of class-riven private domestic spaces. *La mujer sin cabeza* reflects on these intimate spaces of members of the middle class and their privilege that rests on the service provided by the poorer class. The film conceptualises this class en masse, from the point of view of the bourgeois Vero (María Onetto) and her family, for whom they exist purely as servants, and explores the bourgeoisie's complex relationship with them that rests on dependence and rejection. *El niño pez* reveals the same class inequalities determined by society and the family unit as *La mujer sin cabeza*, shown through the contrasting status of Ailín/La Guayi, the family's domestic servant, and Lala, daughter of a well known judge. Nonetheless, the film develops the potential for a utopian queer politics and presents an ultimately egalitarian vision of a relationship built on love, passion and desire between the two women of different ethnicities, national identities and class status. In the analysis that follows, I consider the different political visions offered by the films through affective strategies developed through Martel's pessimistic realism and Puenzo's utopian queer dramatic storytelling.

Patricia White notes that Martel's films 'explore the micropolitics of gender, sexuality and location, rather than national narratives of oppression and collective liberation' (2015: 45). Yet, as I argue here, Martel's achievement is that she reveals (trans)national and trans-historical narratives and the power dynamics on which they rest through the micropolitics found in domestic spaces.[16] These domestic spaces are those inhabited by Vero, a middle-class dentist, following the trauma she suffers after committing a hit-and-run. Paradoxically, the private interior world of a bourgeois Argentine woman is mined to reveal collective truths and to present an anatomy of a sick, traumatised nation, which can be extended to any nation that creates a servant class from its poor. This is not allegory, in that Vero does not stand for something else; she stands for herself, but that private reality is one shared by many others like her, and connects with both historical and contemporary social injustices. It has been noted by critics and by Martel herself that the timescales of the film are rendered deliberately unclear, and include visual, musical and other cultural references to both the 1970s and 1990s in order to connect the human rights abuses of the earlier dictatorship period with the economic structural inequalities of the 1990s (Martin 2016; Quirós 2010: 233–4; Sosa 2009: 258; Taubin 2009).[17]

Martel has explained the intrinsic political intention in *La mujer sin cabeza* and the transhistorical links between explicit human rights abuses and social deprivation:

> What I believe is that an individual will not come out from a situation like that unscathed. This woman is going to carry this on her back like a corpse, like a bag of bones, forever. In Argentina, my country, I see people that still carry the weight of the really bad stuff that they did not denounce back when it happened under the dictatorship. A lot of people decided they didn't want to see, they didn't want to know what was happening. And now the same process is occurring, but it's in relation to poverty. A lot of people pretend they do not see that a huge part of the country is becoming poorer and poorer and is undergoing great suffering. And what we try not to see is that the entire legal system, health system, and education system are structured by social class. (Taubin 2009)

Despite the apparent focus on a private drama and interior spaces, the film 'does deal explicitly with questions of guilt, responsibility, trauma and amnesia, the central themes of post-dictatorship Argentine culture' (Martin 2016: 80). This is seen in the cover-up orchestrated by the key men in Vero's life. While the servants take care of her material needs, the men in her life (husband, brother-in-law/lover, brother) take care of securing her position in society through their connections with the police and judiciary system, by ensuring any evidence connecting her with the hit-and-run disappears.

With the exception of Candita (on whom more below) the bourgeois characters in *La mujer sin cabeza* attempt to reduce the anxieties between the intimacy and distance dialectic discussed above by enforcing strict borders between them and the servant classes. They are not, as in some of the instances previously discussed, seen as part of the family, and emotional connections are not established, as the bourgeois characters can see only their own needs and dramas. Servants are addressed in imperatives and a different tone of voice, and merely told what to do, while the audience learns the servants' names, if at all, only when they are addressed through orders. These orders contrast with the intimacy demonstrated between the bourgeois characters; Vero is frequently kissed when in the company of family members and friends, with her disengaged state highlighting the ritualistic nature of these shows of affection. It is significant that we learn nothing of the servants' lives, as our frame of reference is Vero. Yet, despite the ruling class's best attempts at enforcing separations, Martel refuses clear-cut spaces between them, by creating cluttered *mise-en-scènes* and staging awkward moments with servants in the frame while their 'patrones' continue to live out their dramas. Servants are in a high proportion of scenes, on the edges of the frame, and out of focus, deliberately 'spoiling' the composition of the shot, passing in front of the camera, or behind the protagonists, providing an awkward reminder of their constant presence and the support structures required to keep the ruling class in place, paradoxically visible through their invisibility. Cecilia Sosa (2009: 256) refers to these marginalised figures as 'murky employees of the house [...], eerie spectres who circulate within the space like phantasms'. In this way, Martel demonstrates how Shireen Ally's oxymoronic formula of closeness and distance plays out in the bourgeois provincial Argentinean family, with servants taking over Vero's care and the running of her life, while simultaneously marginalised.

This sense of servants as non-subjects is momentarily interrupted when Vero believes she may have run over a working-class teenage boy and caused his death. The hit-and-run is more than an irresponsible act: it is a deep-rooted response that connects her to her social group and is located in a refusal to see this class as independent subjects or her own role in their oppression. It is telling that we do not know whether or not Vero killed a boy or the German shepherd dog that viewers are shown lying in the road following the collision (or both), as it is suggested that such confusion hints at an equivalence in value placed on their lives. A further key point is that Vero refuses to leave her car and face the consequences of her actions, and her interests and those of her class ensure that there will be no justice available to those of the servant classes.[18]

Patricia White describes Vero's headlessness as 'a severing from intellect, self-awareness, and ethical subjectivity imposed by the mind/body split and a restrictive social order' (2015: 49). Taking this definition, it could be argued that, contrary to most readings of the film, Vero is 'the headless woman' only in her pre-accident state and following her recovery at the film's close, and for the majority of the film's duration she achieves a form of self-awareness and ethical subjectivity. It is interesting to note that, in fact, the film has many full close-up headshots of Vero – her blond head frequently fills the frame – and she is usually shot in focus, while the backgrounds and often the servant class are out of focus (see Figure 5.1).[19]

The boy Vero may or may not have killed subsequently imposes himself on her psyche, despite her attempts to not engage with the consequences of her actions, and as a result causes her momentary breakdown in identity. The initial act of selective blindness means that Vero paradoxically 'sees' the boy everywhere in the period of her identity breakdown following the accident and chronicled by the film, as all that has been repressed returns. As she can never know intimately a boy of this class, all teenage boys of his class come to stand in for him: an injured soccer player causes her to cry and she allows herself to be comforted by a workman; a young lad in search of some cash in return for odd jobs triggers a desire to help

Figure 5.1. Vero's in-focus head fills the screen, while the boy looking for work is cast in shadow (*La mujer sin cabeza*, Lucrecia Martel, 2008).

and she awkwardly offers him a bath, food and old clothes in a clumsy attempt to break the servant/served dynamic. In addition, she is reminded of him in the police road blocks erected when a boy's dead body is found in the canal, and by the worker at a garden centre who cannot reach the high plant pots Vero wants to buy without his missing young helper, later discovered to be dead. Through these apparitions, teenage male members of the servant class acquire a status as subjects, albeit collective rather than individual, not mere functions, and thus succeed in making an emotional connection with Vero.[20] In this way, the film hints that the route to social change lies in precisely these emotional shifts, through a 'politics of situated feeling', to cite Podalsky (2011: 15), and the creation of 'affective alliances' (Podalsky 2011: 8), a potential that is developed in *El niño pez*, as will be seen.

Nonethetheless, any potential for meaningful action/change on Vero's part is limited as her new consciousness is restricted to a private self. She may see and be emotionally moved by the missing boy in numerous incarnations, she may go to the hospital and the hotel when she suspects that her family members are engaging in a cover-up of her involvement, but these are restricted to individual acts of investigation and charity, and she ultimately colludes with the cover-up and returns to being the headless woman. Ultimately, she refuses the agency that comes with consciousness. As White perceptively notes of Martel's films in general, there is no potential for collective political identities (here she is referring to a feminist identity) as 'her heroines are privatized in a familial setting, hysterics who somaticize their predicaments' (2015: 20).

Vero's feelings remain private, and while she may be sensitive to young men of the servant class, she continues to fail to see her own servants as subjects rather than functions. The new way in which she sees the world is thus partial, temporary and pathologised within her family unit as a sickness. Through the attention of her servants and the patriarchy in which she is cosetted, Vero 'heals' and returns to her previous identity; in this case the emotional leakage seen in the feelings towards teenage boys of the servant classes is curtailed before it becomes political or collective. She also never attains a feminist consciousness – she may be a successful professional woman, yet this is a status that relies on the labour of the poor women and men who do the domestic work.

Deborah Martin (2016) notes that, while for *La mujer sin cabeza* the middle-class family unit is seen to be 'a socially regressive institution', another world beyond the family is glimpsed through the relationship between Vero's niece, Candita (Inés Efrón), and her working class girlfriend Cuca (Andrea Verdún):

> Of all Martel's girls, it is they – as a cross-class, cross-ethnic, queer pair – who most clearly offer a metaphor for social change, justice and integration, they who seem most likely to reject and escape the oppressive codes upheld by adult society [...]. These girls and their friends constitute a group that transgresses the social hierarchies that rigidly structure the world portrayed in the film. The film hints at a utopian queer politics, suggesting that queer forms of community transgress previously established social hierarchies of class and ethnicity. (Martin 2016: 97–9)

In the inverse moral world of the film, it is Candita who is sick (she suffers from hepatitis C), a space of illness she temporarily shares with Vero.[21] Yet, as the film suggests through their names (which signify ' truth'), they, in fact, present a potential antidote to a sick society through their willingness to seek cross-class alliances (in Candita's case) or see their role in social inequalities (in Vero's new state of consiousness). As befits its marginality, this grouping is condemned to be at the sidelines of the film in terms of plot and *mise-en-scène*, with the young women taking up little screen time and often seen at the edge of the frame. Nonetheless, this is the only cross-class relationship in the film not determined by a servant/served dynamic. This relationship between Cuca and Candita is foreshadowed in *La ciénaga*, in the unrequited love that Momi (Sofía Bertoletto) feels for the family maid Isabel (Andrea López), another marginalised storyline that is not developed, as Martel's focus is on revealing the flawed point of view of the middle classes.

El niño pez

These lovers from between the servant and middle classes are transplanted to Lucía Puenzo's *El niño pez*, where Candita and Cuca are re-imagined as Ailín (Mariela Vitale) and Lala (Inés Efrón), but placed centre screen, with the intertextual parallels heightened by the fact that Inés Efrón plays the queer middle-class character in both films. In another intertextual reference, the abandoned dead dog seen following Vero's collision in *La mujer* is recast as a family pet in *El niño pez* (also a German shepherd). In both films the dogs act as metaphors for the treatment of the servant classes. In *La mujer*, as seen, the dog is conflated with young working-class boys in terms of value; in Puenzo's film the angelically named puppy, Serafín, was rescued from the garbage by Ailín, and is given as her gift to Lala, becoming a loved member of the family and another unifying element in Ailín and Lala's relationship.

El niño pez is Lucía Puenzo's second feature film and is based on her own novel of the same name. Ailín, also known as La Guayi, as she is from Paraguay, occupies the condition encapsulated by Shireen Ally: she is both domestic servant and part of the family. Like many of the films discussed above, Ailín's position within the family illustrates a conflicting 'dialectic of intimacy and distance' (2015: 51). She came to the household of Judge Bronté (Pep Munné) when she was only 13, and has forged a passionate romantic and sexual relationship with Lala (Inés Efrón), the judge's daughter. She is also seen to be having a sexual relationship with Lala's father, although it is suggested that she has little choice in this, as it is determined by the power dynamic between the two, with possible dismissal and homelessness for Ailín if she refuses.

Judge Bronté's treatment of Ailín rests on the anxieties described by Ally and seen above in her discussion of the dynamic between employers and servants. This is particularly the case when servants live in the home, and their relationship illustrates well the co-existence of 'closeness, familiarity, and intimacy [...] with distancing, estrangement, and dehumanization' (2015: 51). In one telling scene, a special farewell dinner for the troubled son of the family, the judge tells Ailín to join them at the table, as she is part of the family. The fact that this is an exceptional order, and indeed that it is an order, indicates that her position in the family is unclear and muddled, and, as we know, complicated by her sexual relationship with father and daughter. For a moment, Judge Bronté pays her attention, and she becomes a curiosity, and when she tells him that she would really like to be a singer in Guaraní, in an act reminiscent of neo-colonialism he instructs her to sing. He himself draws attention to these neo-colonial parallels, enjoying his position as master in his comments that by singing the Guaraní women enchanted the Spaniards. Significantly, he misinterprets the song as one of seduction, ensuring it conforms to his own fantasies; in fact, Ailín is singing a lullaby to a baby, probably her dead baby.[22] After a 'family' photo with them all together, the judge instructs her to bring more wine to the table, and tells Lala to get Ailín out of there, when she warns her father not to mess with her girlfriend. Bronté thus re-establishes the more traditional master/servant roles, roles that are entirely collapsed in the case of Ailín and Lala.

The film's dramatic energy stems from the love story between the two women, and the narrative energy stems from the action that results from Lala's murder of her father in an act of jealousy after she discovers that he has been having sex with her lover. Ailín is blamed and imprisoned, essentially because of her class status and position as family maid; Lala's mother and the judicial system assume La Guayi's guilt with no direct evidence, an indictment of a system that chooses to punish someone from the servant class over a middle-class girl. As in the case of Vero in *La mujer sin cabeza*, the bourgeois woman is beyond suspicion and, despite their guilt, neither Vero nor Lala is ever even questioned by the police. Once Ailín enters the prison system, the film reveals a corrupt world where the inmates are taken to sex parties at the home of the police commissioner (played by the Spanish actor Carlos Bardem); as with *La mujer sin cabeza*, for those in power the poor exist to service their needs, in this case sexual.

Like Candita and Cuca, Lala and Aílin are used to present a vision where love and sexual attraction provide the force that overcomes social barriers, another example of a political vision located within cross-class alliances found within emotional, intimate and private spaces. As befits Martel's pessimistic realism, the relationships in her films are marginal and never really challenge the dominant social order beyond showing the potential for 'another way to be',[23] yet in Puenzo's utopian queer dramatic storytelling a new social order is represented and the love between the two young women forms the emotional heart of the diegesis. Puenzo's utopianism, achieved through her approach to genre, allows for a wish fulfillment narrative and an anti-realist happy ending, not possible in Martel's more realist, slow art cinema.

Puenzo describes her film as being a mixture of genres (Ranzani 2009) and in the film there are elements of drama, melodrama, lesbian romance and thriller. Storytelling codes found within these genres actualise the improbable and a new social order, also enabled by the fact that the narrative follows a structure of Lala's memories (flashbacks) and dreams built on desires. Thus, despite the miscarriage of justice and the corruption within the police and prison systems, Lala manages to rescue Ailín, shoot the police commissioner and escape to Paraguay with her lover, with the help of Ailín's old friend, el Vasco. As they are on the bus to Paraguay, Lala asks her lover if their story has a happy ending and when Ailín says she does not know Lala asks her to invent something. In the final scene, which has a mid-shot of the two sharing the screen (a common framing device throughout), in a way that would be impossible in the separate worlds of servants and employers in *La mujer*, the two stare lovingly at each other as Ailín imagines for Lala and the audience their happy ending. In this story, they will share a house together by Lake Ypoá, and will swim together to the bottom of the lake.

In this ending there are echoes of an earlier scene where Lala descends to the bottom of the lake and encounters Mitay Pyra, the mythical fish child who takes the drowned to the bottom of the lake, and where Ailín's drowned baby can be found. This scene also departs from any realism and is constructed through storytelling, dream and myth. In her descent, Lala is guided by Ailín's soft voice through the memory, shown in flashback, when the two were sharing a bath. Ailín recounts a dream of when she was taken to the bottom of the lake by Mitay Pyra as Lala enters a magical underwater world adorned by the offerings of the locals to the fish child, with the narration from the earlier scene laid over this scene. Here the visuals are from a fantasy waterscape and are created using CGI technology (see Figure 5.2).[24] Lala wakes up, and thus the two are connected through water (from bath to lake) and through their dreams. Of this scene the writer/director has said:

> I think that the presence of the legend of the fish child in the water, everything related to water and all that is beneath the surface is more closely linked to the emotions than to reason, it's something that belongs to the feminine world. And the two

find themselves from this space, where everything is mixed; their relationship is erotic, maternal and one of friendship. (Bello 2009; author's translation)[25]

This oneiric scene, constructed through the emotions of the characters, has a radical political vision, as it offers the characters a space where they can be together, and where class, ethnic and national distinctions dissolve. It is also a feminine space where new utopian possibilities open up.

Both *La mujer sin cabeza* and *El niño pez* reveal that affective alliances prove to be the most effective way of overcoming social and political divisions, injustices in the home, and the larger-scale legal institutions (police, judiciary and prison), yet, as argued in this chapter, this potential is realised only in *El niño pez*. In this way, rather than the personal acting in opposition to the political, the films connect the intimate and private to the structural and systemic. In Martel's film the conservatism of the bourgeoisie is found in the failure of these alliances and in the failure of the protagonist and her family and friends to engage in any meaningful way with the servant classes or see them beyond their role as servicing their needs. In Puenzo's film, the political radicalism is located in destroying the servant/served dichotomy through a lesbian love story, and creating an equal relationship reflected in the narrative structure, use of myth, anti-realist

Figure 5.2. Lala glimpses Mitay Pyra in the lake (*El niño pez*, Lucía Puenzo, 2009).

generic codes, representational techniques and framing devices. These films as well as the others mentioned present an intimate anatomy of the class system in Argentina, and Latin America more generally, through the most private of relationships – those between servants and the families who employ them.

Notes

1. While the range of recent films merits the notion of 'new', there are important precedents of films that place the domestic servant at their centre; for instance, the Colombian film *Pisingaña/Hopscotch* by Leopoldo Pinzón (1985) tells the story of a young peasant woman and the hardships she suffers while working as a domestic servant following her displacement from rural Colombia to Bogota (I am grateful to Deborah Martin for this observation). There will be other examples that experts in Latin American film history will be aware of.
2. Shireen Ally (2015) discusses this failure to consider dosmestic service as proper employment as a result of its conceptualisation as an extension of women's 'natural' duties in the context of South Africa.
3. It was not until 2011 that the UN body the International Labour Organization established the Domestic Workers' Convention, and signatory countries agreed to implement appropriate working conditions and prevent abuse for those in domestic employment (Haskins and Lowrie 2015: 13). Notwithstanding the Convention, which came into force only as recently as 2013, it is, of course, notoriously difficult to legislate in favour of and to protect those working in such private spheres. For a list of countries that have ratified the Convention, including Latin American states, see http://wiego.org/informal-economy/ratification-countries-domestic-workers-convention-c189 (accessed 12 November 2015).
4. I would like to thank Ilana Dann Luna for the references to *¿Qué le dijiste a Dios?* and *Zona sur*.
5. This filmic exploration of a dialectic fundamental to the master/mistress/servant relationship is clearly not exclusive to Latin American cinema and, for instance, is explored in the most internationally high-profile film of the genre, *The Help* (Taylor, 2011).
6. Muchos dirán que estas películas, como las fotos de *Lugar común*, 'suavizan' el problema de base: la falta de derechos que amparan a las trabajadoras domésticas, el doble filo de considerarlas 'parte de la familia' y la creencia de que el afecto compensa todo lo demás. Les diría que, por el contrario, estos desequilibrios son el elemento más inquietante de sus historias. (Solórzano 2015). I am grateful to Ignacio Sánchez Prado for this source.

7. Another documentary on the same theme is *Empleadas y patrones/Maids and Bosses* (2010), an Argentine/Panamanian co-production directed by Abner Benaim.
8. For a review of the film see Hooper (2014).
9. Available at https://www.iffr.com/en/films/reimon (accessed 15 November 2015).
10. The film was awarded the Golden Bear for Best Feature at the Berlin Film Festival in 2009. It received a number of nominations and awards from around the world in 2009, including a nomination representing Peru for the Best Foreign Language Film of the Year at the US Academy Awards, the Spanish Goyas, the Montréal Festival of New Cinema and the Mexican Arieles. For a full list of nominations and results, see 'The Milk of Sorrow Awards, 2009' at http://www.imdb.com/title/tt1206488/awards?ref_=tt_ql_4 (accessed 6 January 2016).
11. Criollos are Peruvians of Spanish ancestry.
12. Another film that looks at how changing socio-economic structures affect the relationship between classes is *Cama adentro/Live-in Maid* by Jorge Gaggero (2004), which charts the decline into poverty of Beba (Norma Aleandro) and the resulting changes in relationship with her maid Dora (Norma Argentina).
13. There are also a number of films and television programmes that feature Latina/Latin American maids, including the U.S./Mexican co-production *La misma luna/Under the Same Moon* (Riggen, 2007), *Devious Maids* and *Maid in Manhattan*, (Wang, 2002). The figure of the maid/nanny also constitutes a significant storyline in González Iñárritu's *Babel* (2006). However, I am not including discussion of these here, for reasons of focus and length of chapter.
14. Two of his other films, *Batalla en el cielo/Battle in Heaven* (2005) and *Post Tenebras Lux* (2012), have a focus on the character of the male servant and their wealthy employers, and the director places characters in contact zones to highlight social inequalities.
15. I discuss the symbolism and the act itself in more depth in Shaw (2011).
16. For my discussion of the transnational production, exhibition and distribution patterns for Martel and Puenzo's films, with a focus on *La niña santa* and *XXY*, see Shaw (2013a).
17. Martel explains the historical connections in an interview, 'The same mechanism that we used in the past to ignore the suffering of others is still very present today. That's why in the film, I use music from the Seventies at the same time that people use mobile phones and drive contemporary cars. What I wanted to stress with these elements is that the same mechanism that started back then is continuing. So I use anachronisms to create that continuity'. (Taubin 2009).

18. This point is also made very effectively in one of the stories ('La Propuesta'/The 'Proposal') in the multi-stranded *Relatos salvajes/Wild Tales* (Szifrón, 2014) in which a servant is pressurised into taking the blame for a fatal hit-and-run caused by his employer's son.
19. For a discussion of the significance of Vero's pale skin and blond hair see White (2015: 50–1), Martin (2016). Martel herself notes, 'I cast her because of her physical characteristics, because she is so tall and white-skinned and blonde, and I thought that these physical features made her stand out from the people she interacts with (Taubin, 2009).
20. For an enlightening discussion of the figure of the ghost and hauntings in *La mujer sin cabeza*, see Martin (2016).
21. For further discussion of Candita's illness, see Martin (2016) and White (2015: 52). White writes that hepatitis represents 'a vector of contagion that collapses boundaries of gender, bloodline, and generation', while for Martin it represents 'Candita's sexual and social contamination by "undesirable" elements' (2016: 96).
22. The audience knows this through the use of subtitles (at least in the English-release editions), but the judge would not know the meaning of the lyrics.
23. This a phrase most commonly associated with the Mexican feminist author Rosario Castellanos. In her famous poem 'Meditación en el umbral'/'Meditation on the Brink', she writes that women need to search for new forms of identity to free them from patriarchal control and find 'another way to be human and free. Another way to be' (for the full poem, see Ahern 1988: 28–9). Although Castellanos does reject lesbian identity as a solution to women's oppression, 'there must be another way that's not named Sappho' (29).
24. The process for creating the underwater lake scenes, which were shot in a pool using CGI, is discussed on the DVD, in the 'Behind the Scenes' section.
25. 'Creo que la presencia de la leyenda del niño pez en el lago, todo lo relacionado con el agua y lo que está por debajo de la superficie, está ligado más a lo emocional que a lo racional, es algo muy del mundo femenino. Y el encuentro de ellas dos es desde ese lugar, donde se les mezclan todo: su relación es erótica, maternal, amistosa' (Bello 2009).

References

Ahern, Maureen (ed.) (1988). *A Rosario Castellanos Reader: An Anthology of Her Poetry, Short Fiction, Essays and Drama*, Austin: University of Texas Press.
Ally, Shireen (2015). 'Domesti-city. Colonial anxieties and postcolonial fantasies in the figure of the maid', in Victoria Haskins and Claire Lowrie (eds), *Colonialisation and Domestic Service: Historical and Contemporary Perspectives*, London: Routledge, pp. 45–62.

Intimacy and Distance

Barrow, Sarah (2013). 'New configurations for Peruvian cinema: the rising star of Claudia Llosa'. *Transnational Cinemas*, 4.2, pp. 197–215.

Bello, María José (2009). ' El niño pez: una historia de misterio y erotismo'. Available at http://blogdecinelatino.blogspot.co.uk/2009/05/trailer-el-nino-pez.html (accessed 6 January 2016).

D'Argenio, María Chiara (2013). 'A contemporary Andean type: the representation of the indigenous world in Claudia Llosa's films'. *Latin American and Caribbean Ethnic Studies*, 8.1, pp. 5–23.

De Lauretis, Teresa (1987). *Technologies of Gender: Essays on Theory, Film, and Fiction*, Bloomington: Indiana University Press.

Franco, Jean (2002). *The Decline and Fall of the Lettered City: Latin America in the Cold War*, Cambridge: Harvard University Press.

Haskins, Victoria and Claire Lowrie (eds) (2015). *Colonialisation and Domestic Service: Historical and Contemporary Perspectives*, London: Routledge.

Higman, Barry (2015). 'An historical perspective: colonial continuities in the global geography of domestic service', in Victoria Haskins and Claire Lowrie (eds), *Colonialisation and Domestic Service: Historical and Contemporary Perspectives*, London: Routledge, pp. 19–37.

Hooper, John (2014). 'M-appeal swoops on "Hilda"'. Available at http://variety.com/2014/film/festivals/m-appeal-swoops-on-hilda-exclusive-1201160747 (accessed 7 December 2015).

Kuznesof, Elizabeth (1989). 'A history of domestic service in Spanish America, 1492–1980', in Elsa. M. Chaney and María García Castro (eds), *Muchachas No More: Household Workers in Latin America and the Caribbean*, Philadelphia: Temple University Press, pp. 17–34.

Martin, Deborah (2016). *The Cinema of Lucrecia Martel*, Manchester: Manchester University Press.

Podalsky, Laura (2011). *The Politics of Affect and Emotion in Contemporary Latin American Cinema: Argentina, Brazil, Cuba, and Mexico*, Basingstoke: Palgrave Macmillan.

Quirós, Daniel (2010). 'La época está en desorden: reflexiones sobre la temporalidad en *Bolivia* de Adrián Caetano y *La mujer sin cabeza* de Lucrecia Martel'. *A Contracorriente*, 8.1, pp. 230–58.

Ranzani, Oscar (2009). 'Entrevista a Lucia Puenzo, que presenta el niño pez en el festival'. Available at http://www.pagina12.com.ar/diario/suplementos/espectaculos/2-12776-2009-02-06.html (accessed 12 November 2015).

Richard, Nelly (2004). *Cultural Residues: Chile in Transition*, Minneapolis: University of Minnesota Press.

Saito, Stephen (2015). 'Interview: Anna Muylaert on the long birth of "The Second Mother"'. Available at http://moveablefest.com/moveable_fest/2015/08/anna-muylaert-second-mother.html (accessed 12 December 2015).

Shaw, Deborah (2011). '(Trans)national images and cinematic spaces: the cases of Alfonso Cuarón's *Y tu mamá también* (2001) and Carlos Reygadas' *Japón* (2002)'. *Iberoamericana*, 44, pp. 117–31.

—— (2013a). 'Sex, texts and money, funding and Latin American queer cinema: the cases of Martel's *La niña santa* and Puenzo's *XXY*'. *Transnational Cinemas*, 4.2, pp. 165–84.

—— (2013b). *The Three Amigos: The Transnational Films of Guillermo del Toro, Alejandro González Iñárritu, and Alfonso Cuarón*, Manchester: Manchester University Press.

—— (2014). 'European co-production funds and Latin American cinema: processes of othering and bourgeois cinephilia in Claudia Llosa's *La teta asustada*'. *Diogène: Revue internationale des sciences humaines*, pp. 125–41.

Solórzano, Fernanda (2015). 'Patronas y sirvientas'. Available at http://www.letraslibres.com/blogs/en-pantalla/patronas-y-sirvientas (accessed 12 December 2015).

Sosa, Cecilia (2009). 'A counter-narrative of Argentine mourning: *The Headless Woman* (2008), directed by Lucrecia Martel'. *Theory Culture Society*, 26, pp. 250–62.

Taubin, Amy (2009). 'Interview: Lucrecia Martel shadow of a doubt'. Available at http://www.filmcomment.com/article/shadow-of-a-doubt-lucrecia-martel-interviewed (accessed 6 January 2016).

Tronto, Joan (2002). 'The nanny question'. *Hypatia*, 17. 2, pp. 34–49.

White, Patricia (2015). *Women's Cinema, World Cinema: Projecting Contemporary Feminisms*, Durham: Duke University Press.

6

Women's Filmmaking and Comedy in Brazil: Anna Muylaert's *Durval Discos* (2002) and *É proibido fumar* (2009)

Leslie L. Marsh

Introduction

A veteran screenwriter for Brazilian film and television, Anna Muylaert gained attention as a director after her debut film *Durval Discos/Durval Records* won several awards at the prestigious Gramado Film Festival in 2002, including those for Best Film, Best Screenplay and Best Director. Muylaert then further solidified her position as an important voice in Brazilian cinema when her 2009 film *É proibido fumar/Smoke Gets in Your Eyes* swept the awards at the Brasília Film Festival and received top honours from the Cinema Brazil Grand Prize, including Best Film, Best Director and Best Screenplay.[1] In a production context that has witnessed the increasing commercial success of romantic comedies (especially with new middle-class audiences), both films by Muylaert are unique for their dark humour. Humour is a classic strategy for offering critical interpretations of society and the carnivalesque has a rich history in Brazil. However, women artists' use of humour is a generally understudied area in Latin American cultural production. Muylaert joins other contemporary Brazilian women directors who have deployed humour to offer critical readings of contemporary Brazil, yet her use of dark humour lends itself to a critique of post-feminist culture. In this essay, I first position Muylaert and comedy generally in contemporary Brazilian cinema before I turn to examine the social and political meanings of dark humour in *Durval Discos* and *É proibido fumar*. My discussion focuses on the post-feminist female and male singleton, which then leads to a critique of a key theme of post-feminist culture: the assumption that gender equality and free lifestyle choices have been achieved.

Both films portray the seemingly mundane lives of middle-aged protagonists who are nostalgic for the music of the past and who live in middle-income neighbourhoods of São Paulo. The protagonists face a dilemma when benign events go absurdly and violently wrong. Generally, dark humour consists of making light of the 'darker' sides of humanity (murder, insanity, corruption). In *Durval Discos*, incongruity and awkwardness generate the humour that escalates to a tragic ending when maternal impulses go absurdly awry. By contrast, *É proibido fumar* resolves happily when the quirky, romantic relationship between the protagonists is cemented not through honest declarations of enduring love but through tragic irony and deception. In both instances, humour emerges from elements of incongruity and awkwardness in darker scenarios. This combination reveals cultural identities and values to be strange. Dark humour takes on a critique of post-feminist culture in both films as it communicates the disappearance of ideals in familial (*Durval Discos*) and romantic (*É proibido fumar*) relationships without seeking full reconciliation or the substitution of established gender norms. What is more, both films motivate a shift in expectations for contemporary affective relationships and examine the social and economic pressures that shape contemporary forms of masculinity and femininity in Brazil.

Muylaert and Brazilian (women's) filmmaking

A native of São Paulo, Muylaert (1964–) has charted a varied creative path in Brazilian film and television production over the past decades. She started her career in the audio-visual industry as an assistant director for feature films by Julien Temple (*Running Out of Luck*, 1987) and Paul Mazursky (*Moon Over Parador*, 1988) before moving into television, where she participated in creating the highly successful children's programmes *Mundo da lua* and *Castelo rá-tim-bum* for TV Cultura in the early 1990s. She has continued to write for television (*Um Menino Muito Maluquinho* for TVE Brasil, 2006; *Alice* for HBO Brasil, 2008) and collaborated on screenplays with other Brazilian filmmakers, including Karim Aïnouz, Roberto Moreira and three works directed by Cao Hamburger (*O ano em que meus pais saíram de férias /The Year My Parents Went on Vacation*, 2006; *Xingú*, 2012; *Castelo rá-tim-bum – o filme*, 1999). Muylaert's directing credits include six short films, two made-for-television movies (*E além de tudo me deixou mudo o violão*, 2013; *Para aceitá – la, continue na linha*, 2009) and four feature-length films for theatrical distribution (*Durval Discos*, 2002; *É proibido fumar*, 2009; *Chamada a cobrar*, 2012; and *Que horas ela volta?/ The Second Mother*, 2015). Her most recent film, *Que horas ela volta?*, was featured at the Sundance and Berlin Film Festivals before being nominated as Brazil's entry for Best Foreign Language Film for the 2016 Oscars.

Muylaert's talents as a screenwriter come through in the narrative structure and character development of her films. She tends to develop three-part narrative structures in which she pushes her protagonists out of their comfortable (but unfulfilling) routines, forces them to confront some new scenario that serves as the dramatic (and sometimes tragic) turning point and then lets these characters awaken in various respects to a new visibility or way of being.[2] Subsequently, previous social roles and cultural values are made strange and questioned. Thus, plot development is driven less by action sequences and more by how characters react to changes in their environment or how they interact with one another. And, although her films offer a balance of male and female characters, they tend to include strong female protagonists, which is still relatively (and unfortunately) rare in world cinema.

Muylaert's thematic and aesthetic choices gravitate around a common critique of social conventions – especially gender and class relations. With the exception of the film *Chamada a cobrar* and its development of aspects of the road movie, Muylaert has tended to focus on domestic spaces and has been cited by critics as being particularly good at portraying banal aspects of life (Calil 2012). For instance, both *Durval Discos* and *É proibido fumar* primarily take place in interior locations and are filmed with a relatively stable camera (sometimes at a distance) that observes the consequences of characters' actions. Domestic space frequently becomes the context for examining issues such as motherhood and cross-class relationships. Her films also tend to foreground the experiences of female youth as the departure point for offering social critiques. For example, in *Que horas ela volta?* Muylaert explores female domestic labour and changing social class relations in Brazil on the heels of recent economic transformations. Notably, the protagonist's daughter in this film embodies the new sensibilities of the 'emergent citizen' who rejects traditional class-based social restrictions (Marsh and Li 2016: 8-9, 11-13). In this her film joins a number of other recent Brazilian works that have also subtly explored class hierarchies and changing social relations, such as *O som ao redor/Neighbouring Sounds* (2012) and *Casa grande* (2014).

These more intimate portrayals are set against the backdrop of the urban landscape of São Paulo, where her films tend to pick up on the themes associated with urban dystopias such as kidnapping and ransom (*Durval Discos*; *Chamada a cobrar*); homicide (*Durval Discos*; *É proibido fumar*); calculated deception (*É proibido fumar*); alcoholism and family breakdown (*E além de tudo me deixou mudo o violão*); and entrenched class privilege (*Que horas ela volta?*). Both the focus on domestic spaces and the development of darker themes associated with urban living link Muylaert's work to a history of dystopic portrayals of urban São Paulo with notable examples including Rogério Sganzerla's *O bandido da luz vermelha/Red Light Bandit* (1968) of the São Paulo-based 'marginal film' movement (or *cine marginal*) and more recent films like Tata Amaral's *Um ceu de estrelas/A Starry Sky* (1996) and Sergio Bianchi's *Crónicamente inviável/Chronically Unfeasible* (2000). Yet, Muylaert's work differs in that neither *Durval Discos* nor *É proibido fumar* reaches the same degree of disillusionment as these films. Whereas both *Durval Discos* and *É proibido fumar* certainly lean towards tragedy, the combination of the absurd, the incongruous and 'awkwardness' strikes a humorous chord and prevents characters from becoming dehumanised and urban landscapes from becoming abject, fearful locales. For potential audiences of urban, middle-class Brazilian spectators, Muylaert's films shift focus away from the fear, tragedy and cynicism that can prevent viewers from thinking in more critical and nuanced ways about contemporary urban living and the cultural values (especially regarding gender and class) that shape that experience.

A brief overview of Muylaert's career reveals that she has taken on a variety of roles, working in both television and film production and finding synergy between the two fields. This wearing of many hats is not entirely unique. In historical perspective, women have frequently overseen multiple duties in filmmaking in Brazil, behind and in front of the camera. During the twentieth century, women assumed a variety of roles in film production in Brazil in addition to being actresses and 'script-girls'. The lack of codified roles in the first half of the twentieth century allowed women to participate in a variety of ways but it also facilitated forgetting or not recognising their contributions (Marsh 2012: 13–45).

During the twenty-first century, a distinct set of factors has motivated taking on a broad range of roles in audio-visual production. Whereas a previous generation of women directors who established consistent trajectories in Brazilian cinema benefited greatly from Embrafilme (the state-led film agency) in the 1980s, Muylaert began her career in the midst of the Collor administration (1990–2) in which neo-liberal reforms translated into the elimination of funds for cultural production and the closure of cultural institutions. By the mid-1990s, following the Brazilian Cinema Rescue Award (Prêmio Resgate do Cinema Brasileiro), film production had been renewed and several films received international recognition. Thus, a renaissance of filmmaking in Brazil (the Retomada) took place over a ten-year period. The year 2002 generally marks the end of the Retomada as ANCINE (the National Cinema Agency) was inaugurated in late 2001. Programmes were instituted to develop Brazilian cinema (notably the Programa de Apoio ao Desenvolvimento do Cinema Nacional, PRODECINE) and new funding mechanisms were put into place (such as Fundos de Financiamento da Indústria Cinematográfica Nacional, FUNCINES). The period is further punctuated by the release of *Cidade de Deus/City of God* (2002) and the consolidation of Globo Filmes in contemporary Brazilian cinema. Generally speaking, film production and distribution in Brazil in the post-Retomada period has become more market-oriented, with the goal of capturing a greater portion of box office receipts. Whereas the period of the Retomada is characterised by a variety of styles (from the openly commercial to more strictly experimental) and formats (fiction, documentary and mixed films) with no specific genres predominating (Nagib 2003: xviii–xix), the landscape of Brazilian film since the inauguration of ANCINE can be characterised by the rise of the action crime thriller, frequently set in Brazil's urban favelas, as well as the comedy and romantic comedy.[3]

This changing landscape (or 'moment') of film financing and development of Brazilian cinema during the 1990s is an important factor that frames Muylaert's professional trajectory and, consequently, how her work may be approached by scholars. During the Retomada period, when funding was scarce, Muylaert found work and a creative outlet in television and thereby honed her skills in the audio-visual sector. Yet, her debut feature film, *Durval Discos*, released in 2002, places her film career in a new era. Depending on one's emphasis, Muylaert could be seen as bridging two periods of the Brazilian audio-visual industries or more exclusively as a post-Retomada film director. Although Globo Filmes has clearly cultivated a synergy between television and cinema in the post-Retomada period, Muylaert's work in both television and film precedes and coexists with this tendency.

Muylaert's negotiation of an unstable audio-visual landscape is, as indicated above, relatively common when speaking of women's participation in Brazilian filmmaking from a historical perspective. Women have a minority presence as film directors in Brazil (and elsewhere) and, relative to their male counterparts, they have not benefited from consistent access to production funding. Yet, women have historically participated in significant ways in numerous areas of film production (as writers, 'script-girls', editors, etc.). Academic study of women's varied participation in film production (in addition to directing) avoids the continued replication of gaps in film histories. Whether attributed to economic crisis, personal choice or other factors, Muylaert's multifaceted career suggests that scholars approach contemporary Brazilian women's filmmaking in a more intersectional way. In addition to thinking about women *directors* and feature-length *films* we should also consider how women have taken on numerous other roles in film and media production so as not to ignore their significant contributions in the history of Brazilian film and media. For example, Muylaert has established herself as an accomplished screenwriter, yet little research has been undertaken to explore women's contributions in this area.[4] Indeed, Muylaert joins a number of other accomplished yet unheralded women screenwriters for Brazilian film and television, including Adriana Falcão, Elena Soarez, Izabel de Oliveira and Glória Perez, to name just a few. Although it is outside the scope of this essay and the focus of this volume, this is a rich area for investigation of Brazilian women's cultural production.

Women's Filmmaking and Comedy in Brazil

Drawing attention to women directors as a category in cinema is a meaningful political gesture made by scholars but not one Brazilian women directors themselves have always readily embraced (Marsh 2012: 36–9). For instance, when interviewed at Sundance, Muylaert described herself by stating, 'I am a 50-year-old being' among other personal and professional roles (e.g. writer, mother, filmmaker, woman, Brazilian). In the same interview, she recognises that she lives in a chauvinist and unequal country but further explains that she is a woman 'who does not feel worse than man', which suggests that she sees herself as experiencing challenges in life similar to any other person (male or female) (Narasaki 2015). In this, she echoes a perspective put forth by women directors of a previous generation who wished to be seen as people and professionals before their biological sex or gender. Yet, during more recent interviews, Muylaert reflects on feeling treated like a second-class citizen (Thompson 2015) and experiencing overt sexism that has included receiving demeaning remarks from male colleagues, not receiving credit for her accomplishments, a perverse resistance to her (female) authority, and ongoing social barriers limiting women's access to financing (Kang 2015). Muylaert's reflections on her subject position as a female director in contemporary Brazil and at international film festivals suggest that she herself experiences the personal/professional career tensions of post-feminist culture. In the contemporary Brazilian film industry, women may ostensibly have more opportunities but they also face continuing institutionalised sexist discrimination. Muylaert has spoken out against routine chauvinism in the film industry. In this way, she embodies aspects of her own characters Val and Jéssica in *Que horas ela volta?* by becoming more cognisant of social oppression and not tolerating past prejudices.

Muylaert came of age during the period of the second-wave women's movement in Brazil and broad civilian demands for democratisation. Her two films discussed here revolve largely around white, middle-class, urban experiences and do not foreground the most vocal and successful lines of contemporary feminist activism (i.e., regarding domestic violence and racism).[5] Rather, *Durval Discos* and *É proibido fumar* critique contemporary post-feminist culture, defined generally as the cultural space left after second-wave feminism and characterised by individualist agendas and the celebration of choices, sexual freedoms and the presumed triumph of social equality.⁶ In her work on post-femininities in popular culture, Stéphanie Genz acknowledges that post-feminism defies a simple definition but suggests we think about it in terms of a rhetoric of contradictions, conflicts and ambiguity that brings about complex resignification (2009: 22–4).

The idea of a post-feminist culture or period is not a facile Anglo-American transplant to the Brazilian context. Rita Terezinha Schmidt traces a long history of silencing feminism in Brazil primarily through the repudiation of feminist ideas as a foreign imposition. Contrary to this, Schmidt advocates against quick refusals of so-called misplaced ideas and encourages thinking about how ideas – which are rarely pure and homogenous in the first place – have resonance in the Brazilian context (2006). Ana Gabriel Macedo recognises the existence of a post-feminist era emerging in the 1990s but sees post-feminism as one perspective among various modes of contemporary feminism in Brazil (2006). Muylaert has received international attention for *Que horas ela volta?* but her works are not transnational productions; funding largely comes from Brazilian sources and they emphasise Brazilian contexts and characters. However, as discussed below, her films do include a number of themes and tropes associated with transnational post-feminist culture such as the singleton, consumption as liberation, a critique of contemporary masculinity and the assumption that gender equality has been achieved.

Comedy in context

The rebirth of Brazilian cinema in the mid-1990s is frequently associated with the commercially successful historical comedy *Carlota Joaquina, Princesa do Brasil/Carlota Joaquina, Princess of Brazil* (1995) by Carla Camurati. Other Brazilian women filmmakers have also developed the comedy or romantic comedy, including Sandra Werneck, Betse de Paula, Eliane Fonseca and Mara Mourão, to name just a few. The transitional period of the Retomada has gradually given way to a context in which the comedy and the romantic comedy have become increasingly prominent. Data published by ANCINE on the films with the highest number of spectators from 1970 to 2013 show that comedies have been and continue to be significant. In fact, of the top 50 films on ANCINE's list, there are a total of eighteen films with a release date on or after the year 2000, of which nine are comedies (ANCINE 2013).[7]

Although comedy has a rich history in Brazilian cinema, recent trends can be attributed to three factors: the orientation of ANCINE; the move to culture-led regeneration of the Brazilian economy; and a larger Brazilian middle-class audience. First, the inauguration of ANCINE in 2001 signalled the return of state support for the Brazilian film industry. However, as Melina Marson observes, it was with a 'mentalidade empresarial' (entrepreneurial mentality) of cinema as an entertainment product that has to be self-sustainable, that the state renewed its dialogue with filmmakers (2009: 158). There are pressures to secure box office success to ensure future film financing, which contributes to producing less daring, more commercially appealing works.[8] Second, starting in 2003, cultural policies were reformulated to cultivate a creative economy in Brazil in which audio-visual production was identified as a key sector.[9] This shift in policy further contributed to emphasising more commercially successful filmmaking. Lastly, the economic orientation of cultural policy and the film industry coincided with a remarkable shift in Brazilian demographics. Millions of people entered the ranks of the lower middle class (*classe C*), with greater disposable income to participate in aspirational middle-class lifestyle activities like going to the cinema. It is in this context that the comedy in Brazil re-emerges – pressured to perform at the box office and to please (especially new) middle-class audiences.

Yet, there are costs and benefits of cultivating the comedy genre in the current period. Although the turn to comedy may repeat past trends of appealing to domestic middle-class audiences and there have been clear box office successes, greater potential with national audiences may come at the price of more limited international appeal in an era of transnational co-productions. Slapstick, physical and some situational humour may travel well across borders and time but not all jokes can be translated. Whereas an action thriller may require (relatively) little explanation, comedy has culturally specific layers that not all audiences may be able to decode. Even local audiences may not connect fully with a director's comic sensibilities. Such may be the case with Muylaert's films, which had more limited art-house distribution and relatively low box office numbers. For comparison, both *É proibido fumar* and *Se eu fosse você II/If I Were You 2* were released in 2009 and starred the veteran comedic film and television actress Glória Pires. But whereas *Se eu fosse você II* played at 315 cinemas, where it was viewed by over 6 million spectators and was the highest-grossing Brazilian film of 2009 and fourth among the most-seen Brazilian films of all time, *É proibido fumar* was distributed to only 42 theatres, where it was seen by only 33,291 spectators (ANCINE 2009). What is more, *Se eu fosse você II* develops an entertaining but unchallenging mode of humour regarding traditional gender roles and revolves around a traditional trope of the romantic comedy in which there is a misunderstanding that is resolved in the end. By contrast, *É proibido fumar* develops a dark sense of humour that is neither common to the romantic comedy nor the *telenovela*. Although her two feature films did not record great box office numbers, owing in part to their dark mode of humour and critical stance on gendered relations, Muylaert did gain fame in art-house circles.

As they are currently structured, contemporary funding models in Brazil benefit light-hearted (romantic) comedies, action thrillers and tear-jerking historical biopics. In other words, what is fast, funny and familiar seems better positioned to survive in contemporary Brazilian cinema. But *Durval Discos* and *É proibido fumar* do not clearly fall into any one of those three categories. Again, Muylaert's films are funny but they develop a mode of dark humour built upon elements of incongruity and awkwardness. Muylaert's characters are constructed as slightly marginal or social outcasts in some way who become trapped in scenarios of murder and deception. It is this particular sense of humour that lends itself to post-feminist critique, one that examines the tropes and themes of post-feminist culture.

What's funny?

Although there is no overarching theory of comedy or humour, scholars of humour frequently refer to the importance of comedy as offering socio-political and cultural critiques. In their evaluations of humour, scholars variously refer to a range of approaches, including the expression of the unconscious (Freud), the subversion of hierarchies and norms, as in the carnivalesque (Bakhtin), or the deconstructive nature of humour (Derrida). In her study of Latin American women's use of humour in fiction, Dianna C. Niebylski asserts that one of the most salient features of humour is how it forces a shift in expectations, and demands that we re-examine our epistemological and cultural assumptions (2004: 12). A number of scholars have considered humour as a strategy for social interaction and mode of discourse, and note how humour plays an important role in the formation of new gender roles and social relations. For instance, Helga Kotthoff identifies four dimensions in which humour becomes notably gendered, namely status, aggressiveness, social alignment and sexuality (or corporeality) (2006: 8–20). In fact, both *Durval Discos* and *É proibido fumar* develop these four dimensions to varying degrees with the effect of not so much subverting or affirming a particular critique of gendered roles, but rather more to expose and reveal, in an uncomfortable yet funny way, gendered modes of being. In this way, the humour in both films demands a shift in expectations and an examination of cultural assumptions and both also offer an examination of the post-feminist rhetoric of contradictions, conflicts and ambiguity noted above.

In an essay that investigates the mechanisms of humour in film comedy, Vandaele proposes that an interplay of incongruity and superiority structures humorous phenomena. Incongruity is a generalised feature of humour and traditionally refers to a conflict between what is expected and what occurs, and Vandaele suggests thinking of incongruity in terms of 'oppositeness'; superiority refers to a reinforcement of some social functioning or hierarchy (2002: 224). In both *Durval Discos* and *É proibido fumar*, an idealised (i.e., presumed 'superior') version of life comes into conflict with a darker, unexpected (i.e., 'incongruous') portrayal of events.

Durval Discos: looking for meaning in domestic space

In both *Durval Discos* and *É proibido fumar*, Muylaert examines the performance of gendered identities in domestic space. Indeed, a movement from the external, urban sphere into an interior, domestic space structures the opening sequence of *Durval Discos*. A mobile camera explores the streets of São Paulo with opening credits appearing on signs, bar menus and advertisements posted on poles. Viewers are led to a stable shot of a single-dwelling house nestled among high-rise buildings and inter-titles inform viewers that it is the summer of 1995. Thus begins the first of a three-part narrative. Inside, viewers are introduced to Durval, who runs a record shop from a front room, and his elderly mother, Dona Carmen. When Durval realises his mother is faltering (made evident by her not remembering how to make his favourite dessert), he proposes hiring a maid to help with domestic chores. Despite offering a sum far below expectations at the time, a woman named Célia accepts the position and moves in.

All is not what it may seem. Elizabeth, who works at a delicatessen next door, reveals that Célia has been purchasing rather than cooking the food. Then Célia abruptly disappears, leaving behind her daughter Kiki with a note asking that they take care of her while she resolves some undisclosed problems. Although suspicions about Célia are raised, they are conveniently ignored as this allows Durval and Dona Carmen to engage in fun-loving, playful experiences doting on Kiki. The third and final act begins when Durval and his mother see a television news report in which it is revealed that Célia was part of a kidnapping ring and that Kiki is really a kidnapped girl named Christina Botelho. Whereas Durval wishes to call the police immediately, it is too late for Dona Carmen. Her 'mothering instincts' have been switched on and there is no stopping her. What had been an apparently boring yet peaceful, unremarkable domestic life slowly begins to unravel into a carnivalesque tragedy driven by the absurd.

The film's protagonist, Durval, is an awkward, middle-aged, single man who lives at home with his elderly mother and can best be understood as a post-feminist male singleton. Stéphanie Genz and Benjamin Brabon offer the concept of the post-feminist man as a way to explore masculinity and its transformations in the new millennium. Specifically, they suggest the post-feminist man embodies a variety of contested subject positions and is defined by 'his problematic relationship with the ghost of hegemonic masculinity as he tries to reconcile the threat he poses to himself and the social systems he tries to uphold' (2009: 143). Drawing on this work and as a counterpart to the post-feminist female singleton, Brabon (2013: 117) proposes the notion of the post-feminist male singleton in contemporary cinema, where male protagonists confront or avoid a variety of social and economic pressures that shape and challenge their masculinity.

Durval seems out of step with hegemonic masculinity and the changing global economy. At his record store, he disappoints shoppers when he informs them that he only sells vinyl LPs and no CDs, a digital technology he either cannot afford or stubbornly refuses to embrace. Although sales seem to be stagnant, he does not apparently have other gainful employment outside the domestic space of his home. In this, Muylaert seems to be critiquing a 'rhetoric of crisis' found in São Paulo in the mid-1990s during which time urban crime was on the rise, hyperinflation had reduced household incomes and unemployment rates were steadily increasing. Durval is a middle-aged man whose performance of hegemonic masculinity seems thwarted by unfavourable economic conditions. The labour market does not apparently include him and he does not adopt the latest digital technologies, which frequently serve as the tools and signifiers of modern masculinity.

Besides being excluded from technological innovation and, by extension, the shifting global economy, Durval seems to be challenged by independent working women. For instance, Elizabeth, the single, energetic woman who works next door and visits him at his record shop, seems to overpower Durval. He admires Célia while she sweeps the floor and asks if she is married, suggesting that he has sexual desires for her. But his awkward advances fail to gain her attention. This and other desires seem to be frustrated as he is frequently shot in cramped interior spaces, suggesting he is a conflicted, frustrated and incapacitated heteronormative masculine figure. Ironically, suggested imprisonment becomes true imprisonment in the third part of the film when his mother takes the keys to the front door and effectively kidnaps him.

Kiki's presence in the house presents a threat and opportunity for Durval and his mother. Initially, Durval is anxious and jealous that Kiki seems to steal the attention of his mother. As a man-child figure, Durval plays an 'air guitar' in his bedroom and harbours adolescent fantasies of musical stardom. However, jealousy converts into an opportunity to play again like a child. Durval joins Kiki in dressing-up, dances in the living room, indulges her at a toy store and spontaneously takes a carriage ride through the city. The relationship between Durval and his mother improves through their shared laughter and taking care of the small child. Whereas Kiki's presence allows Durval to experience a childlike regression, needing to take care of Kiki in Célia's absence allows Dona Carmen to become once again a devoted and protective mother to a small child. In this, both Durval and his mother evidence a latent nostalgia for past gendered scripts and familial roles. However, scenes of the three having fun convey a paradoxical message. On the one hand, getting out of a present routine or comfort zone can bring great joy. On the other, failure to get out of one's past comfort zone (i.e., gendered and familial roles) can be highly detrimental and problematic, which becomes most evident in the final scenes.

Durval and his mother react differently to the news of Kiki's kidnapping and take divergent paths. What was incongruous and awkward earlier in the film becomes decidedly dark, absurd and hyperbolic. If there had been signs of quirky family dynamics earlier, traditional gender roles go off the rails completely in the end. Dona Carmen thwarts Durval's efforts to do the logical thing and notify the police – at first through gentle means (manipulative persuasion, hanging up a phone call) and then by harsher methods (cutting the phone lines, locking the doors and keeping the key, shuttering the windows). Dona Carmen becomes aggressive in her goal to protect Kiki, (perhaps) accidentally shooting and killing the neighbour Elizabeth, who recognises Kiki as the kidnapped girl. Dona Carmen loses touch with reality and succumbs to a dark fantasy of mothering. An absurd chain of events culminates in a carnivalesque moment when we see gathered in one bedroom Elizabeth's dead body, a white horse brought in from the street, Kiki dressed as a princess ballerina painting the wall, Dona Carmen dressed up and organising her armoire and Durval, who nervously paces back and forth (see Figure 6.1).

Patrick O'Neill suggests that dark humour (or 'black humour') is articulated in five basic modes – satiric, ironic, grotesque, absurd and parodic – and that the absurd mode of dark humour 'registers the disappearance of the ideal' (1983: 160). The dark humour that appears in the final act of *Durval Discos* certainly exposes and makes fun of urban violence, kidnapping and lingering problems with equality in the domestic sphere, and challenges acritical assumptions concerning motherhood. In the carnivalesque scene above, humour emerges from the absurd as well as what is incongruous. Dona Carmen goes overboard with performing the role of the protective mother and eventually becomes an aggressive, dominating and unreasonable kidnapper. Indeed, she does the opposite of what one expects of a protective, caring maternal figure. This escalation of the absurd exposes the fantasies of motherhood and makes fun of this idealised role.

Figure 6.1. The carnivalesque scene of the crime(s) in *Durval Discos* (Anna Muylaert, 2002).

O'Neill also asserts that dark humour engages in an unravelling of social structures, norms, traditions and hierarchies and, thus, can be considered a comedy of entropy (1983: 160). The film's ending refers to this notion of a comedy of disorder when viewers see the final image of a construction crew razing the house in which Durval and his mother had lived. Handheld camera shots of the house being demolished function as a coda to the film; they serve to shift cinematic registers to a diegetic moment outside the film and raise questions about contemporary society. Here, the use of dark humour with its associated unravelling of norms affords a critique of post-feminist culture, and exposes the incomplete project of gender equality and the failed assumption that individual liberty prevails. The final scenes of the film propose that the social and economic topography of late capitalism demand the abandonment of old gender scripts and subject positions uncommitted to change.

É proibido fumar: infantilised singletons and the romantic dark comedy

Muylaert followed her debut feature film with the 2009 romantic comedy *É proibido fumar*. Romantic comedies have been relatively successful and prominent in recent years in Brazilian cinema; examples include *Meu passado me condena: o filme* (Júlia Rezende, 2013), *De pernas pro ar/Head Over Heels* (Roberto Santucci, 2010) and its 2012 sequel, *Se eu fosse você/If*

I Were You (Daniel Filho, 2006) and its 2009 sequel, and *S.O.S.: Mulheres ao mar* (Cris D'amato, 2014) and its 2015 sequel. While highly successful at the box office, these films deploy humour in ways that largely sustain rather than change the way we think about heteronormative relationships, sexuality and gender roles. By contrast, Muylaert's *É proibido fumar* adds elements of tragedy to the romantic comedy genre and shows the ugly, darker side of romance. In the process, the film makes love a little less normative while critiquing post-feminist culture, especially the trope of the personal makeover (alongside other neo-liberal regimens of self-improvement) and the assumption that women are free to make lifestyle choices.

Set in São Paulo, *É proibido fumar* follows the trajectory of romance between Baby and Max. Similar to *Durval Discos*, a stable camera frequently lets actions unfold in domestic spaces and the plot is driven by characters and their reactions to situations. Baby is a middle-aged woman living alone in an apartment where she gives private guitar lessons. When Max moves in next door with a guitar, Baby's interest in him is instantly piqued. The two begin a romance and their most significant obstacle is not unrequited love or external forces working against them, but surmounting their own character flaws and misunderstandings. For instance, Max speaks highly of his ex-wife, Estelina, in front of Baby and seems helpless with domestic chores but manages enough expertise to critique an elaborate dinner Baby prepared. Meanwhile, Baby embodies the stereotypical insecure female companion given to suspicion and jealousy. To secure Max's devotion, she attempts to fulfil a number of expectations for women (learn to cook, clean house, be well manicured) and engages in various self-disciplining regimes. When Max asks her to not smoke, Baby interprets this as a deciding factor for their budding relationship and begins an arduous cessation programme. In a moment of weakness, she heads out in her car late at night to buy cigarettes but accidentally hits and kills Estelina, which becomes the secret that strengthens the romantic bond between Max and Baby.

At some point in the narrative structure of a traditional romantic comedy, the romantic pair faces an obstacle that they overcome and, subsequently, romantic ideals of true love prevail. This is not quite the case for Max and Baby. Their romantic partnership is cemented in the end but done so through bribery and deception. Apart from the tragic and ironic clarification at the end when Max shares that he really is not that bothered by Baby's smoking, there is no moment of shared confession and clarification commonly found in the traditional romantic comedy. Baby understands Max's dedication to her when she discovers he has acquired and hidden the incriminating surveillance tape that captures her running over his ex-wife. But she keeps this knowledge secret. Theirs is not an edifying story of romance where misunderstandings are fully resolved. Rather, being fully transparent and honest with one's partner is more or less overlooked.

The misunderstanding between Baby and Max is an incongruity that is funny but also tragic and absurd. In his work on the romantic comedy, Celestino Deleyto underscores the importance of thinking more about humour as an agent in a film genre that examines affective human relationships and discourses of identity (2009: 18–54). Whereas Deleyto uncovers aspects of the romantic comedy in suspense thrillers, we need to consider the effects when dark humour is mobilised in the romantic comedy. Drawing again on O'Neill, I add that dark humour merged with romantic comedy shifts expectations about gender and heteronormative romance. It de-idealises views of romance and the discourses surrounding sexuality and gendered identities. In sum, dark humour significantly modifies the romantic comedy as a generic framework for examining affective human relationships.

Similar to Durval, Baby is an awkward character who finds herself unexpectedly mired in murder and deception. She is also a middle-aged character whose name suggests she has skipped several stages of psychosocial development. This lack of synchronicity calls for an exploration of contemporary politics of lifestyle and gender. Notwithstanding the jitteriness of nicotine withdrawal, the anxieties of new romance or the guilt of involuntary vehicular homicide, Baby seems consistently in tension with her surroundings. If Durval is the male singleton, Baby can be understood as a post-feminist female singleton, which Stéphanie Genz defines as an unattached, city-dwelling woman who experiences various contradictions, being bold and ambitious as well as neurotic and insecure and caught between enjoying her independence and a yearning to find 'Mr Right' and settle down (2009: 134–6). Although Baby does not embody the same level of boldness and career ambition notable in various Anglo-American singleton characters, she is a contemporary urban Brazilian woman who lives the tensions between independence and wanting a rewarding home life. Baby's life is presented as lacking and, ostensibly, her greatest desire before Max appears is for a stable, domestic relationship, which is expressed as wanting an aunt's sofa.

Baby and her sisters Teca and Popi present a range of contemporary lifestyle options. Teca, who is married with children, criticises Baby for not being able to catch a man, fall in love and get married (like her). Popi, whose marital status is not revealed, criticises Baby for not studying to become a successful career woman (like her). That Popi appears so much taller than Baby when they talk asserts Popi's presumably more powerful position and further infantilises Baby as the younger, insecure, unaccomplished sister. The three women embody the presumed post-feminist free life choices available to women, yet Baby, as the contemporary female singleton, is not presented as particularly happy. By comparison with her sisters, she has apparently 'failed to launch'. In her critique of the range of contemporary post-feminist subject positions, Genz asserts that the female singleton character frequently moves across binaries and walks 'a tightrope between professional and personal success/failure' (2009: 135). Yet, there is little celebration in the film of Baby's unwed freedom or independence as is found with the protagonist Laura of the Brazilian film *Avassaladoras/ Overwhelming Women* (2002), the English literary and filmic character Bridget Jones or the American women of HBO's series *Sex and the City* (1998–2004).

Not fitting in, or being slightly out, of step cultivates a sense of humour and demands exploration of the social and economic pressures that shape contemporary forms of femininity in Brazil. As noted above, Kotthoff defines incongruity as an important factor in gendered humour. In terms of the body and gendered identities, incongruity becomes reframed most effectively as awkwardness, which suggests a strangeness that disagrees with expectations or norms. For some scholars of contemporary feminism and gender studies, awkwardness has become a rallying cry for feminist activism and interpretation. For example, Carrie Smith-Prei and Maria Stehle draw on the fundamental definition of awkwardness as lacking harmony and underscore the political facets of standing out and not being in harmony with one's surroundings.[10] What is more, Smith-Prei and Stehle underscore how awkwardness draws attention to what is 'normative' and how awkwardness implies a self-awareness of 'doing gender' (2014: 213–18). Indeed, it is through Baby's awkward experiences that formulaic female identities and assumptions about women's life choices are humorously exposed.

Baby undertakes a transformation that affords a critique of heteronormative romance and the contemporary consumption practices that produce femininity and ostensibly liberate women. Overall, Baby undergoes an evolution in the film, dressing better and becoming more domestic (i.e., cooking and cleaning). At first, Max shows little domestic know-how and seems non-committal, needing to 'work through issues' (i.e., have sex) with his ex-wife despite dating Baby. Eventually, he becomes a loyal, respectful partner. In other words, we see gendered performances 'being done' but these are not uplifting or model representations. Rather, these performances reveal anxious and negative aspects of affective relationships in a humorous way that in turn critiques discourses of gendered identity and heteronormative sexuality.

More specifically, Baby undergoes a makeover where her self-improvement becomes a project and potential undoing. She begins a smoking cessation programme and engages in greater self-care (exercising and grooming). In a particularly significant scene, Baby prepares for the possibility of having sex with Max and visits a salon to have her legs and bikini area waxed. There a friend asks her to select the type of waxing she wants, such as the most fashionable genital area manicuring known as 'the Brazilian' (see Figure 6.2). This provokes their laughter, partly owing to this practice taking on a sort of national brand and being reintroduced to them. This scene in the salon affords a unique critique of the production of formulaic femininity. On the one hand, Baby acts as an outsider being introduced to what is presented as a common practice for Brazilian women. On the other, she is cast as an outsider to international notions of producing femininity. Albeit brief, this moment subverts an authenticity presumed locally and internationally and draws attention to the limits of post-feminist culture in which consumption – especially of beauty services and products – is construed as a path to self-improvement and liberation. This critique of post-feminist culture and consumption as a mode of self-fashioning is further underscored by commercials on Baby's living room TV. At various moments, we see broadcast infomercials of a shopping

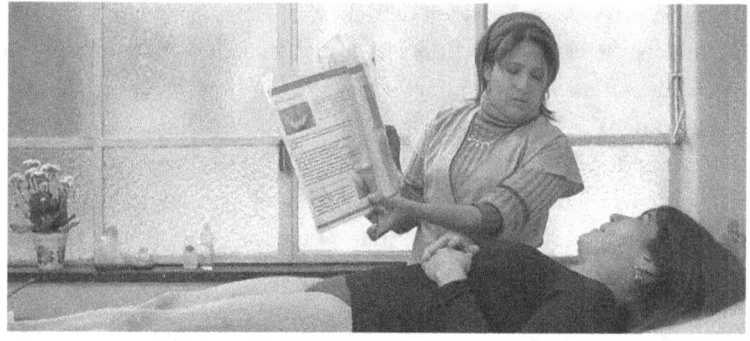

Figure 6.2. The 'Brazilian' wax in *É proibido fumar* (Anna Muylaert, 2009).

channel and style reports on plastic surgery. The disjuncture between what is on TV and the reality of how Baby lives offers a critique of consumer self-fashioning as omnipresent yet also slightly absurd and excessive.

Concluding remarks

The comedy and the romantic comedy will certainly continue to be important genres in contemporary Brazilian cinema. Studies of the film industry can reflect on the economic imperatives and audience demographics that drive this phenomenon. Yet, also at stake is a consideration of how comedic films engage and contribute to discourses of identity. *Durval Discos* and *É proibido fumar* differ from more commercially successful character-driven comedies in that they introduce dark humour as an agent to de-idealise heteronormative romance and call attention to constructions of gendered identities. Awkward characters and elements of incongruity bring about a critique of post-feminist culture – the contradictions experienced by male and female singletons, consumption of goods and services as gendered production of the individual, and the mistaken assumption that gender equality has been achieved. If genres like the comedy and the romantic comedy are historically and culturally mediated and offer frameworks for looking at human relationships in particular ways, then Muylaert's use of dark humour demands thinking differently about contemporary affective relationships.

Notes

1. The Cinema Brazil Grand Prize is the Brazilian Academy's award ceremony. The film also won honours from the ACIE Awards (Brazil), the Prêmio Contigo Cinema and at the SESC Film Festival.
2. For more on this tendency, see Trajano Pontes' review of *Chamada a cobrar* (Pontes 2012).
3. The role of Globo Filmes in the production of some of these comedies has prompted Brazilian film critics to coin the term 'Globo chanchada', making historical reference to the commercially successful film comedies (i.e., the *chanchada*) of the mid-twentieth century in Brazil.
4. Two works that explore women screenwriters in the developing area of screenplay studies are those by Jill Nelmes and Jule Selbo (2015) and María Teresa DePaoli (2014).
5. Regarding the more recent directions of feminist activism in Brazil, see Matilde Ribeiro (2006).
6. In the introduction to their volume, Yvonne Tasker and Diane Negra advocate defining post-feminism not as a line of activism or politics but as a culture (2007: 1–25).
7. Notably, only one of these is directed by a Brazilian woman, Julia Rezende's romantic comedy *Meu passado me condena* (2013), which follows the television series (2012–13) airing on Multishow and of which Rezende also directed several episodes. Rezende has also directed the romantic comedies *Ponte aérea* (2015) and *Meu passado me condena II* (2015).
8. For example, RioFilme established an important line of production funding that is 'automatic', meaning proposed projects are not judged by subjective measures such as the script or a synopsis. Rather, projects by Rio-based producers and national distributors are selected on the basis of their commercial and economic potential according to the number of tickets sold for previous productions.
9. For an overview of contemporary Brazilian cultural policy in English, see Silveira *et al.* (2013).
10. I wish to thank my colleague Dr Faye Stewart for introducing me to this text on awkwardness.

References

ANCINE (Agência Nacional do Cinema) (2009). *Informe de acompanhamento de mercado – 2009*. Available at http://oca.ancine.gov.br/media/SAM/Informes/2009/InformeAnual2009.pdf (accessed 20 September 2015).

────── (2013). 'Filmes Brasileiros com mais de 500.000 espectadores – 1970–2013'. Available at http://oca.ancine.gov.br/media/SAM/DadosMercado/2105.pdf (accessed 15 July 2015).

Bakhtin, Michel (1968). *Rabelais and His World*, Cambridge: MIT Press.

Brabon, Benjamin. A. (2013). '"Chuck flick": a genealogy of the postfeminist male singleton', in Joel Gwynne and Nadine Muller (eds), *Postfeminism and Contemporary Hollywood Cinema*, Basingstoke: Palgrave Macmillan, pp. 116–30.

Calil, Ricardo (2012). 'Crítica: diretora usa o extraordinário para sublinhar o banal na vida', *Folha de São Paulo*, 25 October 2012. Available at http://www1.folha.uol.com.br/ilustrada/1174580-critica-diretora-usa-o-extraordinario-para-sublinhar-o-banal-na-vida.shtml (accessed 10 June 2015).

Deleyto, Celestino (2009). *The Secret Life of the Romantic Comedy*, Manchester: Manchester University Press.

DePaoli, María Teresa (2014). *The Story of the Mexican Screenplay: A Study of the Invisible Art Form and Interviews with Women Screenwriters*, New York: Peter Lang.

Derrida, Jacques (1976). *Of Grammatology*, Baltimore: Johns Hopkins University Press.

Freud, Sigmund (1960). *Jokes and Their Relation to the Unconscious*, trans. James Strachey, New York: Norton.

Genz, Stéphanie (2009). *Postfemininities in Popular Culture*, New York: Palgrave Macmillan.

────── and Benjamin A. Brabon (2009). *Postfeminism: Cultural Texts and Theories*, Edinburgh: Edinburgh University Press.

Kang, Inkoo (2015). '"The Second Mother" director Anna Muylaert speaks out about film-festival sexism', *Indiewire*, 30 September. Available at http://www.indiewire.com/director/anna-muylaert (accessed 20 November 2015).

Kotthoff, Helga (2006). 'Gender and humor: the state of the art', *Journal of Pragmatics*, 38, pp. 4–26.

Macedo, Ana Gabriel (2006). 'Pos-feminismo', *Estudos Feministas*, 14.3, pp. 813–17.

Marsh, Leslie L. (2012). *Brazilian Women's Filmmaking: From Dictatorship to Democracy*, Urbana: University of Illinois Press.

────── and Hongmei Li (2016). 'The global middle classes: towards the study of emergent citizenship', in Leslie Marsh and Hongmei Li (eds), *The Middle Class in Emerging Societies: Consumers, Lifestyles, Markets*, New York: Routledge, pp. 1–16.

Marson, Melina Izar (2009). 'Loucura, morte e resurreição do cinema no Brasil: cineastas, estado e política cinematográfica nos anos 1990', in Lia Calabre (ed.), *Políticas culturais: reflexões e ações*, Rio de Janeiro: Observatório Itaú Cultural, pp. 146–61.

Nagib, Lúcia (2003). *The New Brazilian Cinema*, London: I.B.Tauris.

Narasaki, Rosie (2015). 'Meet the 2015 Sundance Filmmakers #31: Anna Muylaert questions social convention in "The Second Mother"', *Indiewire*, 25 January. Available at http://www.indiewire.com/article/meet-the-2015-sundance-filmmakers-31-anna-muylaert-questions-social-convention-in-the-second-mother-20150125 (accessed 15 July 2015).

Nelmes, Jill and Jule Selbo (2015). *Women Screenwriters: An International Guide*, New York: Palgrave Macmillan.

Niebylski, Dianna C. (2004). *Humoring Resistance: Laughter and the Excessive Body in Contemporary Latin American Women's Fiction*, Albany: State University of New York Press.

O'Neill, Patrick (1983). 'The comedy of entropy: the contexts of black humour', *Canadian Review of Comparative Literature/Revue Canadienne de Littérature Comparée* 10(2), pp. 145–66.

Pontes, Trajano (2012). 'Novo filme de Anna Muylaert une crime e descoberta pessoal', *Folha de São Paulo*, 25 October.

Ribeiro, Matilde (2006). 'O feminismo em novas rotas e visões', *Estudos Feministas*, 14.3, pp. 801–11.

Schmidt, Rita Terezinha (2006). 'Refutações ao feminismo: (des)compassos da cultura letrada Brasileira', *Estudos Feministas*, 14.3, pp. 765–99.

Silveira, Sérgio, Murilo Bansi Machado and Rodrigo Tarchiani Savazoni (2013). 'Backward march: the turnaround in public cultural policy in Brazil', *Media, Culture and Society*, 35.5, pp. 549–64.

Smith-Prei, Carrie and Maria Stehle (2014). 'WIG-trouble: awkwardness and feminist politics', *Women in German Yearbook: Feminist and Gender Studies in German Literature and Culture*, 30, pp. 209–24.

Tasker, Yvonne and Diane Negra (eds) (2007). *Interrogating Postfeminism: Gender and the Politics of Popular Culture*, Durham: Duke University Press.

Thompson, Anne (2015). 'Fest hit "The Second Mother" brings success – and pain'. *Thompson on Hollywood*, 27 August. Available at http://blogs.indiewire.com/thompsononhollywood/fest-hit-the-second-mother-brings-success-and-pain-20150827 (accessed 20 September 2015).

Vandaele, Jeroen (2002). 'Humor mechanisms in film comedy: incongruity and superiority', *Poetics Today*, 23.2, pp. 221–49.

7

Young Women at the Margins: Discourses on Exclusion in Two Films by Solveig Hoogesteijn[1]

Constanza Burucúa

In 1991, when the Third Cinema paradigm was clearly showing its limitations to comprehensively account for the new films that were being produced in Latin America, well renowned bilingual journal *Iris* (published in English and French) dedicated its thirteenth issue to the cinema of this region, setting up the grounds for new approaches and novel avenues of investigation. Among papers by some of the most influential scholars working on Latin American cinema at the time, such as Kathleen Newman, Ana María López, Zuzana Pick, Randal Johnson and Robert Stam, two are of particular interest in terms of the subsequent development of feminist conceptualisations concerning this cinema and the work of Latin American women filmmakers: B. Ruby Rich's 'An/other view of New Latin American Cinema' (1991) and Karen Goldman's 'A "third" feminism? Solveig Hoogesteijn's *Macu, la mujer del policía*' (1991).

In 'An/other view of New Latin American Cinema', Ruby Rich argued that, unlike the films that had formed the canon of the New Latin American Cinema, those that were being produced in the politically and socially shifting Latin American scene during the 1980s asked to be read more as chronicles than as epics and that, as more intimate and personal texts, they offered new forms of looking inward, while their political appeal, although present, was far less explicit. Still very much a cinema of the dispossessed, in Rich's argument, '[s]uch a shift has also, not coincidentally, opened up the field to women' (Rich 1991: 281), whose films explored and denounced the condition of women in Latin America as one form of social precariousness. It is in the light of these ideas that this chapter will look at the work of Solveig Hoogesteijn, by focusing on two of her most significant films: the successful *Macu, la mujer del policía/Macu, the Policeman's Wife* (1987) and the more recent *Maroa, una niña de la calle/Maroa* (2006). To that end, it seems pertinent to begin by introducing a brief contextualisation and frame of reference for the most salient aspects of Venezuelan cinema and the associated national film industry during the last couple of decades.

Venezuelan cinema: formation of a national film industry

In general terms, even if the first piece of legislation concerning the industry was not sanctioned until 1993, with the Ley de Cinematografía Nacional (National Law of Cinematography), the links between the state and the film sector were first established in Venezuela at the beginning of the twentieth century. Subsequent to the discovery of oilfields in 1914, the state acquired the technology needed for the production of short propaganda documentaries about the regime of Juan Vicente Gómez (1908–35). Thus, as explained by Michelle Leigh Farrell, the relationship between film and the state was, from the very beginning, mediated by oil and conditioned by a national economy based on this particular resource (Farrell 2011: 21–9). However, it was not until the 1970s that the support of the state for the film sector was consolidated as a consequence, on the one hand, of sustained efforts by filmmakers and producers to establish and develop a national film culture from the late 1950s and, on the other, of the economic prosperity that followed the oil boom at the beginning of the decade (King 2000: 215–16). Between 1975 and 1980, the state financed 30 films (King 2000: 219) and in 1981 it created the Fondo de Fomento Cinematográfico (Film Development Fund) (FONCINE), an entity that, by means of a budget allocated by the legislature, raised the average number of films produced per year from seven (in the 1970s), to ten and occasionally twelve during the 1980s (Getino 2007: 175). In 1993, together with the sanctioning of the law, the Centro Nacional Autónomo de Cinematografía (National Film Centre) (CNAC) was established, replacing FONCINE; since 2004, it has operated as the regulatory entity of Venezuela's Plataforma del Cine y Medios Audiovisuales (Platform of Film and Audio-visual Media).

The Plataforma was established during the presidency of Hugo Chávez as part of the so-called Misión Cultura. In Farrell's words, the initiative was intended 'to bring people on board with the ideas of the revolution while also democratizing the filmmaking process of representations of Venezuela' (2011: 1). To that end, the Plataforma comprises five organisations, each one of them associated with the different sectors within the industry: the CNAC, which operates not only as its financial and strategic centre, but also as the promoter of all activities related to the film industry at a national level, as well as of all aspects concerning the formation and training of young directors and screenwriters; Amazonia Films, concerned with distribution; the Cinemateca Nacional, which attends to questions of both exhibition and preservation; the Centro Nacional del Disco (CENDIS), in charge of the production and distribution of audio-visual works in digital format; and, finally, the Villa del Cine, which offers both production and post-production services. According to Octavio Getino, its inauguration in 2006 was followed by a sustained increase in national production (2012: 56). However, it is worth noting that the growth of the sector is both the consequence of the continued efforts of the CNAC, which could be thought of as the big state-owned co-producing partner of everything that is being filmed in Venezuela, as well as the result of a fluid system of co-production, fundamentally with Spain, thanks to the ubiquitous Ibermedia programme led by Spain and including other countries of the region such as Colombia, Cuba, Argentina and Mexico.

Solveig Hoogesteijn: the early works of a female auteur

With this broad contextualisation in mind, and before getting into the analysis of Hoogesteijn's work, it is worth noting that the films under scrutiny in this chapter were produced not only during two different periods, but also according to distinct producing schemes: while *Macu* was made with a modest subsidy granted by FONCINE, *Maroa* was a Venezuelan and Spanish co-production, in which Macu Films – Hoogesteijn's own company – partnered both with Ibermedia, during the early stages of development, and with CNAC for its completion.

Women have across the generations played active and, in some instances, prominent roles in the changing landscape of the Venezuelan national film industry (Schwartzman 1992). In this sense, Margot Benacerraf was certainly a pioneer: having directed two documentaries, *Reverón* (1952) and *Araya* (1959) – which was awarded the Cannes International Critics Prize, shared with Alain Resnais's *Hiroshima, mon amour* (1959) – she dedicated the rest of her professional life to the creation and consolidation of the Cinemateca Nacional.

Throughout the 1960s, politically committed documentary became a privileged site for both artistic and political explorations across Latin America; a group of women were integral to the national iteration of this pan-regional movement in Venezuela. Between 1968 and 1973, three filmmakers with a clear political and feminist filiation formed the collective Cine Urgente (Urgent Cinema); its founders – Josefina Acevedo, Franca Donda and Josefina Jordán – were militants of the MAS (Movimiento al Socialismo), as well as members of the Grupo Feminista Miércoles (Wednesday Feminist Group). In the words of Julianne Burton, Cine Urgente was 'a particularly interesting group experiment in the education and mobilization of marginal sectors through cinematic intervention' (1990: 413).

Without belonging to this group, Hoogesteijn shared with these women a strong belief in the importance of a filmmaker's social and political commitment, as made evident in an interview with Keith Richards in which she declared that, '[w]e belong to the generation of 1968, a politicised generation, committed to the conviction that social and economic changes are possible and for that reason we meditate about polemical themes in our films' (Richards 2011: 82). Unsurprisingly, then, Hoogesteijn's *opera prima* was a documentary called *Puerto Colombia* (1975), a film that she completed as the graduation project for the Munich Film School (Germany), where she studied and received 'a very solid political education', as she herself has pointed out (in Trellez Plazaola 1991: 175). Still, after her return to Venezuela she abandoned documentary filmmaking and concentrated, from then onwards, on the production of socially committed and critically aware fiction films.

Her next two films, *El mar del tiempo perdido* (1976), a short film edited first in German and then in Spanish, and *Manoa* (1980), were internationally acknowledged: the former was awarded the Coral Prize at the 1981 Havana Film Festival, whereas the latter was screened in the Section Parallèle at Cannes in 1980. The subsequent *Macu, la mujer del policía* (1987) became not only a box office hit – to date, it is the film with the second highest number of tickets sold (1.1 million) in the history of Venezuelan cinema[2] – but also the film that gained Hoogesteijn the recognition of scholars who, like Rich, were beginning to approach Latin American cinema from a gender perspective around those years.

However, it would be partial not to read Hoogesteijn's work in dialogue with that of two other female filmmakers of the period, Fina Torres and Haydée Ascanio. According to Burton, *Macu*, together with *Oriana* (Torres, 1985) and *Unas son de amor* (Ascanio, 1987), are all films that offer 'polished screenplays, impressive performances, and high production values with a commitment to exploring women's subjective experience in the context of a broad social composite which is both effectively localised and also regionally, culturally, or politically emblematic' (Burton 1990: 413–14). In other words, these three films – each one in its own way but almost simultaneously – articulate a strong critique of a traditionally patriarchal, and clearly *machista*, Venezuelan society: *Macu* by means of the re-creation of a crime chronicle, *Oriana* through the portrayal of the customs and manners of a traditional, rural family, and *Unas son de amor* by daring to deal, for the first time in Venezuelan film, with abortion. Therefore, we can read these films as symptomatic of new discourses about gender identity (and the associated race and class components) which were emerging in the context of the 1980s and which were certainly challenging the status quo.

Moving from the general frame of reference to the case study in question, and returning to Rich's ideas, her reformulations of notions on Third Cinema associated with both feminist film theory and feminist film practices were continued and applied in Karen Goldman's piece, 'A "third" feminism?' Solveig Hoogesteijn's *Macu, la mujer del policía*'. Today, this article should be acknowledged as one of the earliest examples of how much a methodical feminist reading could contribute to the study of Latin American cinemas. Based on a rigorous practice of textual analysis, Goldman articulated her reading of this particular film (*Macu*) and the director's oeuvre with the wider context of a specific film culture (Venezuelan cinema in the 1980s), in relation to the most relevant ideas and debates concerning Latin American cinema at the time. Similarly, a couple of years later, Karen Schwartzman offered a very thorough analysis of the same film in 'The seen of the crime' (1994). Both these articles, together with the attention paid to Hoogesteijn's work in Julianne Burton's entry on Venezuela in *The Women's Companion to International Film* (1990) are evidence of the interest that both the film and its director raised among feminist scholars working on Latin American cinema in the early 1990s. However, despite the attention paid to Hoogesteijn and to her work, and regardless of the fact that hers seemed like a promising career, after *Macu*'s hit at the box office she released only two more titles: *Santera*, in 1994, and *Maroa, una niña de la calle*, in 2006 (curiously, and according to CNAC official figures, both these films had just above 45,000 spectators, which means that neither even approached the success of *Macu*).

Revisiting some of the ideas first articulated by Goldman in relation to Hoogesteijn's early work and its ability to offer 'alternative representations of national realities' (Goldman 1991: 87), this chapter aims to compare *Macu, la mujer del policía* and *Maroa, una niña de la calle* by looking at how more or less 'alternative' Hoogesteijn's representations of these 'national realities' were in the 1980s and at how much these representations have changed in her more recent film. The comparison between *Macu* and *Maroa* will allow for an appraisal of Hoogesteijn's trajectory as a female director, with a particularly critical gaze, in the context of Venezuelan cinema from the mid-1980s to the first decade of the new century. By observing her itinerary and her oeuvre, this chapter advances a new approach to the study of the space occupied by women in contemporary Venezuelan cinema, both in representational terms and in those concerning their agency as filmmakers, producers and scriptwriters. Like Hoogesteijn, who not only directed but also scripted, produced and even distributed all her films through her own company (Macu Films), other renowned Venezuelan women filmmakers, such as Fina Torres and Mariana Rondón, usually pen their own films and produce them.

In *The Politics of Affect and Emotion in Contemporary Latin American Cinema*, Laura Podalsky understands youth as a particular 'sign of the times' (2011: 102), the representation of which varies according to 'differential socioeconomic conditions, specific historical trajectories and local institutional genealogies' (2011: 104). By comparing *Macu* and *Maroa* and by reading them as symptomatic of discourses on (national, class and gender) identity at different moments in time, it will become evident that, although they share certain thematic concerns, they also offer quite opposing interpretations of a shifting national vision: one critical and bleak, the other almost submissively optimistic. In other words, and building upon Vicky Lebeau's (2008) seminal interrogation about what exactly it is that cinema wants of the child, this chapter will investigate what it is that the films of Hoogesteijn want of their young female protagonists. What does *Macu* denounce? What does *Maroa* confess? What happened between the unabashed pessimistic ending of *Macu* and the uplifting finale of *Maroa*? The answers to these questions will be progressively articulated through the analysis of the films, which will in turn provide both the textual and the contextual keys of interpretation. In other words, and in line with the previously mentioned objectives, a detailed reading of the films will necessarily lead to more general considerations about the state of affairs in recent Venezuelan cinema and about the space that women occupy in it, both on and off screen.

Macu, la mujer del policía

Based on real events, *Macu, la mujer del policía* retells, from the eponymous character's point of view, what became known as 'el caso Mamera'/ 'the Mamera case': jealous of his teenage wife's flirtations with some neighbours, *el Distinguido* Ledezma (*Distinguido* – Distinguished – refers to a police rank in Venezuela) murdered three young men and 'disappeared' their bodies. As Goldman has pertinently noted, what sets *Macu* apart from other, previous filmic accounts of the events, and what makes the film a relevant text in terms of a feminist critique, is the fact that by focusing on Macu (María Luisa Mosquera) and by privileging her point of view, alternating between Macu being the object and the subject of the gaze, the film poses some key questions concerning visual identification – an inescapable locus in feminist film analysis. As a consequence of this gendering of the enquiring gaze, the film demands an interrogation about whose history is being narrated and about who is interpreting this history, and how. Thus, on one hand, the film offers no solutions to the real conflicts: whereas the murder case is solved, the real problem, the one concerning this girl who was 'sold' as a bride (as Macu points out), at the age of 11 by her grandmother to her mother's lover, is left unresolved. On the other hand, *Macu, la mujer del policía* exposes and challenges Venezuelan cultural attitudes, social structures and the institutions of marriage and the family (see Figure 7.1). It does this by choosing to focus on the story of this girl's exploitation and, through hers, of countless others. As Schwartzman notes, '[a]t the same time that the film interrogates the social, it also interrogates the Law, that which culturally defines gendered identities, with women as commodities and men as their armed custodians' (1994: 141).

Only a couple of years before the release of *Macu*, Fina Torres had done something very similar, both in terms of the inscription of a feminine point of view and in relation to the question concerning a woman's regaining of memory. In *Oriana*, the almost literally buried story of her aunt Oriana is reconstructed through María's memories and recollections. Defying the orders of her father, a powerful landowner with an uncanny resemblance to Venezuelan dictator Juan Vicente Gómez,[3] Oriana falls in love with her adoptive *mestizo* brother. Although she loses him when her father beats him to death, she retains his child, who is kept hidden until her own death. Thus, both in *Macu* and in *Oriana*, the gaze that structures the narrative is invested in femininity and the films therefore raise the question of whose story is being recounted (to whom does the story 'belong'?). Likewise, by having a woman as both protagonist and discursive subject, they offer what can be understood as a revisionist approach to history. In this sense, these two films are also in tune with other Latin American films of the period, such as Suzana Amaral's *A hora da estrela/The Hour of the Star* (1985) and María Luisa Bemberg's *Camila* (1984), *Miss Mary* (1986) and *Yo, la peor de todas/I, the Worst of All* (1990).

In *Childhood and Cinema*, Lebeau argues that 'the topic of sexuality has [...] been vital to explorations of how the image works on film: the forms of looking it provokes [...] the pleasures and anxieties it solicits' (2008: 99). Going back to the question about what it is that Hoogesteijn's films want

Figure 7.1. Macu's wedding portrait (*Macu, la mujer del policía*, Solveig Hoogesteijn, 1991).

from these girls, we can argue that it is around Macu's sexuality that the film articulates the possibility of, if not solving, at least naming and rendering visible the history of all those who, like Macu, are marginalised within the margins (to the lower-class background, her gender and her age should be added). Thus, throughout the film and guided by Macu's journey of self-discovery, the spectator is asked to look at her sexuality, and to think about it, from her perspective.

In *Child Brides and Intruders*, a study that looks at this particular kind of heroine in North American literature, Carol Wershoven characterises the child bride as untouched by experience, blind (since, 'to see, to question, to grow would be to diminish her marketability' [Wershoven 1993: 11]), innocent – sexually, emotionally and intellectually – and, at the same time and as a consequence of these features, as an inevitably destructive force. In Wershoven's words, 'the endless desires of the perpetual child become an active force for evil' (1993: 12). Unlike her North American literary counterparts, none of these descriptors would be easily applicable to Macu. She is sexually experienced and, moreover, at least up to a certain point, she seems eager for more. As previously stated, the film is basically about Macu's ability to gain a gaze and, with it, the possibility to see – therefore, to understand – by herself. It is eventually this acquired gaze that she uses as a challenging tool to claim responsibility from her mother and grandmother, to accuse her husband and even to directly address the spectator, when, in the final shot of the film, with the credits already rolling, Macu looks straight to the camera, breaking the fourth wall and, with it, the 'illusion' of reality. Macu's 'innocence' in terms of her sexuality is certainly debatable – with the consent and the encouragement of her elders, she has learnt how to effectively use her sexuality from a very young age – and, as the film progresses, she grows out of any residues of emotional and intellectual innocence. Finally, although in the film she is held responsible for causing the death of the three young men by their relatives, the neighbours and the ever-present TV news reporters, it would be a complete misunderstanding to read Macu as a destructive force rather than as an abused victim of a muted system of subjection that is the sum of different levels of oppression based on age, gender and class abuse.

In 'The young and the damned. Street visions in Latin American cinema', Geoffrey Kantaris distinguishes two phases within a tradition of social realism in Latin American cinema that centre around what he refers to as the 'particular phenomena of street children and urban youth culture' (2003: 178). With Luis Buñuel's *Los olvidados* (1950) and Héctor Babenco's *Pixote* (1981) taken as canonical examples, the first phase is composed of films made before the 1990s, films that invite a psychoanalytical and national reading:

> Psychoanalytical because they invoke a Freudian framework of disturbed family structures [...] and national because,

although each director virulently questions the dominant discourses and images of the nation [...], the critique of dominant national images still posits the nation as its ultimate framework. (Kantaris 2003: 182)

The films in the second phase, comprising contemporary films like Adrián Caetano and Bruno Stagnaro's 1997 *Pizza, birra, faso/Pizza, Beer, and Cigarettes* and González Iñárritu's *Amores perros* (2000) among others, 'hint at the linkages [...] between crime–violence–poverty in one place and global flows of wealth in another; they engage in a "global sense of place"' (Kantaris 2003: 182-3). With this distinction in mind and even if, ultimately, both *Macu* and *Maroa* expose the wider geographies of exclusion (Kantaris 2003: 177) and their embedded violence (Podalsky 2011: 101), it would be productive to read them as respectively pertaining to the former and latter group.

Thus, *Macu, la mujer del policía* can be easily read within Kantaris's first phase, of psychoanalysis and the nation. In it, Hoogesteijn focuses on the microcosm of the family unit as a means to denounce an oppressive and abusive patriarchal system that is, in turn, closely related to the composition of longstanding and wider discourses on Venezuelan national identity. In other words, and paraphrasing Kantaris, the film's critique of dominant national images is metonymically structured around Macu's (disturbed and disturbing) family. In the light of these ideas, then, the presence of *el Distinguido* Ledezma (Daniel Alvarado) is doubly ominous: on the one hand, because he has married an 11-year-old girl and he is capable of sexually exploiting the women in the family on the basis of his power to financially provide for them; on the other, because of the way in which he systematically abuses another form of power, the one allegedly conferred on him by his status as a civil servant in the uniform of a police officer.

Maroa, una niña de la calle

Maroa, una niña de la calle (2006) can be placed within Kantaris' second phase, which includes films that underscore the troubled and often uneven links between national and transnational or global contexts. In Tamara Falicov's terms, the bi-national nature of this Venezuelan Spanish technical-artistic co-production (a notion that 'implies that the amount a country invests determines the percentage of actors and/or technicians that will work on a film' [2012: 301]) is echoed in the film's narrative (302). In Falicov's argument, the character of Joaquín, the music teacher played by Spanish actor Tristán Ulloa, is the epitome of one (among four) common tropes of how Spaniards are portrayed in Latin American films produced under the Ibermedia programme or format, that of the 'sympathetic Spaniard' (302). However, regardless of this particular trait – he is 'sympathetic' – his very presence introduces the question about how the 'economic imperatives of funding can shape film narratives in specific ways' (303). Moreover, the unsettling – yet not completely unfounded – accusation of paedophilia that causes Joaquín's expulsion from Venezuela further troubles the interpretation of this character in terms of imbalanced relationships, at both the diegetic and the extra-diegetic levels.

Beyond Joaquín's character arc, and in more general terms, in *Maroa, una niña de la calle* Hoogesteijn revisits some of the questions on childhood and sexuality, power and violence that she had already tackled almost 20 years earlier, with the explicit aim of addressing the matter of street children as the embodiment of the ultimate threshold of social exclusion. At the time of the film's release, the topics of both children and marginality, as well as the themes of power abuse and an out-of-control urban violence, were not only recurrent in Venezuelan films but they also seemed to be favoured by the public. This is demonstrated by films like *Secuestro express* (Jonathan Jakubowicz, 2005), the biggest box office hit in the 1996–2005 period (Getino 2007: 176), and the very successful *Huelepega: ley de la calle* (2000) and *Punto y raya/A Dot and a Line* (2004), both directed by another woman: Elia Schneider. Her creative partnership with her husband, José Ramón Novoa, also produced *Sicario* (1994), the second best-selling film of the 1990s, with more than 450,000 tickets sold (according to CNAC).

Maroa is very different from *Macu* in terms of its narrative structure, given that its temporality is almost completely linear, with only one exception. Unlike in the earlier film, there are no flashbacks here or, in other words, the story that is being narrated does not have a past and so, without a past, there is nothing to be revised or revisited. Without any textual indication that could be in any way identified as the inscription of the protagonist's point of view (as was the case, in *Macu*, with the subjective flashbacks through which history was reinscribed), the only temporal leap in *Maroa* occurs at the very end, when a flash-forward takes us to an indeterminate 'years later'. In it, any traces of poverty, abuse, delinquency, corruption and promiscuity – all of which constitute the present of the film – have disappeared. And Maroa (Yorlis Domínguez), who was last seen as an 11-year-old child being separated by the police from Joaquín, her male music teacher with whom she had been living in hiding, is now a young woman, a clarinet soloist playing in a Madrid theatre, accompanied by star orchestra conductor Gustavo Dudamel, embodiment himself of the world renowned Sistema Nacional de Orquestas (known in English as El Sistema). It is around this particular appearance that the film articulates its ambiguous 'finale', but only a closer look at how time is constructed will allow for a better understanding of the film's ending.

Thus, there are two temporalities in *Maroa*: without a past, the film is mostly set in the present and, thanks to the flash-forward at the end, the future. Even if it is not possible to date this future with precision, it can be deduced that the film's present is situated between 1999 and 2006 (year of release), thanks to a comment made by Maroa's grandmother (Elba Escobar) at the beginning of the film, when she complains about 'all the misery on the streets while the president dances and sings on TV'. She is clearly referring to Venezuela's former President Hugo Chávez's TV and radio show *Alo' Presidente*, a weekly live broadcast that lasted between 1999 and 2012. As per the future, it is impossible to specify when those 'years later' are situated. If Maroa is clearly above the age of consent by the end of the film, this 'years later' as a precise point in time is not much more than a projection of a promising, bright future yet to come, an optimistic prediction of something approaching but, still, far detached from the film's present, as reflected in Figure 7.2.

This temporal indeterminacy, which could be read as an escapist strategy to get from a problematic present to an idealised future, is somehow echoed in Hoogesteijn's words when she tried to predict an impending box office success by arguing that:

> [E]ste es un tema esperanzador y *Macu* no lo era. En *Macu* la protagonista se ve obligada a regresar con el policía para sobrevivir; en cambio aquí la protagonista adquiere una herramienta

Figure 7.2. Maroa looking through a window (*Maroa, une niña de la calle*, Solveig Hoogesteijn, 2006).

> con la cual triunfa. Yo creo que ese mensaje positivo va a atraer mucho a la gente.
>
> [T]his is a hopeful topic and *Macu*'s was not. In *Macu*, the protagonist finds herself forced to go back to the policeman in order to survive; in this case, the protagonist acquires a tool with which she succeeds. I believe that such a positive message will be very attractive to people. (Espinosa 2006)

A first reading of this statement may suggest that what the filmmaker is referring to concerns her young female character's earlier powerlessness (Macu) and the subsequent possibility of gaining some sort of agency (Maroa). However, there is something here, perhaps the excessive appeal with heartening words such as 'hopeful', 'positive message', 'attractive', that makes us mistrust such a naively rosy statement in the guise of a feminist enticement. Or, in other words, something in her statement seems to suggest that Hoogesteijn's feminist stance has shifted from one film to the other. Interestingly, though, audiences did not seem to particularly appreciate this shift: despite the director's predictions (or hopes), spectators did not flock to see *Maroa*. According to CNAC's statistics, only 45,000 tickets were sold, placing it in seventh place among all Venezuelan films released in 2006. The top spot was occupied by Diego Rísquez's *Francisco de Miranda*. But perhaps more relevant is that right before *Maroa*, at number six in the list, we find *Tocar y luchar/To Play and to Fight*. This documentary, while projecting and reinforcing, both nationally and internationally, the official narrative about el Sistema and its alignment with the Bolivarian cultural policies,[4] also cemented the career of its director, Alberto Arvelo, and his ascendance as the director *par excellence* of the Chávez regime. He not only further exploited this found niche in *Dudamel, el sonido de los niños/Dudamel, Let the Children Play* (2011) but he went on to direct – among other titles – the biopic *Libertador/The Liberator*, based on the life and deeds of Venezuela's founding father, Simón Bolívar, significantly released shortly after Hugo Chávez's death, in 2013.[5]

In the late 1980s, in the wake of *Macu*'s box office success and its critical acclaim, Julianne Burton noted that Hoogesteijn's work was committed to 'exploring women's subjective experience in the context of a broad social composite which is both effectively localised and also regionally, culturally, or politically emblematic' (1990: 413–14). The question that needs to be answered, then, concerns precisely this exploration of the 'women's subjective experience': what happened to it in the director's latest film? How is it inscribed in *Maroa*? Is it in any way present in the film? As suggested in the previous analysis, the lack of point-of-view shots which could be attributed to the title character and a narrative structure in which the only temporal leap is a final flash-forward that privileges the point of view of Joaquín while focusing on Maroa, who is literally staged as the object of his/our gaze, imply that her experiences are hardly treated in relation to her own subjectivity throughout the film. Unlike Macu, Maroa never gets the chance to examine her life; the only partial instance in which she seems to speak for herself is in the letter that she sends to Joaquín 'years later' ('años más tarde') but, then again, this is read out loud by him. Maroa is never given the possibility to interpret her past or intervene, in any way, in the narrative of her own memories, as Macu was. Her origins, her past, as well as her future, are thoroughly narrated by others: by her grandmother, who explains at one point who her parents were and how they abandoned her to the care of this unloving woman; and by Joaquín, who voices her letter at the end of the film.

These divergences between the films' narrative structures and the unequal sense of agency attributed to the two leading characters, and consequently the differences between the two films, should be read as central to the construction of what was earlier on referred to as the 'alternative' representations of a changing national reality. Key to the comparison between such representations is the analysis of the differential use that Hoogesteijn makes of the flashback and the flash-forward, in *Macu* and *Maroa* respectively. By focusing on these markers of narrative self-reflexivity, the ideological implications and consequences of their use in each film will come to the fore. And, in so doing, they will reveal the ways in which film, as a medium, has itself been alternatively used, in these two instances, as a tool to either subvert – or at least challenge – the established order of things, or seemingly comply with it.

Historically dealt with as complementary narrative devices, the flashback and the flash-forward signal narrative alterations of the temporal order of the events by which their presentation in the plot does not correspond to their chronological progression in the story. The flashback presents events that belong to the past of the story being presented; the flash-forward, in turn, pre-announces future developments. But, as film historians and scholars have shown, their use serves radically different purposes. Whereas in narrative fiction films, flashbacks are conventionally read as the cinematic means to represent memory and history, generally from a character's perspective or subjectivity, flash-forwards can hardly be attributed to a character's subjectivity. As David Bordwell explains, flash-forwards 'constitute self-conscious narrational asides to the spectator … [they tend] to be highly self-conscious and ambiguously communicative. This is doubtless why classical narrative cinema has made no use of it and why the art cinema, with its emphasis on authorial intrusion, employs [them] so often' (1985: 79). It is precisely around this oscillation between a text that privileges the main character's subjectivity and another one that articulates its conclusion around the intrusion of the filmmaker in the narrative that Hoogesteijn's films reveal their ideological differences, in terms both of the interpretations of particular social contexts and of the use of film as a medium.

In *Macu, la mujer del policía* the temporal segmentation of the plot adds two different layers of the past to the linear course of the chronicled events: the present of the film is set in the aftermath of the young men's disappearance and during the investigation of the crime; the first set of flashbacks recreates the build-up that led to the confrontation between *el Distinguido* Ledezma and Macu's paramour (Simón, played by Frank Spano) by focusing on the young lovers' time together; the second set of flashbacks recreates the circumstances around Macu's elopement (or rather kidnapping, as she is an 11-year-old girl) with her mother's boyfriend. This last group of memories is unmistakably attributable to Macu's subjectivity: triggered by the contemplation of her wedding portrait, the path to this troublesome past is introduced by a highly self-reflexive image, in which the face of the staring protagonist is visibly reflected on the glass that protects the framed photo. Thus, in this case, the self-reflexivity of the image, clearly aligned with the character and with her point of view (literally inscribed in the image), exposes the film's intention to open up in order to include, and privilege, the young woman's exploration of the past. In so doing, the film becomes a space in which history is not just revisited but, moreover, rendered as multifaceted, troubled, unstable. In this light, the crime against the young men is not simply a crime of passion, but the result of an intricate net of intertwined causes related to gender, social, economic and age exclusion and marginalisation. As suggested at the end of the film, when the protagonist looks with anger at the camera, while frustrated when waiting in line to visit her imprisoned husband, justice may have been partly served but history is clearly unfinished, contentious and still to be challenged.

As previously mentioned, *Maroa, una niña de la calle* finishes with a flash-forward that provides a hopeful ending to an otherwise hopeless story. Leaving aside the content of the flash-forward, which has been presented already, what is worth signalling is that what this leap in time follows is the most desperate moment in the story, its dramatic climax. Subsequent to her grandmother's death and having escaped from the reformatory school where she was being musically trained by Joaquín, Maroa moves in with him, living in hiding from everyone, especially from Ezequiel (Luke Grande), the corrupt policeman who wants her to reveal the whereabouts of a gang of young criminals. The secret does not last for long and, after a birthday celebration that includes Maroa's gift to Joaquín in the form of Yuleisi (Greisy Mena), her equally young prostitute friend, the police raid the place. Joaquín and Maroa are separated by force: he is handcuffed, accused of child abuse and extradited to his native Spain, while Maroa is taken by one of the female guards of the same institution that she had previously fled. It is at that point, when Joaquín and Maroa go their separate ways and her future could not be any bleaker, that the story is abruptly interrupted and subsequently continued by the projection, detailed in the flash-forward, of her future stellar career as a musician.

The impending questions, then, are pretty straightforward. How should this flash-forward be read? What are its consequences and implications? Why the decision to silence the hardships endured by Maroa in a place that was previously shown as filled with hostile students and equally adverse teachers and guards? And, moreover, why is this young woman's later professional achievement presented almost as the result of the workings of a *deus ex machina* instead of choosing to show it as the product of her own hard work, commitment and effort? The answers to these questions can be structured around some reflections on the use of the flash-forward as the 'authorial intrusion' that Bordwell alludes to.

Thus, whereas in *Macu, la mujer del policía* the flashback served, as previously pointed out, to inscribe the young protagonist's point of view, connoting its subjectivity in terms of a subaltern and marginalised identity that gains, throughout the film and thanks to it, a visibility and a voice that are usually absent from mainstream discursive interpretations of the social fabric, in *Maroa, una niña de la calle*, such possibility is systematically denied. In this film's linear progression, Maroa is not only deprived of the possibility of acquiring a gaze or constructing her own memory but, moreover, the flash-forward imposes a fairy-tale resolution. In it, Joaquín chivalrously steps aside as if not wanting to interfere with Maroa's promising career. Said conclusion is as arbitrary as it is acquiescent with those ideologically dominant discourses which, while allegedly acknowledging the existence and the rights of subalterns, cannot avoid speaking on their behalf, appropriating their voices, shaping their (hi)stories.

Conclusion: different contexts, different endings

Discussing the complexities entailed in the representation of violence and its spectacularisation in Latin American films, Kantaris argues that: '[i]f the films attempt to engage with an *other*, invisible scene, it is logical that they can only do so through a questioning of their own mode of expression' (2003: 178). To bring the ideas so far discussed to a close, and in line with Kantaris's argument, it seems pertinent to conclude that, while in *Macu* Hoogesteijn skilfully managed to use and even subvert filmic conventions – as when Macu directly addresses us with her resentful and heated gaze – with the aim of transforming the 'invisible scene' at stake into a visible and contested space, in the case of *Maroa* the director did not equally succeed at using the medium as a tool for social critique. On the contrary, by resorting to the flash-forward, a device that clearly highlights the filmmaker's control over the narrative, Hoogesteijn may have yielded, more or less voluntarily, to the same univocal, monological discursive strategies that she had so successfully challenged two decades earlier.

Now, why this ending? Could the film have finished differently? Did Hoogesteijn surrender to the commercial imperative of a happy ending? Or are there other elements that should be factored in, as a means to provide a wider and more comprehensive explanation, one that would account for the film and/in its context? The key to answer these questions is provided in the flash-forward and, more specifically, in Dudamel's appearance as himself in it. Thanks to his talent and masterly management, and combined with the appropriate media exposure, el Sistema is recognised, worldwide, as Venezuela's most valuable cultural asset and, as previously pointed out, Arvelo's *Tocar y luchar* was instrumental in the legitimation of el Sistema's official narrative and Dudamel's consecration as its international ambassador. However, critics have not failed to question to what extent el Sistema, established in 1975 by José Antonio Abreu and funded almost in its entirety by the national state since the late 1970s, should be taken as representative of the country as a whole and of the successful implementation of the Bolivarian government's (cultural) policies. As stated in an article that appeared in *Intelligent Life*, the lifestyle magazine accompanying *The Economist*: 'It is precisely [el Sistema's] imponderability ... that disturbs some observers, especially those who see a contradiction between the policies of Chávez and the positive message of El Sistema's success' (Burton-Hill 2013: 58). Geoffrey Baker offered a thorough, as well as much tougher and quite controversial, analysis of this cultural phenomenon in *El Sistema: Orchestrating Venezuela's Youth* (2014). With statements like 'Abreu has a near monopoly on the classical musical sphere in Venezuela' (2014: 13) and 'El Sistema not only takes a zero-tolerance approach to criticism but also has a formidable PR machine to keep information under tight control' (13), he systematically contested and challenged the official narratives (until recently, the only existing ones) about el Sistema, irrevocably unsettling them.

But, before Baker's book, could *Maroa* have unwillingly operated a fracture within these legitimate and almost hagiographic accounts of el Sistema? What if the ending of the film, that flash-forward set in an indeterminate future, was a 'necessary' addition? A closer look at the film's production history reveals that Ibermedia committed its support to the development of the project in the year 2000 (see programaibermedia.com). We can assume that between then and the film's release in 2006, the script underwent a process of several revisions; to argue that, at any point, Abreu had a say in this story about a street girl rescued by a music teacher, who is eventually accused of corruption of minors, would be pure speculation. However, whereas on the one hand it is undeniable that *Maroa* does not share *Tocar y luchar*'s sheer optimism, not even after the intervention of Dudamel embodying the aforementioned *deus ex machina*, on the other hand the state funding and the financial participation of Ibermedia may have had a more or less direct impact in the 'sanitisation' of the image of Venezuela operated in the flash-forward that brings the film's narrative to a close.

Hoogesteijn was capable of conceiving and completing a film like *Macu* in the 1980s, yet could not replicate its bravado in the later *Maroa*. Ironically, the financially precarious production conditions of the earlier film implied fewer constraints in terms of the possibility of articulating a critique of the status quo and a denunciation of the conditions of some of the more marginalised and excluded victims of society: girls who eventually become young women, like Macu and her younger alter-ego Maroa. It is that space for a cinema of dissent that did not comply with official narratives but rather defied them, the one that people like Rich celebrated in the 1980s as an opening up of the field and an opportunity for women filmmakers, that is difficult to find and to envisage in Hoogesteijn's more recent film.

Notes

1. A version of this article has been published in Spanish in: Gabriela Copertari and Carolina Sitnisky (eds). (2015). *El Estado de las Cosas. Cine Latinoamericano en el Nuevo Milenio*, Madrid: Iberoamericana – Vervuert.
2. The number one spot in the ranking is occupied by *Homicidio Culposo*, directed by César Bolívar, which premiered in 1984 (CNAC).
3. Rafael Briceño, the actor playing Oriana's father, was in fact well known for playing Juan Vicente Gómez in the TV series *Gómez I* and *Gómez II*, broadcast by Radio Caracas Televisión (RCTV) in 1980, with high audience ratings.
4. Soon after the release of *Tocar y luchar*, Chávez launched Misión Música, with the aim of politically consolidating the alliance with el Sistema (ZGM 2014).
5. In relation to Arvelo's *Libertador*, Chávez's successor, Nicolás Maduro, has argued: 'Tienen que ver la película "Libertador", es el Bolívar más Chavista que ha existido, es volcánico y revolucionario. Chávez redescubrió a Bolívar y las tesis que el lanzó, fueron colocadas en la película' ('You have to watch the film *Liberator*, it is the most Chavista Bolívar that ever existed, it is volcanic, revolutionary. Chávez rediscovered Bolívar and the theses that he proposed were placed in the film') (in Parada 2014).

References

Baker, Geoffrey (2014). *El Sistema: Orchestrating Venezuela's Youth*, Oxford: Oxford University Press.

Bordwell, David (1985). *Narration in the Fiction Film*, Madison: University of Wisconsin Press.

Burton, Julianne (1990). 'Venezuela', in Annette Kuhn and Susanna Radstone (eds), *The Women's Companion to International Film*, London: Virago Press, pp. 412–414.

Burton-Hill, Clemency (2013). 'After the whirlwind', *Intelligent Life*, March /April, pp. 50–61.

Espinosa, María Elisa (2006). 'Yorlis Dominguez es Maroa', *Revista Estampas/El Universal*, 16 July. Retrieved from www.eluniversal.com/estampas/anteriores/160706/encuentros2 (accessed 7 July 2013).

Falicov, Tamara (2012). 'Programa Ibermedia: cine transnacional Ibero-Americano o relaciones públicas para España?', *Revista Reflexiones*, 91.1, pp. 299–312. Retrieved from http://kuscholarworks.ku.edu (accessed 27 November 2015).

Farrell, Michelle Leigh (2011). *A 'Revolution of Consciousness': Redefining Venezuelan National Identities Through Cinema*, PhD thesis, Georgetown University.

Fundación Musical Simón Bolívar. Retrieved from: www.fesnojiv.gob.ve (accessed 7 November 2013).

Getino, Octavio. (2007). *Cine Iberoamericano: los desafíos del nuevo siglo*, Buenos Aires: CICCUS.

—— (2012). *Estudio de producción y mercados del cine latinoamericano en la primera década del siglo XXI*, La Habana: Fundación del Nuevo Cine Latinoamericano.

Goldman, Karen (1991). 'A "third" feminism? Solveig Hoogesteijn's *Macu, la mujer del Policía*', *Iris*, 13, pp. 87–95.

Ibermedia. Available at http://www.programaibermedia.com (accessed 27 January 2016).

Kantaris, Geoffrey (2003). 'The young and the damned. Street visions in Latin American cinema', in Stephen Hart and Richard Young (eds), *Contemporary Latin American Cultural Studies*, London: Arnold, pp. 177–89.

King, John (2000). *Magical Reels: A History of Cinema in Latin America* (second edition), London: Verso.

Lebeau, Vicky (2008). *Childhood and Cinema*, London: Reaktion.

Parada, María Elena (2014). 'Maduro: "Libertador" de Alberto Arvelo presenta a un Bolívar épico y revolucionario', *Correo del Orinoco*, 5 August. Available at http://www.correodelorinoco.gob.ve/politica/maduro-libertador-alberto-arvelo-presenta-a-un-bolivar-epico-y-revolucionario (accessed 26 January 2016).

Podalsky, Laura (2011). *The Politics of Affect and Emotion in Contemporary Latin American Cinema*, New York: Palgrave Macmillan.

Rich, B. Ruby (1991). 'An/other view of New Latin American Cinema', *Iris*, 13. Reprinted in Michael Martin (ed.) (1997), *New Latin American Cinema, Vol. I*, Detroit: Wayne State University Press, pp. 273–97.

Richards, Keith (2011). *Themes in Latin American Cinema: A Critical Survey*, Jefferson: McFarland.

Schwartzman, Karen (1992). 'A descriptive chronology of films by women in Venezuela, 1952–92', *Journal of Film and Video*, 44.3/4, pp. 33–50. Available at http://www.jstor.org/stable/20687982 (accessed 2 February 2016).

—— (1994). 'The seen of the crime', *A Journal of Women's Studies*, 15.1, pp. 141–82. Retrieved from http://www.jstor.org/stable/3346617?seq=1&cid=pdf-reference#references_tab_contents (accessed 2 February 2016).

Trellez Plazaola, Luis (1991). *Cine y Mujer en América Latina*, San Juan de Puerto Rico: Editorial de la Universidad de Puerto Rico.

Wershoven, Carol (1993). *Child Brides and Intruders*, Bowling Green: Bowling Green State University Popular Press.

ZGM (2014). 'En 2007, Líder Hugo Chávez ideó la misión música'. Available at http://www.vtv.gob.ve/articulos/2014/11/23/en-2007-lider-hugo-chavez-ideo-la-mision-musical-8875.html (accessed 27 January 2016).

III

Key Agents

8

Re-framing Mexican Women's Filmmaking: The Case of Marcela Fernández Violante

Niamh Thornton

Research on women's filmmaking in Mexico has been a combination of important acts of recovery that pinpoint pioneering women from the first half of the twentieth century (Tuñón Pablos 1999) and celebrations of the varied and incremental growth in numbers of women filmmakers since the 1980s (Rashkin 2001). The first group of directors were part of a studio system that supported genre cinema and they became filmmakers against the odds, while the second group have had to navigate complex and precarious funding regimes to make films with feminist approaches. Within this historiography, Marcela Fernández Violante (1941–) is an anomaly. She does not belong to the first wave of pioneering women, nor can her work be described as 'feminist', as that term was defined to describe the work of the 1980s generation. Yet, she is both feminist and pioneering in ways that complicate both categories.

She is a formidable and noteworthy presence in Mexican cinema and a woman of many firsts. In 1969, she was one of the first graduates of the Centro Universitario de Estudios Cinematográficos (CUEC). In 1977, she was the first woman admitted into the film directors' union and she was the director of the CUEC from 1984 to 1988. She had a notable start to her career: her first film, *Azul* (1967), a short about Frida Kahlo, won her an Ariel – a Mexican industry award – while still at film school. She subsequently made eight features up to her 2002 film, *Acosada: de piel de víbora/Accosted: snakeskin*, as well as a 30-minute episode on pioneering Mexican director Matilde Landeta (1910–99), as part of the television documentary series *Los nuestros/Our Own* (1987). Despite this body of work and her influential position in central filmmaking roles, there is little critical analysis of her work. Conversely, her centrality and renown mean that there are numerous interviews. These are illuminating because she does not deploy the usual diplomatic language of someone in filmmaking, a field that relies on goodwill and teamwork, and where it is rare to get a full account of what went wrong in a project. They are forthright assertions of her career goals, where she feels she belongs, and who and what came between her and greater success (Mosier and Gonzales 1983; Burton 1986; Horton 1987; Pech Salvador 1997; Blanco Figueroa 2001).

Her direct, sometimes spiky, approach in interviews makes her voice a fascinating source for Mexican film history, and as a woman she is perforce a marginal figure, which makes writing about Fernández Violante an act of recovery in alternative history telling and a challenge to conventional narratives. Therefore, given the paucity of critical analysis of her work, I shall make reference to the interviews because of the unique insights they give into film education, the industry and her process. This chapter is also about recovering the untold by looking at two of her feature films, *De todos modos Juan te llamas/General's Daughter* (1975) and *Misterio* (1980). Both of the films analysed here are individually significant because they mark different modes of filmmaking and exemplify the developments both in her career and in the Mexican film industry, which I will consider here. The former is a personal project that was supported by the CUEC and she was a hired director for the latter. This chapter is also about asserting the need to reconsider how Mexican film history is told. Inserting Fernández Violante into the history of Mexican cinema shows that the current framing of that history has significant gaps, omissions and oversights. Some of these are a consequence of gendered assumptions and others are because Fernández Violante is difficult to fit into the existing parameters.

Film historians have different accounts of Fernández Violante's significance. For Patricia Torres San Martín, Fernández Violante 'marca la transición entre la generación de las pioneras del cine sonoro mexicano y la generación que incursiona en la década de los setenta' (2004: 69) ('marks the transition between the generation of the pioneers of sound cinema and the activities of the 1970s generation'). Yet, as one of the first generation to go to film school in the 1960s, this should place her alongside 1970s filmmakers such as Paul Leduc, Jorge Fons and Felipe Cazals, who had similar concerns and, like her, had to navigate a difficult period when the industry was moving from being studio-based and supported by the government to a free-market model mostly funded by private finance (Mora 1989: 116–41). Torres San Martín's reading of Fernández Violante as being at a remove from this, mostly male, generation is easy to dismiss as simply erroneous, but it is rather a reflection of how Fernández Violante occupies a curious inbetween-ness. In line with the archetypal narrative of male endeavour, these contemporaries are read as operating more clearly outside of the studio system, and their work and many of their statements about their work are seen in opposition to the old guard, that is, the studios and the unions (Treviño 1979).

The context for this framing of film history is significant. From a peak in the 1930s through to the 1950s, the studios were in decline by the 1960s. Given the nature of the clientelist Mexican model of governance, film unions were often closed shops unwilling to change and slow to admit new members. At their peak, this meant little advancement but, as the studios declined, a change in the relationships between workers and the state in the 1960s led to a shift in admission. While this was being worked out, the emergence of university funding for filmmaking meant that many new directors, impatient with the slow pace of reform, sidestepped the unions altogether. By the 1970s a new generation of filmmakers working with a different model of financing, often preferring to shoot on location or using studio lots, but not employed by a studio, were making films that were different from and sometimes in direct opposition to what had come before.

The growth in Mexican film criticism and historiography coincided with the emergence of these male 1970s filmmakers. The journals that were launched at this time were highly supportive of their work and framed them in opposition to the studio system, which was seen by a new generation to be too closely allied to the government and not sufficiently critical of the regime's many shortcomings (Thornton 2013: 73–8).

By becoming a member of the directors' union, Fernández Violante was admitted into an organisation that some of her (male) contemporaries felt no longer served their interests. Simultaneously and conversely, as a woman her admission was a radical step but, for those who could choose whether to belong or not, membership allied her with the past. She did not fit into the career trajectory of the independent filmmakers, with independence often associated with male young auteurs, as evidenced by the success of the Mexican directors cited above and by the New Hollywood directors of the 1970s such as Martin Scorsese, Brian De Palma and Francis Ford Coppola. Neither was she a traditional studio filmmaker, as it was heretofore understood. This conundrum is typical of the difficulties Fernández Violante has had to navigate as a pioneering woman of her generation, and means that she has not been included in the accounts of the period alongside her contemporaries.

These industry changes and the debates around the new directions film should take were determined by a context of protest and state violence. A key formative moment for many of the 1970s filmmakers was the student protests in 1968 in the lead-up to the staging of the Olympic Games in Mexico City. On 2 October 1968 in Tlatelolco Square in Mexico City, after months of protest, students were massacred under government orders (Brewster 2005). The numbers and those responsible are still not fully determined, but it was a shocking and defining moment for this generation. Influenced by this event, able to access equipment from the universities and eager to find ways of articulating this new political landscape, some made documentaries, other filmmakers played with genre, thereby disrupting conventions by taking the old and making it new, and still others made experimental art-house films. Although funding came from public and private sources, because they were making films outside of the studio system, these filmmakers are described as 'independent'.

It was also against the backdrop of the rising activism in the 1960s and Tlatelolco that critics and filmmakers were honing their craft and establishing the parameters of the field. Given that this was also a time when the feminist movement in Mexico was consolidating its position, it could be expected that women's voices would be part of this discussion. This was not the case, principally because many of these filmmakers tended to come from film schools, but only two women studied at the CUEC between 1963 and 1970 (Rashkin 2001: 68), and the only one to complete her degree at this time was Fernández Violante. Therefore, women lacked a significant presence in the discussion.

Fernández Violante participated in filming the protests and in the university occupations (Pech Salvador 1997: 103), like many of her male contemporaries. When interviewed, she emphasises that these took place out of a need for social and political change, which, for her, includes a need to challenge patriarchal power in Mexico. She criticises familial and state relations marked by 'una autoridad muy irracional' ('a very irrational authoritarianism') (Pech Salvador 1997: 103). This anti-authoritarianism does not clearly place her politically, but it does suggest some common ground with her contemporaries. Her feminist politics are also difficult to precisely define. She rails against gender inequality and details the struggles she has had to face in her career as a woman (Horton 1987: 4), yet repeatedly distances herself from being labelled as someone who should be seen solely in terms of her gender. This means that she can seem contradictory in response to questions about whether she is a feminist filmmaker. When Andrew Horton asked her this question, she replies, 'I am feminine, that is, I am a woman [...] I am interested in the problems of all people not just one group', and then asserts that *Azul* and *De todos modos Juan te llamas* are both feminist films (1987: 5). These shifts challenge a clear linear trajectory or a plotting out of her politics in ways that are more evident in the post-1980s generation of women filmmakers.

Consequently, just as it has proven difficult to position her alongside her male contemporaries, her place within the history of women directors is not an easy fit either. There were other female filmmakers before Fernández Violante, such as the aforementioned Landeta and Adela Sequeyro (1901–92), but for many years up to the 1980s there were few recognised by the unions, critics or any of the awarding bodies. As a woman, Fernández Violante is often positioned alongside María Novaro (1951–), Busi Cortés (1950–) and other women directors who came to prominence in the 1980s, yet she was already well established before this later generation and, unlike the others, she does not make women's stories the primary focus of her films. Union membership would prove a controversial subject with this 1980s generation as well. Filmmakers such as Novaro strongly disagreed with Fernández Violante's ambition of making changes from within the unions and felt that they limited their potential to choose the crew they wanted (Arredondo 2014: 19). For such reasons, in her analysis of women filmmakers, Elissa Rashkin describes Fernández Violante as being 'on the borderline between industrial and university cinema. An always controversial figure, [… she] can perhaps best be described as a maverick' (2001: 77). The term 'maverick' works because she does not fit neatly into the 1980s generation of women filmmakers who were more explicitly interested in challenging 'a long-standing cinematic tradition of female objectification, erasure, and displacement' (Rashkin 2001: 2) and, yet, her gender and union membership have determined that she is not included in the 1970s group.

Fernández Violante's interstitial position and exceptionalism are underscored by comments made in an interview with John Mosier and Alexis Gonzales in 1983, when she stated that '[i]n Mexico, in feature length films, I am the only one [female director], I am the only survivor' (185). She further elaborates on how few women directors there were more generally in the rest of Latin America in the early 1980s. Like many who operate within a male-dominated context, she shies away from being pigeonholed as a director who perforce tackles feminist issues:

> I am a woman […] most women directors use their scripts to talk about being women. Most of them belong to women's lib movements. I don't know what they are capable of doing if they are offered a script that doesn't talk about women specifically but jsut [sic] about things in general. (Mosier and Gonzales 1983: 185)

It is worth teasing out how troubling a statement this is. It is indicative of an approach that is integral to the few women directors who found success in the Mexican film industry up to the mid-1980s. The implication is that women and their stories are not 'things in general'; they are a marginal particularity, a common perception and one that deserves to be unpicked. Additionally, many Mexican feminist filmmakers of the 1970s and 1980s were engaged in non-mainstream, mostly low-budget experimental filmmaking that has a different set of skills, artistic engagement, intended audience and outcome from the commercial (albeit of an independent aesthetic) filmmaking of Fernández Violante. Therefore, her comments, which can be read as harsh and dismissive, are also reflective of someone negotiating a difficult moment in Mexican cinema for women.

She is aware of the critical context in which her films are received and of how being a woman determines her own experiences, yet she struggles against this. But she did not see herself as engaging in feminist filmmaking and, in fact asserts her place in opposition to feminist filmmaking practices. Nonetheless, a feminist reading can be applied to her career as she breaks through where others have not and there are often strong female roles in her films. At the same time, although she is a woman, she does not conform to the filmmaking modes of those who emerged in the 1980s. This anomaly makes her difficult to categorise within current frameworks and has resulted in critical neglect.

Two films that function as useful case studies and which should help to understand Fernández Violante's output are *De todos modos Juan te llamas* (1975) and *Misterio* (1980). The first is a war film centred on a foundational period of the modern Mexican state, a preoccupation of many of her contemporaries, and the second is an adaptation of an experimental novel, following a long tradition of such work by respected auteurs. These illustrate some of the reasons why her recuperation is complicated. Where her contemporaries made films about the Revolution (1910–20), she set hers during the more challenging period of the Cristero Rebellion (1926–9) when there were violent skirmishes that attempted to disrupt the new democracy. This period is still seldom filmed and when it is it has been largely by those sympathetic to the Catholic Church. This then becomes a period tarnished by conservative representations. *Misterio* is an adaptation that Fernández Violante was hired to make. The implication attached to this is that she had little freedom to express her own creativity and, thus, cannot be read as an auteur. *Misterio* was made when other women filmmakers, such as Novaro, were filming women-centred narratives, which distances her from their work. To challenge the assumptions attached to both projects and to reclaim Fernández Violante as an important figure in Mexican cinema, I shall carry out close analyses of key features in the creative process as articulated by the director and draw on these in a close reading of the texts.

De todos modos Juan te llamas (1975)

De todos modos Juan te llamas is Fernández Violante's first feature as well as being the first by a woman in Mexico since Landeta's *Trotacalles/Streetwalker* in 1951 (García Riera 1994: 96). Shot with financial support from the Universidad Nacional Autónoma de México (National Autonomous University of Mexico), starring professional actors, and mostly crewed by students and staff from the CUEC, Fernández Violante describes *De todos modos Juan te llamas* as semi-autobiographical, 'una metáfora del 68 – que coincidía con un episodio familiar –, la disolución de una familia por diferencias ideológicas en su propio seno' (Blanco Figueroa 2001: 222) ('a metaphor for 68 – that coincides with a family episode –, the dissolution of a family because of ideological differences within it'). The internal rifts caused by 1968 are what link this film to its setting (Mosier and Gonzales 1983: 16). Fernández Violante explains, 'I knew that I couldn't make a film about 1968, since it was so recent that I wouldn't have the proper perspective, but I asked what happens in the same situation when religion is the main source of the conflict?' (Mosier and Gonzales 1983: 16). The Cristero Rebellion was a religious war that took place in central Mexico, motivated by repressive rules against the Catholic Church (Meyer 2008), at a time in which the promises of the Revolution were being tested by a government which was still heavily influenced by military leadership. Issues that feature most significantly in *De todos modos Juan te llamas* are around land redistribution and tackling rural poverty; ownership of oil and mining rights; and post-Revolutionary corruption.

Episodic in nature, with temporal and narrative leaps, *De todos modos Juan te llamas* is centred on the family of General Guajardo (Jorge Russek – voiced by Federico Romano), an authoritarian figure who has a difficult relationship with his wife, Beatriz (Patricia Aspillaga), and three children, Armanda (Rocío Brambila), Andrés (uncredited) and Gabriel (uncredited). Seen as an intermediary between the church and state via her husband, Beatriz is mistrusted by the local women in the small village setting. The first act of Cristero violence in the village takes place when the women are roused by the priest's call to arms; then they assert Beatriz's complicity with the military, by saying, '¡tú que fornicas con Lucifer, maldita seas!' ('damn you for fornicating with Lucifer!'), and beat her to death in the church in front of her children. These local women are conservative supporters of the Cristero Rebellion and target Beatriz for her class and educational differences, and as a provocation to instigate further violence and state reaction. Therefore, there is space for different political positions, as not all women are understood to be reactionary. Most attention is given to the impact this has on the eldest child and only daughter, Armanda, who has a close relationship with her older cousin, Colonel Gontrán Bonilla (Juan Ferrara), in whom she has a growing sexual interest, and from whom she learns about foundational Revolutionary concepts that challenge the political actions and speeches of the priest, the local women and her father. Bonilla, in turn, frequently challenges Guajardo on the many ways he is turning his back on Revolutionary ideals, which eventually leads to Bonilla's death at the orders of Guajardo. In revenge, Armanda drags Bonilla's body into the stables and sets fire to the building with her father's prized horses inside. She plans to die with Bonilla, but is saved by one of the farm labourers. The film ends with Armanda banished to the capital city, Andrés about to go to study in the US-based military academy Westpoint, and Gabriel in jail for participating in a protest as a member of the Communist Party. The family is dispersed.

As in the war films by her male contemporaries, the narrative moves between public and private concerns. There are also frequent scenes of brief battles, skirmishes and assassinations, which mean that the film cannot be viewed solely as a domestic drama. It opens with a sequence that mirrors that of *La sombra del caudillo* (Julio Bracho, 1960), with several men driven out to wasteland by the military and summarily executed. The parallels between the openings of *La sombra del caudillo* and *De todos modos Juan te llamas* have been noted by Fernández Violante. She states that prior to making the film she had not seen *La sombra del caudillo* as for many years it was subject to a form of delayed release that amounted to censorship (Velazco 2005) and she ascribes this coincidental opening to her reading of Mexican history (Pech Salvador 1997: 125). Comparisons between her work and a widely studied canonical text are a strategic move on Fernández Violante's part in this interview. She is clearly asserting an equivalency in quality, a necessity for someone whose work has been largely overlooked, unlike the attention garnered by Julio Bracho's controversial film.

Where *La sombra del caudillo* has the build-up to the assassinations as the focus of the film and is a pessimistic realisation of the violent corruption and political machinations involved in a presidential campaign, *De todos modos Juan te llamas* never fully explains this incident. As an opening scene it establishes the tense mood of the film, the military's disregard for the rule of law and, as is evident from the other incidents in the film, is to be understood as a break in linear time. It takes place after the rest of the events in the film and represents the escalation of military terror after the Cristero Rebellion. The arrival at the scene of the sinister looking US consulate, Harry Lynch (Ramón Menéndez), to ensure that the task has been carried out completely, implicates the United States in Mexico's violent corruption, which is another significant strand in the narrative. While Armanda is integral to the plot, this is a film that makes the wider context integral to her world. Power structures are multilayered. Her father as a military commander is deeply integrated in a regime that imposes controls at all levels of her public and private world. This is a feminist film that places Armanda's coming of age in a pivotal historic moment.

As previously mentioned, 1968 was a foundational and deeply formative moment for filmmakers of Fernández Violante's generation. She was not part of the student organising committee, but was an active participant in marches and in their filming and reporting. Her then partner, Roberto Jaime Sánchez, collaborated closely with Leobardo López Aretche, who made the documentary drawn from students' films of the protests, *El grito* (1968) (Blanco Figueroa 2001: 221). Additionally, her brother was very active in the movement and their father turned him out of the house for this (Blanco Figueroa 2001, 221). This biographical detail has significant parallels with Guajardo's attitude to his rebellious communist son, Gabriel. Fernández Violante describes her father, a specialist in military law and employee in the national oil company, as a considerable inspiration for this film (Pech Salvador 1997: 126). Indeed, her reflections on this film make her one of the few filmmakers of her generation to repeatedly draw this comparison between the films of the Revolution produced in the 1970s and the student movements.

The use of music in *De todos modos Juan te llamas* is a significant referent in this regard. It creates further layers to the representation of women in the film and opens up further interpretive spaces to understand the contrasting characters. As many of the documentaries reveal, the student protestors in 1968, in line with others in Latin America, were drawing on traditional folk music forms and inflecting these with the political energies of the present, which resulted in the *nueva canción* folk music movement. She describes herself as part of 'una generación de radio. Nuestro bagaje es más auditivo que visual' ('a radio generation. Our baggage is more aural than visual') and asserts that musical awareness is integral to this sensibility (Blanco Figueroa 2001: 218). Song has a grassroots political function that signals solidarity with the labouring class and is allied to the appeal of popular forms to Fernández Violante's generation. In the film this is manifest in the ways that music is employed throughout. The acoustic space at the burial of Beatriz is filled by the diegetic singing of the mourners burying those murdered in retaliation for her death as they process past the Guajardo family. In this way, the small numbers at Beatriz's burial, their silence and isolation from each other and from the villagers is made more acute through this use of song just as, conversely, the villagers' solidarity with each other and their deceased is made explicit. On another occasion, Cristero songs are sung by those following the priest in an attack on the mining company and even as they flee from the army who defend it. The power of the song and the banner with the image of the Virgin of Guadalupe carried by the Cristeros means that the foot soldiers initially refuse to defend the mine. Thus, Fernández Violante demonstrates the power of the audio-visual markers of religious and folk tradition over the soldiers, who are clearly identified as lower ranking and of humble origin. She captures the multifaceted experience of the Rebellion and sonically posits the potential for folk music to be a force of reactionary rebellion as well as radical change. This is an unconventional approach and contrasts with the use of such music as co-terminous with a challenge to conservative power and the status quo.

The use of the word 'our' in the above quotation is not incidental. Just as reference to *La sombra del caudillo* asserts value, 'our' is inclusive and collective, and identifies a generational trait that has significance in her work. At the same time, her choice to focus on the Cristero Rebellion sets her apart from the majority of her contemporaries who ignore this battle in favour of the earlier Revolution. The Cristero Rebellion is an unusual event to choose to draw parallels with the student movement. Rarely represented on film, it is a historical episode that was characterised by reactionary politics, unlike the radical leftist politics of the students. But, demonstrating her unique perspective, Fernández Violante sees it as a similar moment of power games (Pech Salvador 1997: 126) when a considerable shift was taking place in the relationship between the people and the state.

Commonalities can be seen in the tensions, power plays and the imposition of military might on grassroots activities of both eras. In *De todos modos Juan te llamas* she also drew on Spanish history under Francisco Franco (1936–75), where, she contends, priests acted as spies for the military (Pech Salvador 1997: 126). In the film this is made explicit when, at the end, the priest, despite his repeated rhetoric against the government, is shown laughing and celebrating with Guajardo. Thus, she makes a potent point about the relationship between the church and state while also making international connections.

For Fernández Violante the family is the unit of society where its dysfunctions are both played out and impossible to sustain in the face of 'tanta corrupción' ('so much corruption') (Pech Salvador 1997: 127). The dispersal of the family and its breakdown are shown to be a direct consequence of Guajardo's authoritarian actions. Therefore, in *De todos modos Juan te llamas* she works this out through an exploration of the inter-relationship between family, community and the state, and how political ideologies work on and through these.

Bonilla has numerous functions within this family, community and ideological terrain. He is the voice of Guajardo's conscience, which makes his assassination meaningful in its/his silencing. For Armanda, he is the focus of her burgeoning sexuality and their conversations both facilitate her ideological coming of age and act as a means of bolstering her challenges with her father. Bonilla also signals a link with Fernández Violante's next film, *Cananea*, a fictional biography of the leading Mexican anarchist and intellectual originator of the Revolution, Ricardo Flores Magón (1874–1922). When Bonilla is packing up to leave the village, the camera focuses in on a copy of Flores Magón's influential collection of political essays, *Semilla libertaria* (1923).

Dedicated to her mother, who died during the shooting of the film, *De todos modos Juan te llamas* is an ambitious semi-autobiographical first feature (Pech Salvador 1997: 135). It shares many commonalities with films by her contemporaries in its preoccupation with abandoned Revolutionary promises. Given the originality of her approach and focus, it is remarkable that this film has been ignored. In its decision to shift the focus to the aftermath, she asserts that this is 'the first film to put the armed forces on the screen', that is, their political manoeuvrings and domestic life. It avoided the censorship that befell other projects, such as *La sombra del caudillo*, because of the university support. *De todos modos Juan te llamas* is critical of the regime, but 'with the university behind me [...] I had the freedom to attack two of the most powerful institutions in Latin America, the military and the clergy' (Burton 1986: 198). Authoritarianism stemming from these is shown to be destructive for all. The film's episodic narrative has the family as a central defining connection and it traces out its collapse. Armanda's point of view is privileged, thus focusing our attention on her experiences and coming of age sexually and ideologically. How this is done is consistent with feminist film praxis. Her losses and coming of age are the emotional centre of the film, but she is not the sole focus; nor do we filter everything through her point of view. Therefore, while Armanda and Bonilla are given considerable agency and attention, there is space for critical engagement and ambiguities with regard to other characters. This distance and interpretive space can also be found in *Misterio*.

Misterio (1980)

Misterio is a very different project, but one that challenges how the 1980s in Mexican cinema are to be understood and understandings of what it meant to be a female filmmaker at this time. *Misterio* was adapted from the novel *Estudio Q* (1965) in collaboration with its author, Vicente Leñero, an experimental author and prolific scriptwriter. It is a farce about process, production and power in the television industry. The narrative follows a television star, Alex (Juan Ferrara), whose own life becomes the subject of a soap opera. He realises this early on in the narrative when he is told that his first holiday in a decade cannot go ahead because this decision to convert his life into televisual spectacle has been taken by the producers and station owners. He is never a willing participant in this experiment and the lines between truth and fiction are continuously blurred through dialogue and audio-visual technique. For example, the set is deliberately lit in a flat soap opera fashion, the *mise-en-scène* appears typically stylised to resemble a set even in the outdoor scenes, and the characters make value judgements about specific scenarios based on whether their dialogue appears convincing. Comparisons could be drawn to *The Truman Show* (Peter Weir, 1998), which is about a reality television show that observes an individual's every moment from birth. Unlike Truman Burbank (Jim Carrey) in *The Truman Show*, however, Alex is aware from very early on that his life is being mined for entertainment value in *Misterio* and responds negatively to it. His fellow actors treat it as another job. At several points, characters assert that a fellow actor's or character's lines must be false because they appear too *cursi* (trite or tacky), after the fashion of the scriptwriter, Gladys (Beatriz Sheridan), yet it is frequently unclear whether we are watching the truth of the actor's or character's story or the scripted enactment for the television. This is because they are never sure of where the boundaries between truth and fiction lie.

Misterio was made in the 1980s, which is, according to Mexican film histories, a supposed lost decade (Hershfield and Maciel 1999: 193–6). Already in decline in the 1970s, the studios had lost their power, some were in financial ruin and government support for filmmakers was waning. At the same time it was a period during which there was a very high level of production, most of which was low budget and intended to go straight to video distribution. Therefore, it is an era that has become synonymous with trash cinema (Sconce 1995), or *Latsploitation* films as they have been labelled by Ruétalo and Tierney (2011) in the Latin American context. Accepted assessments of the decade suggest that because audience attendance was greatly reduced as a result of the poor condition of cinema theatres and the increase in home video viewing, little of consequence was made. However, such an assessment ignores filmmakers such as Fernández Violante, or her contemporaries, such as Felipe Cazals and Luis Alcoriza, who continued to make challenging films that play with form and narrative. There is critical space for further explorations into the blanket disavowal of this period of auteurs. In part, it is a question of taste because most were shot on video, which has not withstood the passing of time. In the case of *Misterio*, filming on video a story that draws on narrative tropes and audio-visual structures from the telenovela, with its formulaic conventions, works at a meta-textual level. The use of video simultaneously draws on and critiques the aesthetic choices and narrative structure. Fernández Violante thereby becomes both creator and cultural critic.

From the opening scene, the film is meta-fictional in ways that comment on the means of production and repeatedly draw attention to it. It opens with Alex being instructed on his movements through a voice-over that is revealed to be the director (Víctor Junco) when he says 'perfecto, graba' ('perfect, print') and in reverse shot we see the crew and set. At first, this set-up suggests that it is just going to be a film about the making of a television soap opera. Gradually, it becomes about the collapse of fact and fiction in Alex's world, which has sinister elements of surveillance culture, where the director is acting as omnipotent and willing to kill those, such as Gladys, who do not conform to his wishes. When Alex is told that the soap opera is to be about his life, the director shows him that the conversation they are having is already written down and the outcome is decided. Alex believed it to be a spontaneous real-life event. When the director reveals it to be scripted he is confused and tries both to puzzle through what is his real life and what is soap opera and to resist being controlled by the director.

The character of the director is integral to a political reading of this film in his sinister capacity to control the fate of the characters. He repeatedly orders the actors and crew to perform their roles in specific ways, and punishes individuals such as Gladys with death, as an example to others of the consequence of disobedience. Surveillance is an important component of his control. This is revealed in ways that are impossible according to conventional understandings of space and time and are unsettling for the characters. Dialogue is repeated, scenes are repeated and the cast appear not to remember events that have just taken place. These breaks are a comment on patriarchy and authoritarianism, which, from her interviews, Fernández Violante sees as indelibly interlinked (Pech Salvador 1997: 103).

It is Ellen McCracken's contention that the source novel is typical of the boom in Latin American literature of the 1960s and 1970s, in that Leñero and his contemporaries (such as Gabriel García Márquez and Carlos Fuentes, who also wrote for the big screen) 'strongly asserted their identity as practitioners of high culture' (McCracken 2010: 210) and that while they were 'fascinated with the mass media and constructed their work with many elements of mass culture, [… they] never allowed their texts to *become* mass culture' (2010: 210, italics in original).[1] This assertion is a more complicated one when the inter-media relationship between television and film is not so distant, especially in the 1980s, when films were frequently shot on video and, therefore, have the same aesthetic traces (Hershfield and Maciel 1999: 193–6). It is in the meta-textual awareness, collapse in time and space, and the frequent pulling back and revealing of the means of production, visually and through both dialogue and effects, that *Misterio*'s challenges to convention lie. These techniques and their experimental nature should have been lauded. However, given the scant critical attention this period of filmmaking has received, the use of a much-derided form (telenovela) and shooting on video have resulted in *Misterio* being overlooked. This neglect is further compounded by the fact that it was also made by a filmmaker difficult to pigeonhole.

McCracken uses the term 'meta-telenovela' to describe the film and discusses the use of paradigmatic substitution in the adaptation process and how it 'teaches that none of its signifiers can be trusted because new signifieds are constantly being substituted' (2010: 209). The novel is multi-layered in its textual referents in ways that have much to do with the formal aspects of fiction writing and many of its conceits are highly text-based. For example, much space is given over to detailed classifications of Alex (also referred to as Alejandro in the novel). This begins with the minutiae of his birth registration (Leñero 2007: 22–4); exhaustive measurements that include his height, length of his legs to his knees, and even the number of hairs on every part of his body (34–7); his medical history (39–42); phrenological analysis (44–6); and so on. This information is mostly dull to read and disrupts the flow. It also functions as a reflection on the impossibility of knowing a character through facts and (pseudo-)scientific analysis. *Misterio* has none of this detail. Instead, it draws on the transcriptions of direction; dialogue between actors in their roles and of characters from the novel; passages taken from scripts; and descriptions of action. It plays with these in ways that are possible using conventional televisual language. The film changes the order in which some events take place and, unlike the novel, where it is often unclear who is speaking to whom, the actors' physical presence obviates confusion in the same ways: the tactic used in the film is that they sometimes change roles, blur the lines between being characters and performers, or speak dialogue that is against type and sometimes self-reflexive. *Estudio Q* is a novel about writing as much as it is about television. In *Misterio*, form and content make the film a meta-narrative but also make broader points about power, control and surveillance in everyday life. Again, as in the case of Fernández Violante's contemporaries, politics continues to be an important component of the narrative.

If we are to read Fernández Violante as an auteur with a significant and consistent voice, she deals with power, its potential to corrupt and how destructive it is for others. Yet, she does not ascribe full ownership of any of these projects to herself, thus undermining the auteur label, a gesture which can be read as inherently feminist. For example, she is credited as a scriptwriter for *Misterio*, but in interviews she is clear that the script is Leñero's and that she took on the film as a jobbing director (Pech Salvador 1997: 146). In interviews she is unusually honest about the frustrations and challenges posed by the industry, lack of finance and the effect individuals' decisions have had on her career that have sometimes impeded her realising her vision, but also generously ascribes skill and talent to those she is collaborating with on her films. Her blunt statements about producers and their impositions have also worked against the distribution of her films. All of these elements have resulted in her work being largely overlooked.

Conclusion

It is important to recover Fernández Violante's filmic output and see it beyond and within gender. Her gender must be taken into account, given the pioneering nature of her work and the limitations and constraints that her gender has entailed on how her work is distributed and seen. However, to read her only through this lens, according to current framings of Mexican film history, is not to see her in the light of her 1970s contemporaries who have been lionised by earlier generations of critics who, in turn, ignore her work, primarily because she is a woman, but also because her status as an auteur is more ambiguous than is the case with her contemporaries. Her interviews illuminate what analysing her work demonstrates, that she makes a fascinating case study in the evolution of the Mexican film industry as a director, a worker, an influential industry professional and a gendered subject. She is also someone whose work and her assertion of where it should be placed indicate that there are significant flaws in how Mexican film is read.

To return to Rashkin's contention that Fernández Violante is controversial, this is due to her repeatedly very forthright and critical statements about others in interviews, as is evident in her description of her pathway to inclusion and acceptance within the industry. For her, these are twofold. Firstly, 'after six years in the union of being treated like the worst boy in class, they accepted me. You know why? Because I take shorthand and type! But this is very useful to me' (Horton 1987: 4). Her pragmatism and disappointment in the means of attaining recognition through having secretarial (read feminine) skills in the male-dominated industry are evident here, and can also be found in the second reason she gives: 'in order to have power and to be respected in Mexico, you must be well known internationally' (Horton 1987: 4). Serving on the jury of the Moscow and Havana Film Festivals fulfilled this function. She is highly self-reflective in these interviews. Her reading of her career is clear: she has carefully manoeuvred her way through a system that was stacked against her. She is very aware of the limited chink of possibility her success has afforded her and other women, '[s]o I am an important person for the industry. They feel it is best to work with a well-known "prestigious" woman director and then they are able to say how pro-feminist they are because they support me' (Horton 1987: 4). Her example does not necessarily lead to radical systemic change because she becomes the exceptional woman. The scare quotes in her remark reflect an awareness of what she represents, and work to ironise the notion of value in the word 'prestigious'. Her gender has determined how she has gained access to institutions, such as the directors' union, and she has made considerable moves to pave the way for others, who then chose alternative routes. There is a directness in the interviews that unmasks the conservatism of the context in which she was making films and the resistance she experienced as a woman in trying to succeed in the industry.

Fernández Violante has been in the unusual situation of being simultaneously inside the structures of the studio system and signalled as a marginal subject because of her gender. She became a director at a transitional moment and has been highly influential due to her various professional roles in education and direction. Her first feature, *De todos modos Juan te llamas*, was made shortly after graduation and won significant industry awards. Being asked to make *Misterio* resulted in an experimental adaptation of a post-modern text. These shifts and changes are not a story of linear progression and upward trajectory. They are the account of someone who has had to navigate an industry in crisis and one in which her gender has been a significant impediment to renown and acclaim.

Fernández Violante has worked within and outside the studio system to make ambiguous, politically complex films ambivalent about many of the grand narratives. An analysis of her filmmaking foregrounds the difficulties in taxonomy, challenges how Mexican film histories are conventionally told and highlights the ways in which the intersections of gender and generation serve as simultaneously exclusionary and inclusionary. Her career is disruptive to current narratives regarding Mexican film history and demands that it be retold. Historically, she belongs to the 1970s generation, yet she is left out of critical studies. As a woman she was pioneering and should be read as such, but her lack of clear feminist aesthetics means that she is excluded. Her work challenges us to consider what it means to be a woman filmmaker trying to make her way in an industry that was resistant to her presence, among contemporaries who did not accept that what she made was worthy of inclusion in their canon. Fernández Violante's output creates a dissonance in the neat categories heretofore used about gender and independent filmmaking in Mexico, which suggest that they do not work. She and others who fall between and outside of the current frameworks, deserve their place in history

Note

1. For more detail on García Márquez's writing for cinema as well as the adaptations of his work, see del Río (2013).

References

Arredondo, Isabel (2014). *Motherhood in Mexican Cinema, 1941–1991: The Transformation of Femininity on Screen*, Jefferson: McFarland.
Blanco Figueroa, Francisco (2001). 'Desde todas las coordenadas del cine: Marcela Fernández Violante', *Mujeres mexicanas del siglo XX*, 2, pp. 215–27.
Brewster, Claire (2005). *Responding to Crisis in Contemporary Mexico: The Political Writings of Paz, Fuentes, Monsiváis, and Poniatowska*, Tucson: University of Arizona Press.
Burton, Julianne (1986). *Cinema and Social Change in Latin America: Conversations with Filmmakers*, Austin: University of Texas Press.
del Río, Joel (2013). *El cine según García Márquez*, Havana: Ediciones ICAIC.
García Riera, Emilio (1994). *Historia documental del cine mexicano, Vol. 17, 1974–76*, Guadalajara: Universidad de Guadalajara.

Hershfield, Joanne and David R. Maciel (1999). *Mexico's Cinema: A Century of Film and Filmmakers*, Wilmington: SR Books.

Horton, Andrew (1987). '"We are losing our identity": an interview with Mexican director Marcela Fernández Violante', *Literature Film Quarterly*, 15.1, pp. 2–7.

Leñero, Vicente (2007). *Estudio Q*, México DF: Joaquín Mortíz.

McCracken, Ellen (2010). 'Proto-hypertextuality in late modernist Mexican culture: from avant-garde novel to meta-telenovela', *Interdisciplinary Journal for Germanic Linguistics and Semiotic Analysis*, 15.2, pp. 203–12.

Meyer, Jean (2008). *The Cristero Rebellion: The Mexican People Between Church and State 1926–1929*, Cambridge: Cambridge University Press.

Mora, Carl J. (1989). *Mexican Cinema: Reflections of a Society 1896–1988*, Berkeley: University of California Press.

Mosier, John and Alexis Gonzales (1983). 'Marcela Fernández Violante on Mexican cinema: interview', *Studies in Latin American Popular Culture*, 2, pp. 182–9.

Pech Salvador, Cynthia Eugenia (1997). 'El cine de Marcela Fernández Violante', Undergraduate dissertation, UNAM.

Rashkin, Elissa J. (2001). *Women Filmmakers in Mexico: The Country of Which We Dream*, Austin: University of Texas Press.

Ruétalo, Victoria and Dolores Tierney (eds) (2011). *Latsploitation, Exploitation Cinemas, and Latin America*, London: Routledge.

Sconce, Jeffrey (1995). '"Trashing" the academy: taste, excess, and an emerging politics of cinematic style', *Screen*, 36.4, pp. 371–93.

Thornton, Niamh (2013). *Revolution and Rebellion in Mexican Cinema*, New York: Bloomsbury.

Torres San Martín, Patricia (ed.) (2004). *Mujeres y cine en América Latina*, Guadalajara: Universidad de Guadalajara.

Treviño, Jesús Salívar (1979). 'The new Mexican cinema', *Film Quarterly*, 32.3, pp. 26–37.

Tuñón Pablos, Julia (1999). *Women in Mexico: A Past Unveiled*, Austin: University of Texas Press.

Velazco, Salvador (2005). '*Rojo amanecer* y *La ley de Herodes*: cine político de la transición Mexicana', *Hispanic Research Journal*, 6.1, pp. 67–80.

9

Bertha Navarro and the Remapping of Latin American Cinema: Markets, Aesthetics, Cultural Politics

Marvin D'Lugo

Remappings

For general audiences, Bertha Navarro's most prominent achievement has been her collaboration with one of the three 'amigos' of contemporary Mexican cinema, Guillermo del Toro. What is less well understood is that her collaboration with del Toro is part of her long-standing engagement with Latin-American trans-national cinema largely through a double emphasis on international co-productions and the cultivation of the critical presence of the film auteur.

Navarro observes to an interviewer: 'at the time I began, in the 70s, it was more the era of the director, the director-driven films. Now it's the era of the producer. It has become more oriented to having the director work more closely with the producer; the producer in many cases is driving the film. I'm the producer that leads the film, I find the project, I find the money, I finish it' (Jordan 2012). That conception is rooted in her efforts to bring Latin American filmmakers to reconceive their work in trans-border contexts through the scriptwriting seminars she organised in Mexico beginning in 1993 under the auspices of the Sundance Film Festival.

Although not especially identified with women directors, as for instance is Lita Static in Argentina, Navarro has nonetheless demonstrated through her own exemplary career a model of the possibilities for women within Latin American film industries. Ana Cruz is a Mexican filmmaker, fellow film producer and coordinator of the Guadalajara Film Festival's commemorative volume to honour Navarro. She says: 'It doesn't seem relevant to the young women filmmakers of today to emphasise their gender in order to open the way to the world of filmmaking, but for Bertha's generation and mine, it seems fundamental. As a producer, Bertha has had to fight two or three times more than any of her male colleagues to be where she is, and even harder than the current generation of women producers to achieve what she has achieved'[1] (Cruz 2008: 73).

Navarro's particular sensibility to questions of gender has not translated into any explicit political agenda in the films she produces but she is suggestively ambivalent. This is not unlike the strategy of contemporary Mexican women filmmakers like María Novaro and Dana Rotberg, for whom the questions of gendered narratives of the national community are generally not openly framed through the plotting of their films. Indeed, in the evolution of women's filmmaking in Mexico, as Elissa Rashkin observes, there has often been a subtle dynamic at work through which they 'expressed feminism less as an explicit stance than as a visceral extrapolation of lived experience' (2001: 221). This may well be due, as Rashkin reasons, to 'the impossible models of Womanhood that uphold national and patriarchal ideologies at the expense of female agency and autonomy' (2001: 33).

Navarro is a self-defined 'child of the sixties'. Born in Mexico City in 1943, she spent part of her early youth in the United States, where, besides perfecting her English, she became immersed in counter-culture (Vietnam, student protests); in the mid-1960s, she studied French and art in Paris, returning to Mexico in 1967. During this period she worked as assistant producer to Manuel Barbachano Ponce, who had been involved in a number of important Mexican–Spanish co-productions of the previous decade (Carlos Velo's *Torero/Bullfighter*, 1956; Juan Antonio Bardem's *Sonatas*, 1959; Luis Buñuel's *Nazarín*, 1959*)*. During this same period she met Paul Leduc and became involved in the alternative filmmaking collective Cinema70, working on a series of documentary shorts related to the upcoming Mexican Olympics (Cruz 2008: 19).

She entered film production in the aftermath of the first major challenge to the Mexican authoritarian state that erupted around the 1968 Olympic

Games, at a time when local resistance movements across Latin America found unprecedented solidarity and common cause. Navarro's embrace of internationalism in her filmmaking would later be reflected in her own documentary work in Nicaragua, most notably in her feature-length documentary of 1978, *Nicaragua, los que harán la libertad/Nicaragua, Those Who Will Make Freedom* (Cruz 2008: 31–41). Her subsequent engagement in private, international co-funding of films beginning in the early 1980s arose in the context of the Mexican government's intensified neo-liberal practices (Sánchez Prado 2014: 112–13) and deepened in the aftermath of the Zapatista uprising of 1994, which, as Roger Bartra has argued, marked the demise of Mexico's revolutionary national myth of origins and the beginning of post-national Mexico (2013: 23–9). In this regard, we need to see key phases of Navarro's evolving approach to trans-national filmmaking against the backdrop of and as a response to Mexican and Latin American politics.

In the late 1960s, Navarro would identify with ideologically engaged cinema as inspired by the revolutionary cinema of Cuba, which emphasised the primacy of testimonial documentary cinematic practices. When she assumed her first role as producer with Leduc's *Reed, México insurgente/Reed: Insurgent Mexico* (1970), she began to embrace the notion of an experimental political cinema that Leduc had developed through his earlier participation in the Grupo Nuevo Cine. The objective of this approach, as reflected in the script and editing of *Reed*, was to integrate into the viewing experience strategies through which to more actively engage with its audience.

Once *Reed* was completed, Navarro found herself engaged in a new aspect of production: attempting to develop an effective distribution model when previous efforts to engage international distributors for Mexican films had been largely haphazard. The film's successful run in France after its screening at the Cannes Quizaine des Réalisateurs (Directors' Fortnight) provided her with the first understanding of how to package a Mexican film as a cultural product for international audiences and festivals (Cruz 2008: 28–9).[2]

Navarro followed *Reed* with a brief tenure as chief of production at Conacite I, the state-funded film production company established during the presidency of Luis Echeverría, and her own engagement in documentary filmmaking in Nicaragua. Owing to the shifting politics of film production in Mexico under the presidency of José López Portillo, by the early 1980s she was compelled to look beyond national industrial possibilities, to foreign projects (Cruz 2008: 43). In a striking reversal from the alternative film projects with which she had engaged up to this point, she started approaching an emerging form of independent commercial cinema. This would come in a project that she would later describe as ill-defined: Gregory Nava's *El norte* (1983). Despite the filmmaker's claims to the contrary, this was a commercial enterprise, albeit of a modest scale, involving Navarro as the Mexican producer, owing to the necessity of engaging Mexican actors and shooting in Mexico. *El norte* would be her first multinational project with British–American co-productions. Half of the production costs were met by US Public Television's American Playhouse, with pre-sale to Channel 4 London and eventual grants from the Telluride Film Festival (Innsdorf 1984).

Beginning with *Cabeza de Vaca* (Nicolás Echevarría, 1991), which had been gestating since 1984, Navarro embarked on what would be a two-decade cycle of activities that crystallised the potential of a truly transnational cinema. *Cabeza de Vaca* was at first a contingent production, fed by the dubious idea of the celebration of the encounter of two cultures and funded by Spain's Fifth Centenary Commission. The script was inspired by the diaries of the Spanish conquistador Alvar Núñez Cabeza de Vaca and his eight-year captivity among the native communities of what is today the south-western United States. Interestingly, the film is built around a Spanish explorer's cross-cultural contacts in what might appropriately be described as a pre-national narrative and thus, like the earlier *El norte*, coheres as a chronicle of border-crossing.

Navarro's growing dexterity in handling commercial productions, while tied to the need to develop alliances with international funding groups, helped shape a little-noted dimension of the kinds of films to which she would become increasingly attracted, what Thomas Elsaesser, working on European production schemes of the 1980s and beyond, describes as a cinema that holds 'the national as a second-order concept'. These are films in which 'reference to the nation, the region and the local have become second-order realities' (2005: 83). Such films, as Elsaesser argues, provide

> access-points for the international and global cinema markets, which includes the national audience, thoroughly internationalized through the films on offer in cineplexes and videotheques [...]. The films' attention to recognizable geographical places and stereotypical historical periods thus begins to echo Hollywood's ability to produce 'open' texts that speak to a diversity of publics, while broadly adhering to the format. (83)

Misha MacLaird has argued that Navarro and her long-time production collaborator, Jorge Sánchez, provided the model of the producer in a leadership role in the creative and commercial aspects of filmmaking in Mexico, 'reconciling the demands of the artists with those of the financial backers to arrive at something also desirable to audiences' (2013: 66–7). In her own self-description she would characterise her role this way: 'I'm a filmmaker, as a producer. I know the craft very well and I have passion. I became knowledgeable as to every area of filmmaking; and I think that's why I'm a good producer, I decided to focus; it's what I feel that I do best' (Jordan 2012).

Marketing

El norte had involved the participation of television pre-sale arrangements (Channel 4 London and the US-based PBS) for part of the film's direct funding. The subsequent arrangement for *Cabeza de Vaca* was made possible through co-funding with the Spanish government's commission for support of film productions commemorating the fifth anniversary of Spain's acquisition of its American colonies (Comisión del Quinto Centario). Since the 1970s, as Elsaesser reminds us, German television had been actively engaged in developing such auteur film projects (Elsaesser 2005: 213–16). A more immediate model for Navarro was to be found in the decade-long arrangement between the Cuban Film Institute (ICAIC) and Spanish state television (RTVE), an arrangement that effectively provided a showcase for Spanish films at the Havana Film Festival and the subsequent international circulation of a number of Cuban–Spanish co-productions of the period. It was indeed this emerging 'festival circuit' in combination with TV collaborations that was destined to alter the nature of Latin American film productions, and Navarro's work in the 1980s is among the earliest of these multifaceted inter-media and trans-national projects.

What is most significant about such largely improvised production alignments is that they reflect a shift from the conception of cinema as a locally defined enterprise to a broader set of reception networks that effectively erased the borders of what we think of as 'national' cinema in favour of what Will Higbee and Song Hwee Lim term 'critical transnationalism': that is, a continual exploration of the interface of global and local (2010: 10) that eschews the monological geopolitics of the nation for a multifaceted borderless aesthetic/commercial hybridity. The kinds of films to which Navarro is attracted beginning in the 1980s have been small movies generally, which are in keeping with the post-industrial notion of Latin American film (Vargas 2005: 16), that is, a mode of filmmaking and circulation that is built around the tenets of private financing, artistically conceived projects that are independent of state coercion and are also potentially strong box office contenders within both national and international markets.

Navarro's view of her activities ('I'm a filmmaker, as a producer') suggests a reworking of Walter Benjamin's conception of the producer as author, that is, as a creator of forms whose intervention in the market of cultural production generates new aesthetic models that other authors can emulate (Benjamin 1988: 233). This involves strategies to produce and circulate films whose aesthetics allow them both to cross borders within the Hispanic milieu and to penetrate non-Latin American markets, thereby enabling Spanish-language films to stabilise a global presence. She has described herself as a 'boutique producer' (Jordan 2012) involved in a small number of unique and high-quality films.

Her emphasis is on auteur cinema, a feature that initially does not distinguish her from other global art-house producers. But within auteur-based cinema, Navarro has made a striking difference between the role of the filmmaker and that of the scriptwriter. This, in fact, is a critical feature that has led her to focus on the qualities of script as a central framework for the quality film, as distinct from the overall effect of production. Those skills would come to the fore with the first of her collaborations with Guillermo del Toro, whose first feature-length project, a vampire genre story, is reworked through Navarro's help into a workable production script (Cruz 2012: 251).

The script that would eventually become *Cronos* (1993) is a variation of a gothic horror genre film, but one in which, as critics observe, the tenets of genre appear to have been rewritten to accommodate the filmmaker's highly personal 'auteur' perspective. The film's premise is a rhetorical flexibility built on the basis of the global flow of popular culture as well as the potential of audiences, not defined by either nationality or class or even generation, to accommodate themselves within a hybridised version of the genre. Unlike the elitist notion of the 'festival film', *Cronos* is aimed at the cross-cultural spectatorship of popular genre cinema and thus undermines the restrictive frames of reference that would otherwise define the narrow audience of national cinema. In discussing the dynamics of audience viewings of genre films at Sundance in 2000, Daniel Dayan explains, 'Behind each [genre] film one feels more than an author – one feels a constituency' (2013: 52). For del Toro, that constituency takes shape through a trans-border popular cinematic vernacular unencumbered by geopolitical borders.

The immediate result of Navarro's collaboration with del Toro is a work whose script and production values will exceed the limits of the genre and whose extra-textual dimension – shaped by the integration of an international cast – provides the impetus precisely for what film scholars have read as a self-referential interrogation of the borderless flow of cultural tropes that defy the specificities of the national as well as the tenets of established genres (Kantaris 1998; Davies 2008; Shaw 2013). Because of the difficult circumstances of exhibition in Mexico (Cruz 2008: 46), *Cronos* turned out to be a film more seen outside Mexico than within the country. Shown to enthusiastic audiences at Cannes in 1994, the film made possible del Toro's entrance into US filmmaking with *Mimic* (1997).

As *Cronos* circulated beyond Mexico without the need to 'explain' it as a Mexican film, we begin to discern the emergence on a global scale of the unhinging of a certain type of Mexican filmmaking that advances the notion of a marketable Hispanic trans-national cinema. This concept was reinforced by del Toro's next film, *El espinazo del Diablo/The Devil's Backbone* (2001), begun as a collaboration between Navarro's production company, Tequila Gang, co-founded in 1997 with Alejandro Springall and del Toro, and the Almodóvar Brothers' production company, El Deseo. What is significant here is the effort to merge Mexican authorial tendencies with the apparent 'house style' of El Deseo. The most obvious feature of the collaboration is that del Toro and Navarro separately and together benefit from a strategy of international distribution around the Almodóvar brand that would in effect affirm the ubiquity of a different kind of Latin American film, one which integrates Spain into the new trans-Hispanic cinematic cartography.

As she worked on *Cronos*, Navarro successfully negotiated with the Sundance Film Festival to mount a specifically Latin American scriptwriting workshop (Fundación Carmen Toscano undated). This is an activity formalised in 1993 initially operating under the auspices of the Sundance Festival, but run in Oaxaca, Mexico.[3] From this point on, Navarro became aligned with a series of trans-national strategies that would, over time, be identified with the current of Latin American quality films that include both mainstream popular fare (Chilean Andrés Wood's political drama *La fiebre del loco/The Abalone Fever*, 2001; Mexican Antonio Urrutia's black comedy *Asesino en serio/I Murder Seriously*, 2002; Ecuadorian Sebastián Cordero's police thriller *Crónicas/Chronicles*, 2005) as well as more predictable 'arthouse' cinema (Paul Leduc's *Cobrador: In God We Trust*, 2006; Andrea Martínez Crowther's *Cosas insignificantes/Insignificant Things*, 2008).

Among the underlying principles of Navarro's screenwriting workshops as they evolved in the 1990s and beyond was the formation of an informal community of aspiring auteurs brought together to engage in a profound and intimate border-crossing experience involving novices from across the Spanish-speaking world. Moving the individual filmmaker outside his or her comfort zone to collaborate with professionals from other parts of the Hispanic world had the effect of weakening the idea of cinema, very often rooted in their respective formation in a discrete 'national' cinema. The *talleres* not only challenged the sacrosanct notion of a national cinema but helped break down gender barriers through the presence of women filmmakers. Among the workshops' outstanding alumnae are Lola Salvador (Spain), Lucrecia Martel (Argentina), Andrea Martínez Crowther and Patricia Riggen (Mexico).[4]

The central focus of Navarro's work in more recent years has been the expansion of that production model and aesthetic beyond Mexico. This has engaged her with Chilean, Ecuadorian and Spanish co-productions while at the same time returning to the activities of two key Mexican filmmakers: del Toro and Leduc. In all of these works, she has remained faithful to the certain conceptual core that might be described as relocalising the

Hispanic cultural imaginary through the erasure of cultural and political borders of Latin American cinema.

Aesthetics and politics

As part of the Guadalajara International Film Festival's *homenaje* to her, Navarro was characterised as 'una cineasta sin fronteras' ('a filmmaker without borders') (Cruz 2008), a phrase that captures the essence of her aesthetic choices and even her career formation. It is, in a fundamental way, the unpinning of the state-constructed national discourse that for decades defined Mexican cinema which provides the focus on the transnational *mise-en-scène* that is woven into her work.

Her autodidactic formation as a film producer of Paul Leduc's *Reed, México insurgente* remains a watershed experience in her career and shapes her later work. Unavoidably, we need to recognise that the experience of *Reed* is determined by the fact that it is the product of the authorial sensibility of a politically engaged experimental filmmaker of the 1960s, one who eschewed the national precisely in the period of political crisis. Her identification with the film auteur as 'the nominal currency of the film festival economy' (Elsaesser 2005: 100–1) is inflected by the political agendas of Mexico and more generally of Latin America. It combines the romantic view of the filmmaker as resistance fighter, in the spirit of regional filmmakers of the 1960s and 1970s (Argentina's Fernando Solanas, Bolivia's Jorge Sanjinés, Brazil's Glauber Rocha), with the notion of the auteur promoted through film festivals, which often relies on the figure of the producer.

We can recognise this cultural hybridism in the visual style of *Reed*, in Leduc's structuring a narrative of the Mexican Revolution around a foreigner, the American journalist John Reed, whose diaries of his time in Mexico reporting the Civil War become the film's cardinal conceptual gesture. Rather than telling the story from within, the notion of the Revolution as the crucible of the nation is depicted from the outside, in effect, establishing the second-order status of Mexico in what now becomes ostensibly Reed's story. In the first post-credit sequence, in fact, Leduc stages Reed's movement across the border to Mexico as the camera, through a tracking shot, follows the movement of Mexicans fleeing their own country. The centre of attention is thereby shifted from an inward-looking narrative to an outside-looking one, reducing the audience's sense of Mexico by visually guiding them to observe the deflation of the force of borders in defining the national community. The staging of border crossing will in time become a literal and figurate gesture in Navarro's films, giving prominence to characters who are not bound by the geopolitical confines of the nation. It is at the border where identity, imposed on individuals and whole communities, is challenged and refigured.

In his reworking of the historical material, Leduc will emphasise John Reed's liminal status; embedded with revolutionaries and yet an outsider, Leduc chooses to 'Mexicanise' his protagonist by giving him somewhat fluid expressive skills in Spanish rather than to remain faithful to the historical figure, who apparently spoke only a pidgin Spanish (Pick 2010: 79). This simulated linguistic agility and casting (Mexican actor Claudio Obregón plays Reed) facilitates an interpenetration between the insider and the outsider in which mental and cultural borders dissolve. This first linguistic-cultural gesture may speak more directly to the wishful thinking about contemporary Latin American borderless culture than to the historical truth of Reed in Mexico.

Arguably, the most salient feature of *Reed* for international audiences upon its initial release was the film's innovative narrative-visual style, which traces its sources beyond the conventions of Mexican cinema to the patterns of the New Latin American Cinema of the period, specifically the pseudo-documentary immediacy of ICAIC's experiments (films like Manuel Octavio Gómez's *La primera carga al machete/The First Charge of the Machete*, 1969). The film heightens the dissolution of national specificity by displacing the Mexican conventions of representing national history as grandiose myth that had long since been codified as a 'national' style through the cinematography of Gabriel Figueroa. In its place, Leduc utilises static cameras for staging numerous scenes and generally avoids the kind of epic visual strategies that would aggrandise action (Thornton 2013: 82).

Navarro would look back to *Reed* as 'el acto de libertad en donde todo era posible' (the act of liberty in which everything was possible) (Cruz 2008: 29). Since so much of the Leduc film is contingent, based on the limits of the moment, it may seem a risky proposition to project a retrospective conceptual scenario of the film onto Navarro's subsequent career.

Yet, there is an undeniable congruence between Leduc's notion of cinema and the aesthetic patterns of Navarro's later productions. Most prominent among these may be the focus on plot elements that foreground the act of border-crossing and thereby diminish the illusion of fixed 'national' identities.

Guillermo del Toro's *Cronos* (1993) expands those notions of a borderless visual style with an ingenious aesthetic strategy of positing the second-order view of Mexico as a dystopian space perceived from the future (1997 in the film) through the filter of popular gothic horror film conventions, not unlike Ridley Scott's *Blade Runner* (1982). The script that will eventually become *Cronos* is an over-the-top variation of the gothic horror or vampire film, with its overdetermination of genre conventions (lighting, sound, eerie *mise-en-scène*), and becomes a way to address at least one built-in fan base. Yet, as film critics and scholars have generally noted, the film far exceeds those genre expectations, by imbuing its narrative space with a series of cultural and even geopolitical meanings. Geoffrey Kantaris reads *Cronos*'s depiction of the Mexican megalopolis as the dystopian version of the exploitative practices of capitalism in the age of intensified globalisation. In a *mise-en-scène* that anticipates NAFTA, he sees the narrative unfold in a symbolic setting caught between a macabre past and an equally macabre future (Kantaris 1998). Similarly, Ann Davies notes that vampirism is the ideal trope for depicting the crossing of borders (2008: 396). Following that same line of cultural analysis, Deborah Shaw calls del Toro himself an alchemist for the way 'the director alchemically utilises references from across cultural, mythical, and religious texts, from across continents and ages, to create a film which produces a personal and Mexican take on immortality, death, and morality' (2013: 20).

The film's narrative is focused on Jesús Gris (noted Argentine actor Federico Luppi) (Figure 9.1), an antiques dealer living with his wife Mercedes and caring for their granddaughter Aurora. Jesús finds a clock-like scarab, the Cronos device, embedded in the statue of an angel delivered to his shop. The device, invented in the sixteenth century by the alchemist and chief watchmaker of the viceroy of New Spain, provides eternal life by being fed human blood. Along with the device is a book of instructions on its appropriate use. Gris accidentally cuts himself with the Cronos device, mixing his own blood with the liquid from the scarab, and becomes, by progressive stages, addicted to human blood, effectively metamorphosing into a vampire. The device is also being sought by a factory owner dying of cancer, Dieter de la Guardia (Claudio Brook), who sends his nephew Angel (Ron Perlman) on a mission to track it down. A battle between Jesús and the de la Guardias forms the action for the rest of the film.

A totally Mexican film in terms of funding, production and location, del Toro's artistic design for *Cronos* continually foregrounds the ambiguous status of national specificity as the signifiers of Mexican-ness are transformed. He was insistent, for example, that the casting include two key 'foreign' actors – Ron Perlman and Federico Luppi. These actors are joined by Claudio Brook, who, though Mexican, speaks English at certain points, but with a faintly European accent, to undercut any clear linguistic/cultural identity. These moves to disengage linguistic specificity from locale are further coupled with the audio-visual mixing of Mexican space juxtaposed from the opening credits onward of Argentine tango music to provide a score for Gris, an Argentinian who has made his home in Mexico City. As much to accommodate Luppi's appearance, the score functions to disrupt the indexical quality of those spaces by suggestively transposing them to

Figure 9.1 Guillermo del Toro on the set of *Cronos* with Federico Luppi (Guillermo del Toro, 1993).

other milieus, in much the same way that the film's Cronos device, invented during Spanish colonial times, does with the historical body of its alchemist inventor in modern-day Mexico.

For del Toro, genre is not an end in itself, so, not surprisingly, the vampire genre's decentring of cultural rootedness is played out with a certain measure of humour in the foregrounding of languages, presumably a stable indexical marker of cultural identity. Yet, as Shaw notes, 'Dieter de la Guardia has a Germanic/Hispanic name, is bilingual and within the diegesis speaks flawless, Mexican-inflected Spanish with a slight English accent. His nephew Angel addresses Jesús in both flawed Spanish and English. The "American" characters, then, inhabit a bilingual linguistic borderland that characterises a Hispanic American space more clearly than an Anglophone one' (Shaw 2013: 24–5). Thematically, *Cronos* suggests that the dystopian version of the global space is anchored in the world of NAFTA, but derived from the invention whose origins are located in the colony of New Spain, as if to imply the persistence of Mexican subaltern identities. *Cronos* proposes a cultural style of filmmaking that combines a respect for the local with aesthetic strategies that demarginalise the conventional stereotypes of Mexican locales for international audiences.

Sebastián Cordero's *Crónicas/Chronicles* (2005), co-produced by Navarro's company, Tequila Gang, is, in a sense, the conceptual twin to *Cronos* in its embrace of another popular genre and its foregrounding of the trans-national spatial texture of film. *Crónicas* is explicitly rooted in a grim contemporary social reality: the sexual molestation of young children and the mass media exploitation of these events. In what may be taken as a macabre homage to del Toro, executive producer of *Crónicas*, Cordero begins his narrative with a shot of Vinicio (Damián Alcázar), who will soon be revealed to be a serial killer, his head bobbing out of the water of a lake. This image clearly references the imagery of Jack Arnold's 1954 sci-fi cult classic *Creature from the Black Lagoon*. In later scenes the panicked townspeople speak of the serial killer as *el monstruo*, the monster. The epithet echoes the voice-over question in the prologue to *El espinazo*, '¿Qué es un fantasma?' ('What is a ghost?') that accompanies the horrifying images of infant fetuses floating in formaldehyde. Cordero's film thus seems to propose a local answer to del Toro's global questioning of the identity of the monster.

Though *Crónicas* relies heavily on genre conventions, those of the thriller in particular, the horror story which is the response to del Toro's question – 'What is a monster?' – is not based on the conventions of fantasy genres but on mass-mediated exploitation television. The trans-national enters into this formulation by means of the inter-media force of television. As it broadcasts across borders in Latin America, television constructs its commercial and cultural audience, thereby refiguring geopolitical spaces that might otherwise appear fragmented and disconnected. A sensationalist television news programme, *24 horas con la verdad/24 Hours with the Truth*, a not-too-veiled copy of Univision's extraordinarily popular *Primer Impacto: Noticias de Hoy/First Impact: News of the Day*, becomes the technological agency through which to establish a pan-Latino trans-national regional space that crosses borders from Miami to Ecuador and Colombia. The strategy is to play with the geopolitical markers of national identity as these are erased through the commonplace technology of television.

The film, Navarro's first collaboration with Cordero, emerges, as the screen credits indicate, from 'assistance of The Sundance Institute/Toscano Script Lab', from where Cordero originated the script. The cast includes Colombian-born US Latino John Leguizamo, Leonora Watling from Spain and well known Mexican actors Damián Alcázar and José Yazpic; the employment of this range of Hispanic actors suggests, as in *Cronos*, seamless linkages across cultures. The film premiered at the prestigious non-competitive Directors' Fortnight at Cannes, and was later shown at the Rotterdam Film Festival. Similar to Navarro's productions of *Cronos* and *El espinazo del Diablo* before it, *Crónicas* follows the producer's highly successful strategy of embracing popular genre formulas, yet also suggestively integrating themes and plot elements that appeal to film festival programmers (Wong 2011: 74–7, 85).

The plot focuses on the relation between Manolo Bonilla, the anchor of a sensationalist Latino news programme from Miami (Leguizamo), and a serial killer (Alcázar). Through his misguided efforts to free Vinicio for a crime unrelated to the serial killings, Bonilla becomes forced to acknowledge the immorality of his exploitation of the tragedy of the victims' families. Despite the local geographical specificity of the action, the film's central theme of moral complicity is posed as a universal theme. In keeping with the visual filter of television news programmes, the film's camerawork suggests a *verité* style, with hand-held cameras to simulate the activities of the on-site media photographer Iván (Yazpic), but, as Cordero notes, his inspiration for the fast-paced editing derives from the editing style of Hollywood films of the 1970s, specifically Sidney Lumet's *Dog Day Afternoon* (1975) and *Serpico* (1973) (Barisazman 2010).

The narrative foregrounds the inter-media construction of locale. A series of inserts of the television news programme punctuate the action in and around the Ecuadorian village where Vinicio's family lives; we thus come to see local spaces self-referentially shaped by Bonilla and his producer into a virtual trans-border community. Two striking features of the film's stabilisation of this trans-national *mise-en-scène* are notable. The first is the ways in which the film continually jumps across geographical borders to underscore the connectedness among different locales that have been constructed by trans-border media culture. In particular, the linguistic code-switching from English to Spanish by Leguizamo, along with the shifting accents from Watling's Castilian to Leguizamo's Colombian Nuyorican to Yazpic's *mexicanismo*, suggest a Latino lingua franca the effect of which is to affirm a borderless community. The second is the centrality given to the border-crossing protagonist Bonilla, whose origins go back to Leduc's construction of John Reed.

While figures such as Reed or Cabeza de Vaca operate within the fiction to evoke a second-order sense of the nation, Bonilla is a somewhat different character, for a different age. His position as a television news personality (he is more than a reader – he is a celebrity investigator) enables him to move across geographical borders in the virtual space invented by television. Thus freed from the local by the mobility dictated by the news programme, ironically, he finds himself trapped into confronting larger moral questions. The physical stand-in for his transnational audiences, he also becomes their moral conscience. Ultimately, it is Bonilla's moral dilemma that saves the film from being simply an expansion of sensationalist reportage of television news programmes.

Andrea Martínez Crowther's *Cosas insignificantes* (2008) provides an important expansion of the underlying decentrings of the authority of national space that recur in earlier films produced by Navarro. This is, as well, a narrative that intensifies the undermining of patriarchal tropes while drawing a critical spotlight on the representation of women and their own self-representation in a transnational narrative. The film exemplifies what noted Latin American literary scholar Jean Franco describes as the rejection of the narratives and story-telling related to patriarchal power (1989: 182). In her suggestively titled study of gender in Mexican letters, *Plotting Women* (1989), Franco examines the different 'discursive positioning of women in Mexican society' and what she calls the female 'struggle for interpretive power' (xi): 'Women have long recognized the imaginary nature of the master narrative. Without the power to change the story or to enter into dialogue, they have resorted to subterfuge, digression, disguise, or deathly interruption' (xxiii).

Cosas insignificantes is in its own way a 'coming of age' genre narrative. A variant of Franco's 'plotting women', Esme (Paulina Gaitán), Martínez Crowther's teenage protagonist, views everyday life in urbanised Mexico through the filters of a mythology that predates and transcends the notion of Mexican state-orchestrated modernity. From her position on the margins of the contemporary cityscape, she can literally look to the two imposing dormant volcanoes, Popocatépetl and Ixtaccíhuatl, on the horizon and recall the myth recounted by her grandmother in Otomí, one of ancient Mexico's pre-Hispanic languages. This subtly constructed visual narrative counterpoint underscores Esme's struggle for discursive power: she needs to juggle that mythic pre-national past with her own contemporary crisis, which she does by reinterpreting the social myth of the father's power.

In that myth, Princess Ixtaccíhuatl's father sends the young warrior Popocatépetl, who is in love with his daughter, to a war in Oaxaca, promising him his daughter's hand if he returns victorious. The father tells his daughter that Popo has died and she dies of a broken heart. Upon his return, Popo kills Ixtaccíhuatl's father and as a punishment from the gods is turned into a volcano, along with his beloved. As the sole provider for her younger sister Lita (Regina de los Cobos) and her ailing grandmother, Esme must assume the role that would otherwise go to the subaltern father to provide for his family. Her life struggle is thus an effort to maintain the unity of her otherwise fractured family in a plot whose dramatic logic is to show the heroine attempting to accommodate the gaps in the paternal rhetoric of family and even nation.

This was Navarro's thirteenth feature-length film production, but only the first directed by a woman in what by then was a 40-year career.[5] The product of the 2002 Toscano Writer's Lab, its production was delayed some six years, however, as Navarro pursued appropriate financing for the production, which would ultimately be a bi-national collaboration between Tequila Gang, Spain's Manga Films and Warner Brothers Mexicano.

The film opens in a smog-covered Mexico City suburban community from which it is possible still to discern the peaks of the nearby volcanoes. To draw our attention to them, we hear the continual background voice of a radio news reporter describing the dormant Popocatépetl's imminent eruption. These announcements serve as the precipitating mechanism of closure at the film's end, when clouds of ash cover parts of the metropolis from the explosion of the volcano. Against this backdrop, the script proposes an intricate trans-national weave among the contemporary characters and their stories. Of these, Esme's own story of her fractured family is foregrounded. Abandoned by her mother and father, supporting her younger sister and grandmother by working in a Chinese restaurant, Esme suffers from severe migraines. What sustains her is the dream of reuniting with her brothers in Canada where, she believes, her migraines will be cured by the snow. As a diversion in her drab existence, she collects found objects, each of which relates to a different story whose protagonists are the owners of the various objects. These include Augusto, an aging child psychologist (Fernando Luján) estranged from his daughter who ran away from home as a teenager and whom he has not seen in 20 years; and Iván (Spanish actor Carmelo Gómez), a paediatrician who is treating a young boy, Vaquerito (Diego Lanzeta), whom he does not realise is his natural son. The various characters cross paths in and around the Chinese restaurant. It is from these contacts that Esme picks up the found objects she places in a box she hides.

It could be argued that *Cosas insignificantes* comes closest to Navarro's own philosophy of scripting, as it presents, for the first time in her career, the centrality of female narrative agency. Stylistically as well, the film's attention to mundane objects collected by Esme recalls Navarro's 1986 talk at the Havana Film Festival's symposium on women and audio-visual media (La mujer en los medios audiovisuales), when she spoke of the concept of 'la realidad cotidiana' (everyday reality) aligned with women's work, which is generally presented as a series of seemingly inconsequential tasks ('quehaceres intranscendentes') that are nonetheless the cornerstone of society (Navarro 1987: 150).

The film title's reference to supposedly inconsequent things is dramatised in a framing device as we see Esme place each object she finds in a box, thereby leading into a retelling of the story of that object. The framing narrative gives a metonymic coherence to the seemingly unrelated objects and story fragments. Their underlying thematic coherence, however, is to be found in the two interlocking stories of other fragmented families and absented fathers: Augusto embodies the rejected father, while Crowther introduces an Oedipal twist to the plot in Iván, who misrecognises his son. For as much as these are men's stories, the women whose lives are entangled with them provide a strong melodramatic frame: they embody themes of alienation from the family for Augusto's daughter Mara (Blanca Guerra); frustrated maternity for Iván's lover Eli (Lucía Jiménez); and finally adultery and abandonment for Paola (Uruguayan-born Mexican telenovela star Bárbara Mori), the woman with whom Iván fathered Vaquerito.

That these narrative threads all seem to verge on the melodramatic is not coincidental. Formally playing on the broad trans-national popularity of the Mexican soaps both within Mexico and beyond (Sánchez Prado 2014: 222–3), the narrative dynamic generated by Esme's situation gives special agency to the young girl as unifying consciousness to the film as a whole. Though the various women are initially posed as passive, not unlike the character of Ixtaccíhuatl from the Otomí legend, they eventually assume inner strength, as if to rewrite the pre-Hispanic patriarchal myth for a contemporary audience.

By the film's end, the appearance of a magical 'MacGuffin', in the Hitchcockian sense, is a snow globe from Niagara Falls, symbol of the magical 'other place', Canada, where she hopes both to cure her migraines and to be reunited with her family. Esme has been given the snow globe by Augusto, who treats her as the substitute for his estranged daughter. The snow in the globe eventually is mirrored in the film's magical ending, as it appears to snow in Mexico City, now evoking the myth of the volcanoes but updating it as a new myth for the modern world. The final scene of *Cosas insignificantes* is the only point in the film at which characters in the contemporary cityscape acknowledge the sacred legendary *mise-en-scène* of the volcanoes. Standing on the roof of their apartment building, Esme, Lita and their grandmother look toward what they imagine are the volcano peaks. Esme points out to her grandmother that she can see the sleeping princess Ixtaccíhuatl covered in a blanket of snow and Popocatépetl at her side. The nearly blind grandmother cannot see them until Lita points them out. The film ends poetically with the contemporary reaffirmation of the myth now evoked through the agency of the female narrator now in dialogue with the patriarchal past.

Though not commercially successful, the film did compete internationally at the San Sebastián Film Festival in the New Directors series and won the audience award for its director at the Biarritz International Festival of Latin American Cinema. *Cosas insignificantes* remains an important expression of the kind of refiguration of a Hispanic cultural imaginary proposed by Navarro. In particular, it is suggestive of the inclusion of questions of gender in her rejection of the narrow nationalisms that long dominated the international circulation of films from the region.

Conclusion

As the aesthetic underpinning *Cosas insignificantes* suggests, the model of the kind of films Navarro develops is one that seeks to displace from the audience's attention the national as a locus of narrative, social or cultural meaning. As in her earlier work, the film does not so much affirm a new national identity as much as it normalises a different perspective on familiar social representations. The opaqueness of the marks of the national thus returns us to that notion of a second-order depiction of the nation. Such an approach has long been attractive to Navarro, as it accommodates both local and other audiences, thus offering a strategic feature in the film's negotiation of a place in international contexts.

The incomplete erasure of the old high legibility of national tropes of Mexican-ness (the volcanoes that are both backdrop and protagonist to the story) thus constitutes a branding label, a marketing tool 'signifying the local' (Elsaesser 2005: 71) that reflects both the pluralism of contemporary Mexican society as well as the need for filmmakers and producers to open films to other audiences. With *Cosas insignificantes*, we can better understand how Navarro's brand of film production has consistently sought to formulate a cultural style of filmmaking that combines an abiding respect for the local with textual strategies that could de-exoticise Mexican culture for international audiences.

Perhaps the two least understood facets of Navarro's career and contributions to the contemporary development of Latin American cinema relate to questions of politics and auteurism. As the preceding discussion suggests, much of Navarro's career has been a series of creative responses to the authoritarian political culture that historically precedes her entrance into filmmaking but which has at key moments shaped her activities. With the exception of her active engagement as a documentary filmmaker during the Sandinista struggle of the 1970s, local politics has largely been a back-story to her work. Yet, undeniably, the difficulties imposed on filmmaking in Mexico under various presidencies, beginning with that of López Portillo (1976–82), moved Navarro to imagine a notion of filmmaking that could move across borders. Through the neo-liberal push toward privatisation of the film industry, she was forced to seek funding sources outside of Mexico, which motivated her engagement with international financing for her projects.

This in turn led toward her embrace of auteur cinema, a second notion that is essential to the trans-national development of her work but is equally misunderstood. While affirming the artistic centrality of the filmmaker to any film, Navarro's engagement with auteurism has largely been inflected by the need to adjust the presumed artistic exceptionalism of the individual filmmaker and to acknowledge its place in the international commercial networks that involve the marketing of films at film festivals and beyond. For the filmmakers with whom she has worked, the figure of the auteur moves outside the art cinema and becomes, as Elsaesser reasons, 'a stand-in and standard bearer of the values and aspirations of its culture, its better half' (2005: 48). The growing emphasis on genre films in Navarro's repertoire is consonant with that transformation as it expands beyond the mind-set that shapes national cinema and now opens up to borderless communities of hybrid audiences.

This is, in effect, a trans-national vernacular and, not surprisingly, the films of Javier Urrutia, Carlos Carrera and Sebastián Cordero have been marked by visual narrative styles that are consonant with the kind of narrative structures that align most favourably with Hollywood. One need only compare these films with the international success in recent years of a new generation of Mexican art-house favourites – Carlos Reygadas, Amat Escalante, Gerardo Naranjo, Michel Franco and Nicolás Pereda. This group makes films that play extremely well at festivals abroad but have only minimal commercial repercussions in Mexico. By contrast, Navarro continues to promote a broad rather than esoteric art-house approach, especially through her insistent 'genre-crossing' strategies. The underlying agenda of her productions has been a pursuit of a cinematic audience both at home and abroad whose film-viewing habits are both borderless and enlightened, yet rooted in a popular and mainstream cinematic experience which, as it respects the local, also esteems the universality of characters and their circumstance.

On 27 May 2015, Navarro received a lifetime achievement award (Ariel de Oro/Golden Ariel – see Figure 9.2) from the Asociación Mexicana de Artes Cinematográficas (AMAC; the Mexican Association of Cinematic Arts). The irony of the gesture could not be more apparent. Having worked for most

Figure 9.2. Bertha Navarro receives the Ariel de Oro as a lifetime achievement award (public domain).

of her career on the margins of the dominant and mainstream Mexican film industry, her resistance to the imposed constraints of national cinema embodied by the industry represented by AMAC was now being valorised. In her characteristically understated manner, she used the occasion not to reflect on her own life and career but to remind her colleagues what was truly at stake in the Mexican film industry: 'To make films is a privilege and also a great responsibility: what we see, how we see, what stories we are going to tell, how we are going to tell them. As cineastes we should be ready to see – that is our profession. We cannot not see and we cannot not know'[6] (IMCINE 2015).

Notes

1. 'A las jóvenes cineastas de hoy no les parece relevante hacer énfasis en su condición de mujer para abrirse camino en el mundo del cine, pero para la generación de Bertha y a la mía propia nos resulta fundamental. Como productora, Bertha ha tenido que luchar dos o tres veces más que cualquiera de sus colegas masculinos para estar donde está, y mucho más que las actuales productoras para lograr lo que ha logrado.' This, and all subsequent translations from the Spanish, are my own, unless otherwise indicated.
2. It is worth recalling that the non-competitive Directors' Fortnight was established in the aftermath of the 1968 student uprising in France as a way to acknowledge the political contexts in which film culture operated. See Wong (2011: 24, 48).
3. From 1995 till 2009, the scriptwriting workshops would be run through the Mexican Fundación Toscano and IMCINE and conducted in the regional city of Oaxaca. They would subsequently be run in Cartagena, Colombia, under the auspices of CMO Producciones, Laboratorios para Profesionales de Cine y Creación, along with the Sundance Institute and the Fundación Carmen Toscano. For details of the shift in locale and focus see 'Lanza Bertha Navarro convocatoria para Taller para guión cinematográfico', La Jornada Espectáculos 20 diciembre 2009 (electronic edition). Available at http://www.jornada.unam.mx/2009/12/20/index.php?section=espectaculos&article=a09n1esp (accessed 20 September 2015).
4. The participants during the first 15 workshops included young filmmakers from across Latin America and Spain (Daniel Burman and Martín Salinas from Argentina; Juan Carlos Valdivia from Bolivia; Andrés Wood from Chile; Jorge Navas and Víctor Gaviria from Colombia; Eliseo Alberto Diego and Juan Carlos Cremata from Cuba; Jesús Regueiro and Lola Salvador from Spain). Participants were linked to Mexican 'asesores', among them María Novaro, José Luis García Agraz, Laura Esquivel, Vicente Leñero and Alejandro Springall.

5. This fact may owe as much to the still male-dominated nature of the Mexican film industry as to the very nature of Navarro's belief in engaging only in projects that interest her. It raises important questions about the nature of women's cinema within the contemporary structures of Mexican and Latin American filmmaking. See Rashkin (2001: 221).
6. 'Hacer cine es un privilegio y también una gran responsabilidad, qué vemos, cómo lo vemos, a quién nos dirigimos, qué vamos a contar, cómo lo vamos a contar. Nosotros como cineastas debemos estar dispuestos a mirar, esa es nuestra profesión, no podemos no ver, no podemos no saber.'

References

Bartra, Roger (2013). *La sangre y la tinta: ensayos sobre la condición postmexicana*, Mexico: Debosillo.
Benjamin, Walter (1988). 'The author as producer', in *Reflections: Essays, Aphorisms, Autobiographical Writings*, edited with an introduction by Peter Demetz, New York: Schocken Books, pp. 220–38.
Cruz, Ana (2008). *Berta Navarro: Cineasta sin fronteras*, Guadalajara: Universidad de Guadalajara.
––––– (2012). *Antes de la pelicula: conversaciones alrededor de la escritura cinematografica*, Mexico: Conaculta.
Davies, Ann (2008). 'Guillermo del Toro's *Cronos*: the vampire as embodied heterotopia', *Quarterly Review of Film and Video*, 25.5, pp. 395–403.
Dayan, Daniel (2000). 'Looking for Sundance: the social construction of a film festival', in Ib Bondebjerg (ed.), *Moving Images, Culture and the Mind*, Luton: University of Luton Press, pp. 43–52. Reprinted in Dina Iordanova (ed.) (2013). *The Film Festival Reader*, St Andrews: St Andrews Press, pp. 45–58.
Elsaesser, Thomas (2005). *European Cinema: Face to Face with Hollywood*, Amsterdam: Amsterdam University Press.
Franco, Jean (1989). *Plotting Women: Gender and Representation in Mexico*, London: Verso.
Fundación Carmen Toscano (undated). Archivo histórico cinematográfico. Available at http://www.fundaciontoscano.org/esp/oax-historia.asp (accessed 15 September 2015).
Higbee, Will and Song Hwee Lim (2010). 'Concepts of transnationalism: towards a critical transnational in film studies', *Transnational Cinemas*, 1.1, pp. 7–21.
IMCINE (2015). 'Reconoce la AMACC a Bertha Navarro con el Ariel de Oro'. Available at http://www.imcine.gob.mx/comunicacion-social/comunicados-y-noticias/reconoce-la-amacc-a-bertha-navarro-con-el-ariel-de-oro (accessed 18 October 2015).

Innsdorf, Annette (1984). 'El Norte: on screen and in reality, a story of struggle'. Available at http://www.nytimes.com/1984/01/08/movies/el-norte-on-screen-and-in-reality-a-story-of-struggle.html?pagewanted=all (accessed 15 September 2015).

Jordan, Judi (2012). 'Bertha Navarro – leader of the Tequila Gang: the producing partner of Guillermo del Toro talks'. Available at https://judijordanwriter.wordpress.com/2011/09/25/requested-reading-bertha-navarro-leader-of-the-tequila-gang-the-producing-partner-of-guillermo-del-toro-talks (accessed 4 January 2014).

Kantaris, Geoffrey (1998). 'Between dolls, vampires, and cyborgs: recursive bodies in Mexican urban cinema', paper given to the Modern Languages Society, University of Cambridge, November 1998, and to the Society of Latin American Studies conference, Cambridge April 1999. Available at http://www.latin-american.cam.ac.uk/culture/vampires (accessed 25 July 2015).

MacLaird, Mischa (2013). *Aesthetics and Politics in the Mexican Film Industry*, New York: Palgrave Macmillan.

Navarro, Bertha (2012). 'El escritor aporta la semilla', in Ana Cruz (ed.),. *Bertha Navarro: Cineasta sin fronteras*, Guadalajara: Universidad de Guadalajara, pp. 247–52.

—— (1987). 'Una reflexión sobre el papel de la mujer, su compromiso y responsabilidad dentro de los medios audiovisuales y de la comunicación de masas', in *La mujer en los medios audiovisuales: memorias del VIII Festival Internacional del Nuevo Cine Latinoamericano*, México: Coordinación de Difusión Cultural/ Dirección de Actividades Cinematográficas, Universidad Nacional Autónoma de México: pp. 149–61.

Pick, Zuzana (2010). *Constructing the Image of the Mexican Revolution: Cinema and the Archive*, Austin: University of Texas Press.

Rashkin, Elissa (2001). *Women Filmmakers in Mexico: The Country of Which We Dream*, Austin: University of Texas Press.

Sánchez Prado, Ignacio (2014). *Screening Neoliberalism: Transforming Mexican Cinema 1988–2012*, Nashville: Vanderbilt University Press.

Shaw, Deborah (2013). *The Three Amigos*, Manchester: Manchester University Press.

Thornton, Niamh (2013). *Revolution and Rebellion in Mexican Film*, New York: Bloomsbury.

Vargas, Juan Carlos (2005). 'Agonía post industrial: 1990–2005', *Proceso*, 17, pp. 16–17.

Wong, Cindy Hing-Yuk (2011). *Film Festivals: Culture, People, and Power on the Global Screen*, New Brunswick: Rutgers University Press.

10

Planeta ciénaga: Lucrecia Martel and Contemporary Argentine Women's Filmmaking

Deborah Martin

> Para mí lo que Lucrecia ha tenido es un efecto muy liberador en mucha gente... En esa intimidad, en esa observación, en ese momento muerto de la tarde o de la siesta, hay un montón, y creo que ella inauguró una especie de 'planeta ciénaga' que le ha dado el pase a mucha gente.
>
> I feel that Lucrecia has had a very liberating effect on a lot of people... In that intimacy, in the observation, that dead time of the afternoon or the siesta, there is so much going on, and I think that she has inaugurated a kind of 'swamp-world', which has opened the way for many people.
>
> Julia Solomonoff (in Martin 2012)

Lucrecia Martel has been seen as a prominent figure in the experimentalism and aesthetic break with previous Argentine filmmaking that, in the late 1990s and early 2000s, came to be known as the New Argentine Cinema. If that movement has been seen as aesthetically and thematically formed by that period and its context of socio-economic crisis, the increased liberalisation of Argentine law in relation to gender and sexuality since the country's 'progressive turn' has also formed the backdrop to a marked development in cinema's challenging of gender and sexual ideology.[1] This chapter argues that Martel, herself drawing on the legacy of María Luisa Bemberg, has been at the forefront of these challenges in Argentine cinema, and examines the way they have been taken up in subsequent films by Argentine women directors. In addition to the women directors discussed in this chapter, other Argentine women directors of the first decades of the new millennium include Anahí Berneri, Lucía Cedrón, Verónica Chen, Gabriela David, Sabrina Farji, Vera Fogwill, Daniela Goggi, Sandra Gugliotta, Paula Hernández, Ana Katz, María Victoria Menis, Lorena Muñoz, Ana Poliak and Natalia Smirnoff.[2] Martel's work has played a crucial role in the development of a new feminist and queer cinema in Argentina, made by women filmmakers and focused in particular on young characters and girl figures. It has paved the way for a new wave of Argentine women filmmakers making films about children and marginal sexualities, and/or using tactile and immersive film languages and experimentation with sound to destabilise the cultural hegemony of the visual, the masculine and the adult.

Martel's first three features, *La ciénaga/The Swamp* (2001), *La niña santa/The Holy Girl* (2004), and *La mujer sin cabeza/The Headless Woman* (2008), portray the intimate worlds of the middle classes in Salta, a province of north-west Argentina. The films' domestic settings – in which the stories and perspectives of women and children predominate – provide the backdrop for a complex investigation of micropolitics, and of structures of belief, desire and prejudice pervading white, bourgeois family life. Employing an immersive, tactile aesthetics, which emphasises sound over the visual, the films also decentre traditional narrative forms through ambiguity and eventlessness, often featuring a promiscuous multiplicity of narrative directions which are left undeveloped or unconfirmed. In these films, desire has a revolutionary quality and travels wildly in multiple directions: incestuous, inter-generational, lesbian, heterosexual, inter-species, autoerotic and across boundaries of class and ethnicity. Desire is associated with the possibility for radical change that is the thematic undercurrent of these films. In the films' refusal to adhere to a central conflict formula, their insistence on hinting at and alluding to multiple narrative possibilities, along with their multisensory sensuality, there is a queerness, an echoing of the refusal to channel and contain desire. There is a strong emphasis on touch and the tactile in these works, and frequent reference to smell, as well as an unusual predominance of sound – often heightened, hyper-real, acousmatic and/or unidentified – over the visual. Martel's work can be understood as the inception of a tendency in Argentine women's filmmaking which pairs unconventional and transgressive portrayals of gender, of sexuality and of childhood with aesthetic choices which are transgressive of hegemonic visual codes, including the slowing of time and slackening of action, and the privileging of the tactile, the aquatic and even the abject.

In her challenges to reigning gender and sexual regimes, Martel has influenced a subsequent generation of women filmmakers, but she herself was clearly influenced by a pioneer of Latin American feminist filmmaking, María Luisa Bemberg, probably Latin America's and certainly Argentina's most renowned feminist filmmaker, whose work initiated such challenges for Argentine film in the 1970s.[3] Martel compares her first feature, *La ciénaga*, to Bemberg's *Miss Mary* (1986) because of its focus on the decline of a traditional upper-class family (cit. Oubiña 2009: 13). Like *Miss Mary*, *La ciénaga*'s matriarch is named Mecha, and suffers an emotional and mental deterioration brought on (at least in part) by her unfaithful and indifferent husband. Like the earlier film, too, *La ciénaga* explores the relationship of the bourgeois child/adolescent, to live-in employees: in *Miss Mary* this is the eponymous governess and carer of the children, who ends up in a sexual relationship with one of them; in *La ciénaga*, the teenage Momi nurses a passionate attachment to live-in maid Isabel. Both films constitute an exploration of how social and economic structures produce the strange presence of servants within the bourgeois home and the effects of this on the emotional life of the family, a strand within Latin American filmmaking that has important feminist implications and that Deborah Shaw, in Chapter 5 of this collection, links to the increased participation of women in filmmaking.

Like Bemberg, Martel worked with producer Lita Stantic, who had become associated through her work with Bemberg with a tradition of feminist filmmaking in Argentina, and who later worked on some of the most canonical films of the New Argentine Cinema, including *Mundo grúa/Crane World* (Trapero, 1999), *Bolivia* (Caetano, 2001), *La ciénaga* and *La niña santa*.[4] Jessica Stites Mor points out that while Martel does not readily subscribe to a feminist political programme (2007: 149), her work is nevertheless a part of feminist film culture in Argentina, a space

Stites Mor proposes exists thanks to Bemberg. There are several moments of homage to Bemberg in Martel's work. In *La niña santa* there is a pivotal moment on which the film turns dramatically. It is a moment which – as I have argued elsewhere (Martin 2016: 64–5) – figures an act of ideological rupture, a transgression of the intermeshed social conventions of gender, sexuality and childhood. This is the moment when middle-aged Doctor Jano (Carlos Belloso) presses up against the teenage Amalia (María Alché) from behind in the street, and in which she turns around to face him. This turning around and looking at Jano reverses her position as passive female, passive child, and shows her assuming the position of desiring subject; indeed, the subject of a transgressive desire for the older man. This moment plays out to a significant piece of diegetic music, performed by a street musician: 'L'amour est un oiseau rebelle' ('Love is a rebellious bird') from Bizet's *Carmen*, a musical reference to the bodily transgression of the dwarf Charlotte (Alejandra Podestá) in Bemberg's *De eso no se habla/We Don't Want to Talk About It* (1993), where she dances in front of a mirror to the same music.[5] In Bemberg's film, this scene signifies a liberation of the different body which others in the film try to subjugate, closet and repress. Both sequences – linked by the music, of which the lyrics, are, of course, crucial – signal sexual awakenings which society does not deem permissible.

In its strong emphasis on the conflict between desire and social roles and expectations, *La niña santa* also echoes Bemberg's *Camila* (1984), a period drama based on the life of a young socialite, Camila O'Gorman, and a priest, Father Ladislao Gutiérrez, who in Argentina in the mid-nineteenth century embarked on a love affair and were eventually executed by the regime of Juan Manuel de Rosas. In particular, Jano's struggles with his conscience in *La niña santa* echo those of Ladislao in the earlier film. In Jano's case these intensify when he realises that the woman with whom he has been carrying on a flirtation (Helena) and the girl he has groped in the street (Amalia) are mother and daughter, as well as when Amalia starts to pursue him and declare her love for him. Jano's tortured countenance evokes that of *Camila*'s Ladislao, as he battles with the opposing demands of his passionate love for Camila and his religious vows. While *Camila* examines the role of desire in relation to a religious vocation which prohibits any sexual contact, *La niña santa* explores the desire that inheres subtly in the field of medicine, and in doctor–patient contact: Jano assumes a medical relationship with Helena when he turns out to be an expert in a condition which afflicts her and invites her to participate in a doctor-patient role-play at a conference taking place at her hotel. While Bemberg's male subject deviates from the rules of the priesthood, he does so within heteronormative parameters; in contrast, Martel's male subject harbours 'perverse' or more clearly deviant desires for pressing up against underage strangers in the street. Martel's film refuses to pass any judgement on the desire it portrays, while Bemberg creates strong emotional identification with the heterosexual desire of the young couple; however, both films show the desires they portray to be harshly judged by society.

Martel's films, like Bemberg's, stage conflicts between desire and social rules. Like Bemberg's, they also show characters transgressing these rules and focus in particular on the situations and stories of women and girls, examining how they are limited by, or how they transgress, gendered and sexual codes and conventions. Generally speaking, in Martel's work it is young girls who are associated, like Amalia in the example just discussed, with transgressive desires or actions and older women are represented as frustrated by their domestic confinement, their actions thwarted by, or dependent upon, the men around them. For example, the young female characters Momi (*La ciénaga*), Amalia (*La niña santa*) and Candita (*La mujer sin cabeza*) tend to challenge the status quo and have lesbian or intergenerational desires, while their mothers or older relations seem limited in their ability to act, conditioned by patriarchal and bourgeois ideology and to be controlled (in various ways) by the men around them. For Ana Forcinito, however, there is a crucial difference between the feminist politics of Martel's feature films and those of Bemberg. For Forcinito, who discusses *La ciénaga* and *La niña santa*, Bemberg's films offer a more thoroughgoing exploration of feminist possibilities of escape or rebellion, whereas Martel's are more focused on analysing femininity as it exists within confinement and domestic enclosure (2006: 115). We might posit that, in addition to the more limited possibilities of escape afforded Martel's characters, there is a shift also in her films' attitude to moral judgements vis-à-vis those of Bemberg. If Bemberg's films can be associated with a 'second wave' position – 'an exposition of a feminist morality concerned with issues of right and wrong, good and bad' (Shildrick 2004: 70) – then Martel's might be perhaps more easily associated with a 'third wave' ethics, that is, an 'ethics without programmes or rules' (70): Martel's films refuse to pass judgement on characters, have no truck with notions of guilt or innocence, and refuse to paint, for example, Amalia as a victim and Jano as monster. An aspect of third-wave politics that is shared by Martel's work and by Bemberg's last film, *De eso no se habla*, is the way that gendered and sexual liberation is linked to other forms of liberation. Here, feminist politics does not remain narrowly focused on women, but instead begins to recognise and expose the connections between oppressions of gender, class, colour, race and others. In *De eso*, the bodily repression and regulation of the dwarf, Charlotte, come to stand for a whole range of repressions: her love affair with Ludovico for more common forms of sexual dissidence (Foster 2003); and her oppression as female and as having a non-standard body, which is compared with that of ethnic and cultural outsider Mojamé, who we discover at the end has narrated the film, and whose voice is provided by the famous gay actor Alfredo Alcón (Foster 2003: 18). In this way, Bemberg's *De eso* echoes a key objective of third-wave feminism, which is to move women's struggle outwards, looking for the structural links with other forms of oppression based around ethnicity, cultural difference, disability and sexuality.[6]

In Martel, this 'third wave' sensibility is associated with the young girl's (lesbian) desire and its potential to overcome not just her gendered and sexual positioning by the bourgeois family but also barriers of race and social class. The clearest example here is that of Candita and her girlfriend Cuca in *La mujer sin cabeza*, characters which echo Momi and Isabel in *La ciénaga*, all of whom are also strongly echoed by the characters of Lala and Aílin in Lucía Puenzo's *El niño pez/The Fish Child* (2009). To nuance Forcinito's position above, I suggest that Martel's work does strongly *suggest* possibilities of rupture and escape, and that, even though these narrative possibilities are unfulfilled or pushed to the edges of the frame, it is in young girls – increasingly stronger, more rebellious and agentic young girls with each new film – that this potential exists. These girls are the subjects of transgressive desires – for other girls, older women or men; they speak truth to the feckless or irresponsible adults in their lives, the only characters to break with regimes of silence and denial; they are seen as dirty or contaminated by the white, heterosexist, bourgeois order; and they form alliances and romances across racial and class divides. In stark contrast to adult women in the films, they do not conform to cinematic standards of to-be-looked-at femininity: instead, they subvert the codes of conventional cinema by becoming the bearers of the gaze, by existing on the edges of the frame, and by engaging in tactile, sonic and olfactory forms of knowledge. These girls set an important precedent in Argentine filmmaking which is taken up in different ways by filmmakers like Lucía Puenzo, Julia Solomonoff and Albertina Carri, whose own girl characters strongly echo elements of the Martelian girl's subversive behaviour and cinematic positioning. As in Martel and Bemberg, in these later filmmakers there is a 'third wave' tendency to examine gender alongside, and in relationship to, other social oppressions and marginalisations. Citing Karen Warren, Leslie Heywood and Jennifer Drake make the point that 'at a conceptual level the eradication of sexist oppression requires the eradication of the other forms of oppression', and this is a crucial tenet of third-wave feminism (Warren, cit. Heywood and Drake 2004: 21). In Martel's work there is, especially in *La ciénaga* and *La mujer sin cabeza*, a biting critique of white bourgeois Argentina's treatment of the indigenous and *mestizo* poor. It is a committed and sustained critique, which investigates and analyses the denigration and othering of this group through speech, insult, and social and political structures. In Puenzo's *El niño pez* and Solomonoff's *El último verano de la boyita/The Last Summer of La Boyita* (2009), structures of class and ethnicity are brought to the fore and tackled by the narratives which foreground sexual dissidence and difference, and in each case the relationship between these intermeshing structures is scrutinised. In this sense, the work of recent women filmmakers in Argentina can be understood to continue the legacy of class-oriented political filmmaking in Latin America, which was hitherto defined by the late 1950s–1970s New Latin American Cinema. To the long-standing tradition of political cinema in Latin America, these filmmakers bring awareness of debates and struggles around gender and sexuality, as well as a broadening out of these debates to include a new focus on childhood subjectivity and experience.

While in Martel there is a focus on girls, it is also true that her films privilege children in general, gaggles of boys and girls who run wild through the forest in *La ciénaga*, or through the hotel in *La niña santa*. In *La ciénaga* the film's perspective and sensorial charge is strongly aligned with five-year-old Luchi. Martel has spoken about thinking of her camera as a child of 10 or 11, and of valuing the child's gaze for its curiosity and lack of judgement, its ability to perceive more, to perceive what adults have learned not to (Martin 2011). The aesthetics of Martel's films produce not so much a child's gaze but rather a child's sensorium: the experiments with touch and sound which pervade Martel's films are a means of constantly gesturing to what is beyond straight, white, adult, bourgeois subjectivity, that is to say, it is a means of evoking the 'aberrant forms of life and consciousness', which Maurice Merleau-Ponty attributed, among others, to 'children and madmen' (2004: 56), and which are repressed in conventional cinematic forms.

Films about children have become an important feature of the recent Argentine filmmaking scene. Many films which look explicitly back at the period of military rule do so through the eyes of a child, but this strand is not the focus of this essay.[7] I propose there is another strand, a 'swamp-world' of films focused on children and young people, made by women directors. These include the films by Solomonoff and Puenzo already mentioned, as well as Puenzo's *XXY* (2007), Albertina Carri's *Geminis* (2005) and *La rabia/Anger* (2008) and Celina Murga's *Una semana solos/A Week Alone* (2007). In these films, in varying ways, the marginal perspectives and stories of children and adolescents are given prominence, just as 'forms of life and consciousness' which lie outside dominant experience are foregrounded. This focus on childhood and youth in the work of recent Argentine women filmmakers can be read as a continuation of the 'third wave' broadening out of feminist discourse, as women filmmakers, through children, focus on traditionally suppressed or marginalised experience.

Women and children have traditionally occupied comparable positions – of silence, of marginalisation and of subordination – in patriarchal culture. Women writers and filmmakers have often focused on children and child protagonists as a way to explore the domestic realm and family life, and to question and subvert its politics. Because myths of childhood function in similar ways to myths of femininity as a means of structuring and upholding the patriarchal family, and as the sexuality of both women and children has traditionally been negated, women artists often focus on the demythologisation of childhood, especially notions of innocence.[8] In Latin America there is a tradition of women writers, including Silvina

Ocampo and Clarice Lispector, who have written about child protagonists, attempted to create childhood worlds in fiction, or experimented with poetics to suggest a child's perspective. Like many of the films discussed here, Ocampo's work often focuses on children and servants, and the capacity of children to cross class boundaries (Mackintosh 2003: 69) while Lispector's features a series of transgressive young females, 'naughty little girls' (Williams 2013), whom the writer uses to explore the social strictures placed on women in mid-twentieth-century Brazil. In turn, women filmmakers now place child protagonists at the centre of their representations, and these often female child characters both act as vehicles for transgression on a narrative level and generate attempts to mould the cinematic medium to reflect childhood sensorial, psychic and spatial experience. This trend can be aligned with similar attempts in the work of recent European filmmakers. Writing on French culture, Emma Wilson notes the similar importance of themes of child 'autonomy, resilience and resistance' in the work of writers Marguerite Duras, Colette, Amélie Nothomb, Sarah Kofman and Chantal Chawaf (2007: 171), but argues that it is women filmmakers in particular who more recently 'have made the (female) child [...] their sentient, sensing and apprehensive subject' (171).

The child's sensorial world that is created in recent Argentine women's filmmaking has a strong emphasis on touch and the tactile, on sound over the visual, and on embodiment. It is Luchi's little hands in *La ciénaga* as they press up against a dirty window pane; it is Amalia's body as she repeatedly moves in and out of the water in *La niña santa* (see Figure 10.1). These cinematic images and aesthetics are characteristics of the Martelian 'swamp-world', which I offer as a porous, fluid description of Argentine women's filmmaking of the mid- to late 2000s. I borrow the term from Julia Solomonoff's description, in the epigraph to this chapter, of the effect Martel has had on the aesthetics and cinematic visions of some filmmakers that came after her. Solomonoff does not mention women, but this tendency to observe intimacy (rather than simply an observational tendency which would be associated with the New Argentine Cinema more generally), to observe the 'dead time', or seemingly eventless scenes of family and domestic life, is especially associated with *La ciénaga* and with the work of the other women filmmakers discussed here. There is a second aesthetic tendency that is implied but not explicitly stated by Solomonoff, and this is the swampy, wet, sticky and dirty nature of this world, its preference for the aquatic, for swimming pools, lakes and rainstorms. This, in turn, is associated with forms of tactile and haptic filmmaking which decentre the visual and engage the spectator in a physical, bodily relationship to the film world, diminishing the sense, common to conventional visual forms, of perspectival separateness, and producing a sense of embodiment.

An aspect of the 'swamp-world' – exhibited in films like Carri's *La rabia*, Murga's *Una semana solos* and Solomonoff's *El último verano* – is its slowing of time and slackening of action, currently a dominant mode of the global arts cinema which tends to be preferred at international film festivals. In these swamp-world films, though, temporal slowness and eventlessness are in particular associated with the child's gaze, as well as with creating the time in the filmic construction to engage the extra-visual senses. In this sense the films echo Deleuze's proposition that the advent of the time-image was linked to the prominence of the child's gaze in neo-realism (1989: 3), as well as his discussion of how the slowing of time opens up the image to the tactile (12). Although focused on different

Figure 10.1. Watery worlds: Amalia (María Alché) in *La niña santa* (Lucrecia Martel, 2004).

social contexts, *La rabia*, *Una semana solos* and *El último verano* all feature a strong emphasis on idleness, on waiting, or on boredom, which is strongly reminiscent of the atmosphere of *La ciénaga*, and which can be seen as a means of moulding the cinematic medium to the child's perspective, if the child is understood as having a different, less regulated experience of time from the adult experience. Carri's *La rabia* focuses on Nati, a girl of around five or six years of age, mute, perhaps autistic, who lives with her mother and father, *campesinos* (peasants) in La Rabia, an isolated rural community in the province of Buenos Aires (Kairuz 2008: 12).[9] Nati does not speak, but (like girls in films by Martel and others) she is the bearer of a transgressive gaze. She voyeuristically watches acts of violence which take place around her: her mother's brutal sex life with a neighbour, her friend Ladeado being beaten by the same neighbour, his father. The film's aesthetics function to undermine notions of childhood innocence and to communicate the child's embodied experience. The film opens with an idyllic sequence of Nati gambolling through a hazy dawn or twilight landscape, bathed in soft pink light; that is to say, it strongly references the romantic trope of child in the country, a trope which it then goes on to dismantle over the course of the film, showing the country to be a place of degradation and violence, and Nati to be a disquietingly sexual child who is silent, unknowable and uncanny.[10] Nati does not speak, but she does scream, a scream which disrupts the order of family and community: when she screams, she is physically removed from community gatherings and secluded. Her body is the site of a gendered coercion and transgression: we watch as she is pushed and pulled, bathed and dried, instructed in what it is proper for 'las nenas' (little girls) to do (draw flowers). We also witness her physical resistance: her urinating and removal of her clothes outdoors; her desire to play with, clean and fire guns; her strange sexual and violent drawings; her screaming; and her acts of voyeurism. Nati emerges as a radically unknowable child who sees everything but reveals little. For Carri, Nati's drawings 'va[n] en contra de esa idea de los niños como reservorio de la ingenuidad' ('contradict the idea of children as repositories of innocence') (cit. in Kairuz 2008: 13).

In *La rabia*, alongside the slowing of time and evocation of idleness through the use of *temps morts*, Carri also experiments with filmic means of moulding the medium to a child's perception, using heightened and hyperreal sound, tactile images and animation. Nati's drawings have narrative importance: they both reflect and have an impact on the world around her, directly affecting the narrative. They have an impact also on the film language, as the drawings morph into several semi-abstract animation sequences over the course of the film which constitute an attempt to represent the unrepresentable: emotion, reverie, imagination, the inner world of the (mute, autistic) child. These sequences represent an opportunity for filmic experimentation beyond the constraints of mainstream narrative fiction film. Like the rest of the film, these animation sequences are filled with heightened, tactile sound – crunching, cracking – and sound which generates a sense of embodiment, such as breathing. The visual language of the whole film is similarly tactile and visceral, with frequent images of blood, and an important and graphic sequence which features a pig being killed, skinned and eviscerated. The immersive and tactile qualities of *La rabia* are encapsulated in a single image at the beginning of the film, when Nati's friend Ladeado drowns a litter of weasels in a pond: we watch as the animals struggle inside an opaque hessian bag and see their movements inside the bag as it slowly disappears under the water. The image recalls sequences from *La ciénaga*, in which we see Momi plunge into a putrid pool but do not see her emerge, and in which the film returns on several occasions to a cow mired neck-deep in a swamp.

These 'swamp-world' films, importantly, share an emphasis on aquatic environments and, beyond this, a special concern with wetness, stickiness, bodily fluids, the tactile qualities of liquid on skin or of immersion in water. Water is a crucial element of Martel's filmic world and has the capacity to signify both containment and capture, on the one hand, and the transgression of boundaries, on the other. The swimming pool, which appears in all Martel's feature films, signifies the social and economic power of the wealthy white class on whom her films centre to command a resource to which poorer communities nearby have far less access. Martel has commented on the fact that wealthy Argentines have access to swimming pools while poor people on the other side of town don't have enough water to meet basic needs (in Guillen 2009). Murga's *Una semana solos* also makes use of the swimming pool, a focal point of the *country* (country club/ gated community) in which the film is set, to draw out social tensions.[11] In this film, a group of children and adolescents – a mixture of siblings and cousins – are left alone in their country club house with just the maid to care for them, while their parents holiday elsewhere.[12] As Wilson has noted, there is a new emphasis in recent film on children in their own communities, beyond the supervision of adults (2007: 171). The large group of children running wild in *Una semana solos* with little adult supervision has clear echoes of *La ciénaga*, as do other details, such as the incestuous attractions between children. In *Una semana solos*, where the holidays pass slowly and idly, the children pass the time by breaking into neighbouring houses. The maid's brother Juan comes to stay at the house and, being of a similar age to some of the adolescents, tries to integrate into the group, but this is not easy as the white, middle-class kids will not accept the dark-skinned, dark-haired Juan, immediately recognising his lower socio-economic status. He accompanies them on one of their housebreaking escapades, which gets out of hand, with ketchup and shaving cream being sprayed everywhere, wardrobes and cupboards raided. When the group are discovered, they blame Juan. Before this incident occurs, Juan accompanies several of the teenage boys to the club's swimming pool. He tries to lower himself into it, but it seems clear this is not a usual experience for him. As he tries to lounge casually by the pool with the other boys, one of them gets up to buy drinks for the others, but brings back nothing for Juan, signalling his lack of belonging. In this film, water is associated with the creation and display of social and economic power (Strang 2004: 125); the swimming pool – a must in the country club, which segregates the better-off from the rest of society – is used as a marker of social privilege and to reinforce social distinctions.

However, to return to the meanings of water in Martel's work, it is important to note that it is used as a multifaceted image. The connotations of social exclusion are balanced in Martel with more positive associations, as well as with a strong tactile potential which itself has multiple associations, including both pleasure and disgust. In Martel, water's propensity to be contained and channelled – to take the form of its container – as well as its mutability and transformative potential, its capacity to override or transgress physical boundaries and forms through permeation, evaporation and overflowing, make it a versatile image with a range of political meanings. In particular, Martel associates water and desire: that which can be contained and controlled but which also transgresses the boundaries which attempt to contain it. This trope is echoed in films like *XXY*, *El último verano de la boyita* and *El niño pez*, where watery locales and immersion in water give form and tactile resonance to marginalised corporeal experience or forbidden desires, or, as Deborah Shaw argues in her discussion of *El niño pez* in this collection, suggest a utopian space of possibilities (143).

In *XXY*, as the young intersex protagonist Alex – who has been brought up as a girl, and who is played by the actress Inés Efrón – floats on the surface of the sea by her house, she seems both to contemplate her difficult sexual and corporeal situation, as well as to gain some sense of freedom and peace from the sensation of floating and the action of water on skin. *XXY* has been praised for its foregrounding of intersex desire (Mayer 2008: 15) – a marginal desire which had previously received little if any cinematic attention. Alex's desire causes her problems: her anal penetration of the teenage Álvaro does not fit with the feminine role her parents have assigned her. In privileging the desire of an intersex character who seems to be attracted to both boys and girls and who refuses to choose a sex/gender to 'become' (through either hormone therapy or surgery), *XXY* suggests a gender and sexual fluidity which is encapsulated in the image of the watery environment in which Alex peacefully floats. The image is underscored by Alex's association with marine life and the turtle tags she wears around her neck.

Like *XXY*, Solomonoff's *El último verano de la boyita* (released two years later) also focuses on intersexuality, telling the story of Jorgelina, a pre-pubescent girl who visits her family's farm where her old playmate Mario lives. Over the course of the film, she discovers that Mario menstruates, and we come to understand that Mario is a genetic female who was supposed to be male at birth due to a large clitoris and a high level of male hormones, but who is genetically female.[13] The film is radical not only in its figuring of intersexuality through the Mario character, but also of little Jorgelina's fascination with Mario, her childish desire, which can be read as a deviant desire because of Mario's uncertain gender and sexual positioning. In an important sequence, Jorgelina plays in a swimming pool, repeating the word 'Mario' to herself over and over again in a whisper. As she does this, she bobs up and down, in and out of the water (see Figure 10.2). The sequence – which echoes the images of Amalia in *La niña santa* discussed above – strongly connects water and its sensual

Figure 10.2. Water and queer childhood desire: Jorgelina (Guadalupe Alonso) in *El último verano de la boyita* (Julia Solomonoff, 2009).

qualities on the skin to desire, and especially, as here, to the depiction of marginal sexualities and desires which are often beyond representation: the desire of the young child and non-normative desires. Later, as Jorgelina helps Mario unstrap the bandages which he has been forced to wear on his developing breasts, the two children stand in a river, which flows around and through their legs, at once an image of release and freedom as well as of physical pleasure in sensation. *El último verano*, as well as Martel's later films, were produced by the Almodóvar brothers' El Deseo productions, and Pedro Almodóvar himself is known for depicting children as subjects of trangressive desire in *La mala educación* (2004), as do *El último verano* and *La niña santa*.

Lastly, in *El niño pez*, water becomes the psychic and emotional centre of the film, which is a cross-class lesbian romance, with strong echoes of *La mujer sin cabeza* and *La ciénaga*. The resemblance to this theme in Martel is intensified by the fact that Lala, a rich white girl who is in love with her family's Paraguayan maid, Ailín, is played by Inés Efrón, who also plays Candita in *La mujer*. In *El niño pez*, Lala and Ailín bathe together in romantically lit bathroom scenes, and this watery refuge from the external world (in which Lala's judge father will claim his right to sex with Ailín, Lala will murder him and Ailín will be convicted for the crime). This bathroom scene links their tender and erotic relationship with another aquatic environment, the long-lost lake in which Ailín had to drown a baby which she could not keep and to which she and Lala are drawn back over the course of the film. It signals a freedom, and a freedom of desire, which these lovers aspire to and eventually attain. Efrón, through her roles in these films and in *XXY*, comes to stand for a particular rebellious, androgynous 'girl'-hood during this period of the late 2000s, a cinematic symbol of the challenges to gender and sexual norms that were happening in the legal and political spheres. She emerges as the girl-bearer of a transgressive gaze, the blue-tinged, marine (in *XXY*), yellow-tinged (in *La mujer*, where she has hepatitis), sickly or wan-looking girl whose corporeality is coded as abject and who is liminal to and subversive of social structures.

In the 'swamp-world', watery environments and tactile, wet, damp or squelchy filmic aesthetics engender a materiality which may be pleasurable or disgusting. These films, which often also have a strong emphasis on blood and other body fluids, depict transgressive and marginal desires using a liquid, tactile or abject aesthetic which treads a thin line between desire and disgust, and which echoes the films' transgressive subject matter. Indeed, these aesthetic tendencies transgress the rules of dominant cinema, displacing the hegemony of the visual, and subverting Cartesian perspective, which allows the viewing subject to grasp and dominate the image. Instead, the distinction between the film and the viewer's body is undermined, and the viewer invited to undergo the film as an embodied experience. I draw here on the work of Laura Marks and Vivian Sobchack, which proposes that haptic or tactile images may blur borders between film and viewer, inviting embodied spectatorship (see Marks 2000, 2002; Sobchack 2004). Along with the images of wallowing and water play or immersion I have discussed, these films are replete with images and sensory evocations of bleeding (*La ciénaga, El último verano de la boyita, Geminis*), of sweat (*La ciénaga*) and of dirt (*La ciénaga, La niña santa, La mujer sin cabeza, El último verano, Geminis*). They evoke the tactile qualities of sticky, squelchy or swampy places (*La ciénaga, La rabia*) and include visceral images of the corpses of dead animals, complete with blood and innards (*El último verano, La rabia, La mujer*). They use sustained and haptic images of skin or hair (*La ciénaga, La mujer, Geminis*).

In this sense, the films create a kind of abject materiality which refers both to the materiality of the body and its fluids/wastes, as well as to the human body's tactile relationship to the world around it. Kristeva understood the abject as that which is rejected, cast out of the body in order for the subject to assume its status as subject – ultimately the mother's body, for which wastes, fluids and substances generating disgust come to stand. In Kristeva's theory the abject is associated with that which 'disturbs identity, system, order. What does not respect borders, positions, rules. The in-between, the ambiguous, the composite' (1982: 4). It is important to note that, as I have argued, these films tend to represent desires, bodies and experiences that have been traditionally marginalised and/or abjected: they disturb social order or disrespect socially and culturally established borders. In many of these films there is also an emphasis on proximity – the proximity of the camera to its object, the haptic images this produces, and the evocation of a tactile gaze, or images of touch(ing). In this sense, too, the films experiment with creating a filmic language which evokes the experience and perception of the child, for whom the sense of touch may be more important as a way of knowing the world than the visual. These films create a sensory access to childhood through the body, focusing on its relations of nearness and touch to bodies and matter. The child is posited as a subject in these films and at the same time the emphasis on childhood experience and on embodiment destabilises the adult viewing subject. As children are increasingly recognised as subjects on a political and legal level, children's perspectives and experiences enter visual culture in new ways.

Carri's *Geminis* opens with a long take which, in close-up, shows a needle penetrating skin, being drawn back and slowly filling with blood. We see the skin in microscopic detail: its pores, ridged texture and hairs all more visible than they would be to the naked eye. A vial is placed alongside other vials, shown in close-up and encrusted with dried blood. Like Martel's films, *Geminis* contains a strong sense of the horror and the unknown lurking in the middle-class household. In the initial sequences, a disembodied, seemingly subjective camera unconnected to a particular point of view roams the corridors of a well appointed house. We find out that this belongs to a wealthy family whose eldest son returns home with his fiancée, and whose younger twins become involved in a secret incestuous relationship. What in Martel is merely allusion – the hints of desire or a lack of boundaries between family members– is in *Geminis* (released in 2005, four years after *La ciénaga*) the central narrative of the film. The forbidden passion between the twins, Meme and Jere, plays out against the backdrop of normative heterosexuality signified by their older brother's wedding, with which much of the narrative is taken up. *Geminis* shares many characteristics I have identified as part of the swamp-world: it foregrounds the body and skin, as in the opening sequence, as well as acts of shaving and bodily care, and accidents which result in breakages and lesions of the human body; the twins bathe together in a jacuzzi, and creep up on one another in the shower; their writing of each other's names with their fingers in a steamed-up mirror is an image of touch and evokes the sense of wetness. The soundtrack is heightened and hyperreal, giving prominence to sounds of nature, water running and birds, as well as unidentified sounds which do not always support the narrative. Once again, the film foregrounds transgressive desires, as well as using these various images and aesthetic techniques to create an embodied viewing experience which transgresses normative viewing practices, constructing a spectatorial subjectivity in a tactile relation to the body of the film.

This chapter has argued that some significant thematic and aesthetic trends link the work of Lucrecia Martel to that of some Argentine women filmmakers who made films in the years following *La ciénaga* and alongside Martel's later work. Despite differences between the various films I have discussed here, I have highlighted some areas where they coincide, to produce a new critical understanding of Martel's effect on women filmmakers in Argentina. By focusing on intersexuality, on cross-class, cross-ethnic romance, on the subjugation and marginalisation of Argentina's indigenous and poor, and on the marginalised desires and experience of children and sexual dissidents, the work of these women filmmakers suggests an impulse we find in Martel and, before her, in Bemberg. This is the impulse to move beyond a narrow woman-centred focus – even in films which do look at the lives of women and girls and the construction of femininity – in an exploration of the desires, experiences and epistemologies of groups traditionally excluded from a subject position. As Shildrick writes, 'the feminism of the third wave is always intensely concerned with the ethics of the other, whoever that other might be. The figure of "woman" to whom the second wave directed its attention takes her place as just one marker among a multiplicity of significant differences' (2004: 69). The swamp thus comes to signify this tactile and haptic world in which the focus is on intimacy and desire rather than event, and in which the feminist critique merges and mingles with a range of other important political critiques, insights and struggles. The sensory charge of this swamp-world distances it from conventional cinematic aesthetics, destabilising the cultural hegemony of the visual and the adult in favour of a body-centred cinema which both tells stories about different bodies, different desires, and constructs an embodied viewing subjectivity.

Notes

1. In 2010, Argentina became the first Latin American country to legalise same-sex marriage, and in 2012 passed a comprehensive transgender rights bill, allowing transgender people to change their gender on public documents without undergoing surgery and without medical or legal permission. However, a spate of killings of transgender people in Argentina in late 2015 could be considered a backlash against the legal advances. Queer filmmaking is experiencing a boom in Latin America, with acclaimed Mexican director Julián Hernández's *Rabioso sol, rabioso cielo/Raging Sun, Raging Sky* (2009) and the Peruvian *Contracorriente/Undertow* (Fuentes-León, 2009). In Argentina (in addition to the queer-themed films discussed in this chapter) Marco Berger's *Ausente* (2011) deals with a young male student who tries to lure his teacher into a sexual encounter, while the protagonist of Anahí Berneri's *Un año sin amor* (2005) is an HIV-positive writer who tries to find love in S/M bars.
2. Notable in relation to the themes of this chapter are Menis, whose *El cielito* (2004) deals with the relationship of an itinerant man to a baby he steals from a situation of domestic violence, and whose *La cámara oscura* (2008) features a child's perspective and animation. Cedrón also uses a child's perspective and sensory memories as a means of exploring the country's traumatic past in *Cordero de Dios* (2008).
3. For more on Bemberg, see King and Whitaker (2000) and Rufinelli (2002).
4. For more on Stantic, see the Introduction to this volume (12, 26 n. 13).
5. Thanks to Deborah Shaw for this observation.
6. For Shildrick, 'the close attention now paid to global concerns, to non-normative sexualities, to discourses of race and ethnicity, to postcoloniality […] has greatly enhanced not only the political, but also the ethical valency of feminism. These moves to a more out-going and ultimately less self-concerned understanding of the feminist agenda […] have […] mobilised a much richer analysis of the operation of power and difference' (2007: 71).
7. Examples of Argentine films which depict the dictatorship years through the eyes of a child include *Kamchatka* (Piñeyro, 2001), *Cautiva/Captive* (Biraben,

2005), *Andrés no quiere dormir la siesta/Andrés Doesn't Want to Take a Nap* (Bustamante, 2009) and *Cordero de Dios/Lamb of God* (Cedrón, 2008). Other similar Southern Cone films include the Chilean *Machuca* (Wood, 2004) and the Uruguayan *Paisito/Small Country* (Díez, 2008).

8. Gill Rye writes that: 'in their portrayal of children, women authors are attentive to moral and ethical issues, to social, gender and power relations, to memory and history, to plurality and to demythologizing childhood, girlhood and femininity. Ultimately, in portraying the child's voice or viewpoint in their work, the authors examined here are also shown to be reflecting on their own portrayals, challenging the conventional stereotypes and myths of childhood, and creatively engaging with the child as a human subject' (2013: 124).
9. Carri went to live in this region at the age of four, when her parents were 'disappeared' by the military regime (1976–82). The film was shot in Roque Pérez, a village near La Rabia.
10. The director has said that the film '[registra] como se ve el campo desde la ciudad, para luego desarmar esa visión' ('registers an urban vision of the countryside, and then proceeds to dismantle that vision') (Kairuz 2008:12).
11. *Una semana solos* is one of a number of films depicting the growing phenomenon of 'barrios cerrados', or gated communities, in Argentina, especially in the Greater Buenos Aires region. Like others of its type, including *Cara de queso, mi primer gueto* (2006) and *Las viudas de los jueves* (2009), the film is critical of this kind of living, and depicts the threats to its inhabitants as coming from within.
12. Celina Murga has made two other films about children and young people, *Escuela normal* (2012) and *La tercera orilla* (2014).
13. The medical name for this condition is congenital adrenal hyperplasia. 'Intersex' is a general term which refers to a number of hormonal and anatomical conditions in which a person is born with characteristics or anatomy which do not fit the typical definitions of male and female. Congenital adrenal hyperplasia is one of these. See http://www.isna.org/faq/conditions/cah (accessed 22 October 2015).

References

Deleuze, Gilles (1989). *Cinema 2: The Time-Image*, New York: Continuum.
Forcinito, Ana (2006). 'Mirada cinematográfica y género sexual: mímica, erotismo y ambigüedad en Lucrecia Martel', *Chasqui*, 35. 2, pp. 109–30.
Foster, David (2003). 'Introit: queer difference', in *Queer Issues in Contemporary Latin American Cinema*, Austin: University of Texas Press, pp. 1–18.
Guillen, Michael (2009). 'Argentine cinema, *The Headless Woman*: onstage conversation between Lucrecia Martel and B. Ruby Rich', *Twitch*, 30 August.

Available at http://twitchfilm.com/2009/08/argentine-cinema-the-headless-womanonstage-conversation-between-lucrecia-ma.html (accessed 8 October 2015).

Heywood, Leslie and Jennifer Drake (2004). '"It's all about the Benjamins": economic determinants of third wave feminism in the United States', in Stacy Gillis, Gillian Howie and Rebecca Munford (eds), *Third Wave Feminism*, Basingstoke: Palgrave Macmillan, pp. 13–23.

Kairuz, Mariano (2008). 'En el campo las espinas', *Página 12 Radar*, 4 May, pp. 12–13.

King, John and Sheila Whitaker (eds) (2000). *An Argentine Passion: María Luisa Bemberg and Her Films*, London: Verso.

Kristeva, Julia (1982). *Powers of Horror: An Essay on Abjection*, trans. Leon S. Roudiez, New York: Columbia University Press.

Mackintosh, Fiona (2003). *Childhood in the Works of Silvina Ocampo and Alejandra Pizarnik*, Woodbridge: Tamesis.

Marks, Laura U. (2000). *The Skin of the Film: Intercultural Cinema, Embodiment, and the Senses*, Durham: Duke University Press.

—— (2002). *Touch: Sensuous Theory and Multisensory Media*, Minnesota: University of Minneapolis Press.

Martin, Deborah (2011). 'Interview with Lucrecia Martel', 23 October, unpublished.

—— (2012) 'Interview with Julia Solomonoff', 28 April, unpublished.

—— (2016). *The Cinema of Lucrecia Martel*, Manchester: Manchester University Press.

Mayer, Sophie (2008). 'Family business', *Sight and Sound*, 18.6, pp. 14–16.

Merleau-Ponty, Maurice (2004). *The World of Perception*, trans. Oliver Davis, London: Routledge.

Oubiña, David (2009). *Estudio crítico sobre La ciénaga: entrevista a Lucrecia Martel*, Buenos Aires: Picnic Editorial.

Rye, Gill (2013). 'Introduction: writing childhood in post-war women's literature', *Forum for Modern Language Studies*, Oxford: Oxford University Press.

Rufinelli, Jorge (2002). 'María Luisa Bemberg y el principio de la transgresión', *Revista Canadiense de Estudios Hispánicos*, 27.1, pp. 15–44.

Shildrick, Margrit (2004). 'Introduction: sex and gender', in Stacy Gillis, Gillian Howie and Rebecca Munford (eds), *Third Wave Feminism: A Critical Exploration*, Basingstoke: Palgrave Macmillan, pp. 67–71.

Sobchack, Vivian (2004). *Carnal Thoughts: Embodiment and Public Image Culture*, Berkeley: University of California.

Stites Mor, Jessica (2007). 'Transgresión y responsabilidad: desplazamiento de los discursos feministas en cineastas argentinas desde María Luisa Bemberg hasta Lucrecia Martel', in Viviana Rangil (ed.), *El cine argentino de hoy: entre el arte y la política*, Buenos Aires: Editorial Biblos, pp. 137–53.

Strang, Veronica (2004). *The Meaning of Water*, Oxford: Berg.
Williams, Claire (2013). '"When they were good they were very, very good, but when they were bad...": Clarice Lispector's naughty little girls', *Forum for Modern Language Studies*, 49. 2, pp. 154–65.
Wilson, Emma (2007). 'Miniature lives, intrusion and innocence: women filming children', *French Cultural Studies*, 18.2, pp. 169–83.

Index

abject, the 243, 256–7
adaptation 12, 44, 74, 101, 127, 128, 203, 209, 212, 214, 215 n.1
aesthetics *see* poetics, filmic
aesthetics of hunger (Glauber Rocha) 7, 74
Aguiló, Macarena and Susana Foxley
  El edificio de los chilenos 83–4, 86, 87
Amaral, Susana xvii, xviii, 12, 36
  A hora da estrela/The Hour of the Star xviii, 179
Amaral, Tata 35, 36, 42
  Um céu de estrelas/Starry Sky 42, 152
Anzaldúa, Gloria 21, 106, 107, 108, 119
Argentina xviii, 4, 11, 12, 13, 18, 26 n.13, 118, 134–44, 241–60
Arvelo, Alberto
  Tocar y luchar 186, 190
auteur/auteurism xix, 12, 18, 32, 33–4, 36, 50, 77, 82, 90, 200, 203, 213, 217, 222, 223, 225, 236
authorship 32, 36, 40, 41, 43, 44, 45

Badiou, Alain 40, 45
Barreto, Fábio
  Lula, o filho do Brasil 38
Bemberg, María Luisa xvii, xviii, xix, 11–12, 15, 18, 242, 243–6, 247, 258
  Camila 11–12, 244–5
  De eso no se habla/We Don't Want to Talk About It 244, 246
  Miss Mary xviii, 179, 243
  Yo, la peor de todas/I, the Worst of All 179
Benjamin, Walter 18, 222

Birri, Fernando
  Los inundados/Flooded Out 6
border-crossing 18, 24–5, 157, 217, 220, 222–31, 236, 257
Bracho, Julio
  La sombra del caudillo 205, 207, 208
Brant, Beto
  Crime delicado/Delicate Crime 41, 44, 45
  O invasor/The Trespasser 33
Brazil 3, 4, 5, 7, 8, 9, 12, 13, 16, 23–4, 31–46, 126, 129, 131, 149–69
Brecht, Bertolt 40

Caldas, Paulo and Lírio Ferreira
  Baile perfumado/Perfumed Ball 36–7, 41
Carri, Albertina 23, 247
  Geminis 248, 256, 257–8
  La rabia 248, 250, 251, 256
Castillo, Carmen
  Calle Santa Fe 84, 86
censorship 41, 71, 72, 81, 92 n.2, 92 n.3, 205, 208–9
Chicana filmmaking 13, 21, 99–122
Chicano cultural politics 106–10
child, representation of 55–62, 64, 178, 180–1, 183, 242, 243, 244, 247–53, 257
  see also girl, representation of
Chile 3, 10, 15, 16–17, 21, 22, 56, 70–95, 126, 224
Cine Mujer Colombia 9, 10
Cine Urgente 22, 175
Cinema Novo 7, 32, 37, 74
Clariond, Andrés
  Hilda 130

263

Index

class, social 8, 10, 11, 20, 21, 23, 24, 31, 32, 36, 37, 39, 42, 49, 52, 60, 62, 63, 78, 106, 108, 109, 123, 124, 125–44, 149, 151, 152, 155, 157, 176, 178, 180, 181, 207, 223, 242, 243, 246, 247, 249, 252, 255, 257, 258
collaboration 2, 3, 16, 34–6, 42, 43, 72, 73, 74, 75–80, 83, 91, 92 n.5, 108, 151, 209, 217, 221, 222, 223, 224
Colombia 2, 7, 9, 11, 129, 144 n.1
comedy 23, 149–50, 156–9
co-production 1, 13, 14, 66 n.5, 174, 175, 183, 217, 218, 220, 221, 223–4
Cordero, Sebastián
  Crónicas/Chronicles 229–30
Coutinho, Eduardo xx, 35, 42
  Cabra marcado para morer/Twenty Years Later 42
  Jogo de cena/Playing 42
  O fim e o princípio/The End and the Beginning 24, 39
  Santo forte/The Mighty Spirit 42
Cuarón, Alfonso
  Y tu mamá también/And Your Mother Too 133
Cuba xvii, 6, 7, 8, 83, 84, 114, 174, 219, 221

del Río, Dolores 100–1
del Toro, Guillermo 57, 222–4, 227–30
  Cronos 222–4, 227–9
  El espinazo del diablo/The Devil's Backbone 223
Derba, Mimí 4
desire 22–3, 44–5, 242, 245, 246, 254–5, 257, 258, 259
Devious Maids 102, 105–6
dictatorship 12, 13, 17, 19, 32, 42, 70, 71, 78, 79, 81–2, 83, 85, 86, 118, 128, 135, 259 n.7
difference 1–2, 24, 31, 43, 45
disability 23, 44–6, 246
dissensus 32, 38

distribution 9, 33, 71, 73–4, 75, 153, 157, 174, 213, 219, 223–4
documentary 7, 8, 9, 10, 13, 15, 16, 17, 21, 22, 23, 32, 36, 37, 39, 51, 53, 66 n.10, 67 n.19, 70–95, 111–18, 129, 175, 200, 206, 219

Echevarría, Nicolás
  Cabeza de vaca 220, 221
Ecuador 224, 230, 231
editors, female xviii, 16, 36, 77, 84, 85, 112, 154
embodiment 23, 250, 251, 256, 258, 259
ethnicity 8, 10–11, 20, 21, 23, 24, 31, 36, 49, 52, 53, 63, 64, 86, 87, 100–1, 106, 108, 111, 124, 125, 128, 131, 132, 139, 143, 155, 176, 242, 246, 247, 258, 259 n.6
Eyde, Marianne 17, 51, 52–5, 63, 64, 66 n.10
  Coca mama 54
  La vida es una sola/You Only Live Once 22, 53, 63

femininity 5, 43, 71, 79, 91, 143, 166, 167, 201, 245, 247, 248, 254, 258, 260 n.8
feminism 2, 3, 5, 7, 8, 9, 10, 11, 12, 13, 18, 19, 20, 21, 22, 23, 24, 34, 42, 43, 49–50, 70, 79, 80, 81, 82, 84, 90, 106–10, 112, 117, 119, 123, 125, 128, 132, 138, 155, 156, 166–7, 197, 201, 202, 206, 213, 218, 243–4, 245–6
  see also postfeminism; third wave feminism
feminist film theory 31, 43, 44, 176–7, 247
Fernández, Emilio 5–6, 101
Fernández Violante, Marcela xviii, 8, 15, 18–19, 197–215
  De todos modos Juan te llamas/General's daughter 8, 198, 201, 202, 203–9, 214
  Misterio 198, 202, 209–14

264

Index

Ferreiro, Lírio *see* Caldas, Paulo and Lírio Ferreiro
film festivals 13–14, 15, 17, 18, 48, 50, 51, 54, 55, 59, 62, 63–4, 66 n.5, 73, 75, 91, 93 n.10, 149, 214, 219, 221, 223, 225, 230, 235, 236, 237, 250
    Berlin 14, 18, 33, 51, 55, 62, 151
    Havana xvii-xviii, xx, 176, 214, 221, 233
    Rotterdam 14, 54, 130, 230
    Sundance 151, 217, 223, 224
flashback 186–90
flash-forward 186–90, 191
Foxley, Susana *see* Aguiló, Macarena and Susana Foxley
funding 1, 13–14, 17, 18, 32, 49, 50, 55, 63, 64, 66 n.5, 73, 74, 75, 77, 130, 153, 154, 156, 158, 173–4, 183, 191, 197, 199, 200, 204, 213, 219, 220, 221, 228, 236

García Espinosa, Julio xvii, 7, 74
García Montero, Rosario 14, 17, 49, 51–2, 55–62, 64–5
    Las malas intenciones/Bad Intentions 19–20, 22, 49, 55–62, 63, 64–5
gaze 43, 44, 103, 178–9, 181, 186, 189, 190, 247, 248, 250, 251, 256
gender 2, 4, 5, 7, 8, 11, 16, 21, 23, 24, 31, 36, 38, 43, 44, 50, 52, 54, 65, 72, 79, 80, 84, 87, 88, 106, 107, 111, 132, 134, 150, 151, 152, 155, 158, 159, 161, 162, 163, 164, 165, 166, 167, 168, 176, 178, 179, 180, 181, 188, 198, 201, 202, 213, 214, 215, 218, 224, 232, 235, 241, 242, 243, 244, 245, 246, 247, 251, 254, 256
    see also femininity; masculinity
Getino, Octavio and Fernando Solanas
    La hora de los hornos 7
girl, representation of 51–2, 55–62, 64, 65, 178, 234, 242, 245, 246, 247, 249, 251, 256

Gómez, Sara xviii
    De cierta manera/One Way or Another xviii, 6, 7, 8
González, María Paz
    Hija/Daughter 87–8, 89
Gutiérrez Alea, Tomás xvii
    Memorias del subdesarrollo/Memories of Underdevelopment 7
Guzmán, Patricio
    La batalla de Chile/The Battle of Chile 7
Hayek, Salma 101–5
Hollywood 43, 49, 99, 118, 236
Hoogesteijn, Solveig 15, 20, 22, 173, 192
    Macu, la mujer del policía/Macu, The Policeman's Woman 20, 83, 173, 176–82, 185, 186, 187, 188, 190, 191
    Maroa, una niña de la calle/Maroa 20, 173, 177, 182–91
humour, dark 149–50, 158, 162–3, 165, 168

imperfect cinema (García Espinosa) 7, 74
    see also New Latin American Cinema; third cinema
indigeneity, representations of 11, 50, 64, 131, 258
indigenous filmmaking 10–11
intersexuality 254–5, 258

Kristeva, Julia 257

Landeta, Matilde xviii, 5–6, 198, 201
    La negra Angustias 5, 6
    Lola Casanova 5
    Trotacalles 5, 8, 203–4
Largo, Eliana and Verónica Quense
    Calles caminadas/Walked Streets 70, 82
Latinas, depiction of in film and television 99–106
laws, cinema and audio-visual 92 n.2, 173–4
    see also policy, cultural and audio-visual

Index

Leduc, Paul 199, 218, 224
  Reed, México insurgente/Reed, Insurgent Mexico 219, 225–7
lesbian 109, 142, 143, 242, 245, 246
  see also queer; sexuality
Lessa, Bia and Danny Roland
  Crede-mi/Believe Me 37–8, 41–2
Lévinas, Emmanuel 43
Lispector, Clarice 12, 249
Llosa, Claudia 11, 14, 17, 49, 50–1, 62, 64
  La teta asustada/The Milk of Sorrow 17, 49, 51, 62, 130–1
  Madeinusa 17, 49, 51, 63, 64
Longoria, Eva 102–6
Lula da Silva, Luiz Inácio 38
Lund, Kátia *see* Meirelles, Fernando and Katia Lund

Mann, Thomas 37
Martel, Lucrecia xvii, xx, 1, 11, 12, 14, 18, 23, 125, 126–7, 141
  La ciénaga/The Swamp xvii, 59, 126, 139, 242, 245, 246, 247, 249, 251, 252, 256, 257, 258
  La mujer sin cabeza/The Headless Woman 20, 124, 126, 134–9, 142, 143, 242, 245, 246, 247, 256
  La niña santa/The Holy Girl 126, 242, 244–5, 249, 254, 256
Mascaro, Gabriel
  Doméstica/Housemaids 129
masculinity 24, 150, 156, 160–1
Martínez Crowther, Andrea
  Cosas insignificantes 224, 231–5
Meirelles, Fernando and Kátia Lund
  Cidade de Deus/City of God 33, 36, 153
melodrama 5, 22, 38, 55, 105, 142, 234
metafiction 210–12
Mexico xvii, 1–2, 4, 5, 8, 9, 10, 11, 12, 18, 19, 101, 102, 104, 115–19, 123, 132, 133, 197–215, 217–38
  Cristero Rebellion 203, 204–8
  Mexican Revolution 203, 207, 208, 225

student movement of 1968 204, 206, 218–19
studio system of 199, 214, 215
  see also Tlatelolco, massacre of
mimesis 41
Moraga, Cherríe 21, 107–8, 112, 116
Morales, Sylvia 13, 103, 111–19
  A Crushing Love: Chicanas, Motherhood and Activism 21, 99, 112–19
Moreno, Rodrigo
  Réimon 130
motherhood 10, 21, 50, 70, 71, 84, 99, 106–19, 151, 160, 161, 162
Mothers of the Plaza de Mayo, The 13, 118
Mulvey, Laura 34, 43, 44
Murat Lúcia xvii, 24, 42
Murga, Celina
  Una semana solos 248, 250, 251, 252–3
music, 135, 145 n.17, 150, 184, 188, 189, 191, 206–7, 228, 244
Muylaert, Anna 1, 23–4, 131–2
  Durval discos 23–4, 149–50, 152, 154, 158, 159–63, 168
  É proibido fumar 23–4, 149–50, 152, 158, 159, 163–8
  Que horas ela volta?/The Second Mother 23, 131–2, 151, 152, 156, 157–8
myth, pre-Hispanic 104, 142–3, 232, 234–5

nation 5, 6, 50, 60–2, 63, 133, 134, 181, 182
national identity 20, 52, 56–7, 63, 65, 134, 167, 178, 182, 228
Nava, Gregory
  El norte 220, 221
Navarro, Bertha xviii, xix, 15, 18, 217–38
neo-realism 6, 250
New Argentine Cinema xix, 6, 241, 249
New Latin American Cinema xvii, 6–7, 8, 13, 19, 118, 127, 128, 172, 226, 247
  see also imperfect cinema; Third Cinema

Index

Nicaragua 10, 219, 220
Novaro, María xviii, 12, 15, 201, 218

Ocampo, Silvina 248–9

Padilla, Priscilla
   La eterna noche de las doce lunas/The Eternal Night of Twelve Moons 11
Paraguay 14, 140, 142, 255
Peru 11, 17–18, 22, 48–69, 131
Pinochet, Augusto 17, 70
poetics, filmic xvii, 1, 7, 23, 24, 25, 52, 60, 225–6, 231, 233, 234, 242, 248, 249, 251, 256, 259
policy, cultural and audio-visual 32, 53, 153, 157, 173–4
   see also laws, cinema and audio-visual
politics 1, 19–23, 24, 59, 62, 134–5, 201, 211, 212, 219
   feminist see feminism
   left-wing 49, 53–4, 70–1, 114–15, 175
   of the private 1, 6, 7–8, 19–20, 23, 59–60, 172–3
Portillo, Lourdes 12, 13, 118
post-feminism 79–80, 149–50, 153–4, 165–6, 168
producers, female 4, 4, 5, 9, 35, 36, 65 n.2, 67 n.20, 76–7, 101, 102, 103, 106, 118, 152–3, 177
   see also Navarro, Bertha; Stantic, Lita
production 4, 5, 10, 12, 13–14, 18, 35, 36, 49, 55, 71–8, 88–92, 149, 153, 154, 169 n.8, 173–5, 191, 209, 210, 217–38, 255
   see also co-production
Puenzo, Lucía 1, 14, 20, 23, 124, 134, 247
   El niño pez 134, 139–43, 246, 247, 254, 255–6
   XXY 248, 254, 256

queer 80, 110, 124, 134, 139, 140, 141, 242, 255, 259 n.1
   see also sexuality; lesbian

Quense, Verónica see Largo, Eliana

race see ethnicity
Rancière, Jacques 24, 32, 38–9, 41
realism 40, 41, 134
   social 57, 181
Retomada (Brazil) 3, 13, 16, 24, 31–46, 153–4, 156
Reygadas, Carlos
   Japón 132–33
Rich, Ruby xv–xx, 1, 6, 7, 8, 13, 19, 20, 172, 173, 176, 191
Rocha, Glauber 7, 36–7, 74, 225
Rodríguez, Martha and Jorge Silva
   Chircales 7
Rodríguez, Robert
   Desperado 103
   From Dusk Till Dawn 103–5
Roland, Danny see Lessa, Bia and Danny Roland

Saleny, Emilia 4
Salles, Walter 35
   Central do Brasil/Central Station 33, 41, 127
   and Daniela Thomas
   Terra Estrangeira/Foreign Land 34, 35
Santos, Carmen 4
   A inconfidência Mineira/Rebellion in Minas 6
Sarmiento, Valeria
   Un hombre cuando es hombre 10
screenwriters, female 169 n.4, 177, 224
   see also Muylaert, Anna
Sendero Luminoso (Shining Path) 17, 22, 50, 51, 52, 53–62, 64
Sequeyro, Adela 5, 6, 201
servants, domestic 20, 21–2, 123–46
sexuality xvii, 23, 31, 86, 100, 116, 134, 159, 164, 165, 167, 179, 180–1, 183, 208, 242, 243, 254–6, 258
   see also intersexuality and lesbian and queer

Index

silent cinema 4–5, 25 n.1, 41, 100
Silva, Jorge *see* Rodríguez, Martha and Jorge Silva
Silva, Sebastián
   La nana/The Maid 129–30
Solanas, Fernando 225
   see also Getino, Octavio
Solomonoff, Julia 23, 241, 247, 249
   El último verano de la boyita/The Last Summer of La Boyita 247, 250, 251, 254, 256
sound 5, 23, 206–7, 227, 242, 243, 249, 252, 258
Stantic, Lita xvii, xix, 12, 26 n.13, 217

Taller Popular de Video Timoteo Velásquez
   La Dalia 10
Tambutti, Marcia
   Allende mi abuelo/Beyond My Grandfather Allende 87
Teixeria Soares, Ana Carolina 8
television 23, 36, 74, 79, 100, 149, 151, 152, 154, 198, 209–14, 221, 230, 231

third cinema 7, 49, 172
   see also imperfect cinema; New Latin American Cinema
third wave feminism 23, 81, 245–6, 247, 258
Thomas, Daniela *see* Salles, Walter
time-image 250–1
Tlatelolco, massacre of 200–1
Torres, Fina xviii, 176, 177, 179
transnational cinema 1, 13, 18, 49, 55, 63, 63, 65, 65, 66 n.5, 156, 174, 182–3, 217, 219, 220–2, 223–4
trauma 56, 57, 72, 81–7, 91, 128, 134, 135

Valdez, Luiz
   I am Joaquín 110, 112
Vélez, Lupe 99, 101, 111
Venezuela 20, 22, 173–92
video 8, 9, 10, 81, 82, 210, 211, 212

water 142–3, 243, 252–5
women's filmmaking collectives 9, 22, 74, 175

www.ingramcontent.com/pod-product-compliance
Lightning Source LLC
Chambersburg PA
CBHW072128290426
44111CB00012B/1817